D1257663

AMERICAN HERO

THE LIFE AND DEATH OF AUDIE MURPHY

CHARLES WHITING

ESKDALE PUBLISHING

British Library Cataloguing in Publication Data:
catalogue record for this book is available from the British Library

Copyright Charles Whiting 2000

ISBN 0-9538677-0-6

First published in the UK in 2000 by
Eskdale Publishing
Eskdale House
46 St Olaves Rd
York
England
YO30 7AL

The right of Charles Whiting to be identified as the author
of this work has been asserted by him in accordance with
the Copyright, Design and Patents act 1988.

All right reserved. No part of this publication may be reproduced, stored
in a retrieval system or transmitted in any form or by any means,
electronic or otherwise, without prior permission in writing from

Eskdale Publishing, Publishers.

Typeset by Hindley, Corwen, Denbighshire.
Printed and bound in Great Britain by
Mackay of Chatham plc, Chatham. Kent.

ACKNOWLEDGEMENTS

When I first began the research for this book, several of the people I interviewed told me it would be an impossible task. One wrote: 'Anyone who is *crazy* enough to attempt a biography of Audie Murphy needs all the help he can get'. Well, help enough I did receive, and I would like to take this opportunity to thank several people who have given me much valuable aid and assistance. One is Col. Harold B. Simpson, whose research into Audie Murphy's early life has proved invaluable. Another is Roger Bell, an expert on Murphy's combat career in the ETO. As always, Tom Dickinson of the New York Public Library has been outstanding in his support. Carl Swickerath of the Third Infantry Division Association has also given me some valuable leads, Mrs. D Inzer, Texas, Dean Paterson, Hill College, Hillsboro, Texas, John Sneddon, National Secretary, Society of Third Infantry Division, Sam Smith, President, Audie Murphy Fan Club and Marty Black.

But I owe my greatest debt for assistance to David 'Spec' McClure of Hollywood, Audie Murphy's friend and mentor for most of Murphy's adult life. Without Mr. McClure's help, I doubt if American Hero could have been written. This is a posthumous tribute to 'Spec' and his life time hero, warts and all, Leon Audie Murphy.

Charles Whiting
York, England

AUDIE MURPHY

'He is a gentle-eyed little killer'.

- John Huston

'Murphy really knew how to give 'em hell. I guess he was the best soldier we've had since George Washington'.

- President Harry S. Truman

'Audie took the hard way, cutting a swath through the Wehrmacht and then trying to do the same in Hollywood. There, in twenty years as an actor and producer, he found himself outflanked by people he called 'phonies', who wouldn't fight his way. Long before his plane flew into a mountain he was nibbled to death by ducks'.

- Cartoonist Bill Mauldin

'Audie Murphy belonged to an earlier, simpler time, one in which bravery was cardinal and killing was a virtue'.

- Time Magazine

'All men are born to die and if one man must go a few turns of the earth sooner than the rest what has he really lost?'

- Audie Murphy

CONTENTS

INTRODUCTION

I never moved into combat without having the feeling of a cold hand reaching into my guts and twisting them into knots.

Audie Murphy

Two young soldiers in France in the winter of 1945: the one a coward, the other a national hero.

In a strange kind of way, they were to become the two best known young soldiers to emerge from the U.S. Army in World War II. The one because he had run away from battle and *would not* fight, even on the pain of death. The other because he simply *could not* run away. He had to stand and do battle against overwhelming odds, even though he faced almost certain death.

Later, both of them would have hooks written about their wartime exploits. A film, too, would be made of each of their careers in combat. But that was later, long after the events of that winter that decided their fates and after they had gone their separate ways: the one to an unmarked grave in a military cemetery in northern France; the other to become America's most decorated hero, *ever*.

Of course, they never met, the two of them. Even if they had, they would probably have taken an instinctive dislike to one another. After all, one was a hero and the other a coward in the same bitter battle raging in that ravaged, snowbound wasteland. But for one short week in that January of the last year of the war, their fates were almost linked.

The coward met his end at ten thirty on the morning of January 31. 1945. He stood in the ankle-deep snow of the secluded villa where they were going to shoot him in front of his commanding general, huddled in a blanket, his hands free of chains at last. He told the priest who confessed him, 'Father, I'm getting a break that the fellows up on the line don't get. Here I get to sit with you, and I know I'm going to get it. I know I'm going to die in a few minutes. But up there on the line you never know when it's coming, and it's that uncertainty that gets you. I guess that's what I couldn't take that uncertainty'.[1]

A little later, with the priest intoning the Act of Contrition, they bound him to the firing post and shot him to death; the first American soldier to be executed for desertion in the face of the enemy since the Civil War. Afterward, one of the firing squad from his old outfit, the 109th Infantry of the U.S. 28th Infantry Division, commented in bewilderment, 'I can't understand why a man who had the guts to face a firing squad like that wouldn't stay in line with the rest of us'.[2] The priest thought the dead deserter was 'the bravest man in the garden this morning'.[3] The coward's name was Eddie Slovik, the only soldier of the ten million men inducted into the U.S. Armed Forces in World War II to be shot for desertion on the orders of a future president of the United States. *

Five days before, in that terrible last week of January, some twenty miles away from where the coward would be shot by his own comrades, the hero made his last stand. Wounded and limping, his uniform tattered and

---

* Eisenhower, then commanding in Europe.

scorched, he took on a whole company of German infantry, supported by tanks, alone. Balanced on the deck of a knocked out tank destroyer that was smoking and threatened to explode at any moment, the skinny young officer - he wasn't even old enough to vote - fought them off and in the end saved what was left of his decimated company. 'There were times', he said later, 'when our outfit was in battle seventy to eighty days without relief. You got mad and disgusted, and you didn't care what happened to you. This is the way I felt on that tank destroyer They talk about bravery, well, I'll tell you what bravery really is. Bravery is just determination to do a job that you know has to be done. If you throw in discomforts and lack of sleep and anger, it is easier to be brave'.[4] The hero's name? Audie L Murphy, the most decorated soldier in the history of the U.S. Armed Forces.

There, it seemed, the fates of these two young soldiers with such divergent attitudes to war, the one twenty-five years of age, the other twenty, parted. The coward had died violently and suddenly that last day of January 1945. The hero survived for another twenty-six years to attain high honours and national renown. And although he, too, died violently and suddenly in an air crash in 1971, there appears to be no possible link between the two of them.

But there was. Both, in their very different ways, were victims of World War II. Both were fated to die - the coward swiftly when he was young, the hero a more lingering living death over the years until he reached middle age - because of what had happened to them when they had donned the uniform of their country. In retrospect, when one studies the careers of these two very different men, it seems almost as if the war in which they both participated produced not heroes or cowards, but merely victims.

Audie Murphy, the hero, would never have run away in battle, of course. Cowardice, although he was often afraid in combat, was anathema to him. Indeed, once he had appeared for the prosecution in the court-martial of a comrade who had deserted his post during an action. Undoubtedly he would not have hesitated to do the same at the trial of Private Slovik.

Yet as he grew older and wiser, Audie Murphy began to realize that the war and the high honours he had achieved in it had made of him something he had not wanted to become. Just as the coward, Slovik, knew that the war had torn him from the only happiness he had known in his pathetic life, married to a crippled woman in a humdrum, dead-end job, the hero, Murphy, came to understand that the only happiness he had ever experienced had been those thirty-odd months he had spent in combat. In the end, Murphy must have known that being labelled as a 'hero' for all his mature life was just as much a stigma as the epithet 'yellow' applied to Slovik.

Once he had shared in that good feeling of being part of a great mass of human beings, working together, fighting together, suffering the same hardships and simple pleasures to achieve a common goal. The instinct for self-survival had been sublimated to a higher ideal and aim. The individual had meant little. The group, as small as it was - Company B, 15th Infantry, the 3rd Infantry Division - had meant everything. A certain kind of rough and ready idealism had developed.

But then suddenly the war was over. Audie Murphy had found himself thrown back into the world of the civilian, where the old values still held sway - money and position. As he told a friend, David McClure, 'Over there, we really thought we had hold of something. Then we came home to find that it was 'Bang, bang!' How the West was won all over again'.[5]

Or as he once expressed it to a writer from *Esquire* magazine: 'You have a comradeship, a rapport that you'll never have again, not in our society anyway. I suppose it comes from having nothing to gain except the end of the war. There's no competitiveness, no money values. You trust the man on your left and on your right with your life'.[6]

But he had been unable to accept the values of this civilian world. He had treated position and money with contempt, though he forever needed money to buy the 'toys' he required to divert his troubled mind. 'To become an executioner, somebody could and analytic, to be trained to kill', he told the *Esquire* interviewer, 'and then to come back into civilian life and be alone in the crowd - it takes a long time to get over it. Fear and depression come over you'.[7]

The hero's legacy of World War II was what the 'headshrinkers', as he would have undoubtedly called them contemptuously, now diagnose as 'Post Traumatic Stress Disorder'. He had all the classic symptoms. He was an insomniac, eternally restless, suffered from nightmares and hallucinations, was unable to concentrate for more than short periods of time, and seemed apathetic about the values of civilian life. As his friend David McClure has remarked, 'His emotions, with the exception of anger, were practically dead. He had seen too much horror, too much combat, ever to be normal again. His struggle against it was mighty, but he could not win. He probably found more difficulty in the postwar years than he did in the service... *In essence, he was a burned out case!*'[8]

In the war Audie Murphy was wounded three times, killed some two hundred-odd Germans, and won every medal for valour that the United States had to offer (one of them, the 'Silver Star', twice in four days). He became America's most decorated soldier ever, lauded by two presidents and millions of humbler folks. Yet he was unable to sleep, twenty years after the war ended, without the lights on and a loaded Walther automatic pistol beneath his pillow. As he told an interviewer once, who had asked how combat soldiers managed to survive war, 'I don't think they ever do'.[9] In the war he had fought through seven campaigns. The way he visualized what followed in civilian life is indicated by the title he thought of giving to his postwar story. It was *The Eighth Campaign*.

On the same day that the first atomic bomb was exploded at Alamogordo, New Mexico, July 16, 1945, the front cover of *Life* featured a freckle faced young officer smiling out from beneath a tilted, too large cap, headlined 'Most Decorated Soldier'. It was the face of a happy, small town kid, coming home from the wars a hero, with not the least sign of anything remotely resembling a combat neurosis or trauma. Here was the stuff that the American Dream is made of. A sharecropper's son, later an orphan, who had overcome all kinds of obstacles and had won glory before he was old enough to vote.

Murphy was a bright, very witty hero, in much the same mould as World War I's Sergeant York, who when asked how he managed to capture 132 Germans single-handedly, replied, 'I surrounded them'. It can also be argued that he was the last American military hero. Neither Korea nor Vietnam has been productive of the breed - at least in the eyes of the public. Moreover, Murphy's feats did not disappear into the history books of World War II or into the yellowing pages of old newspapers kept in the files. For a quarter of a century after he had gained his military honours for valour in action, he was constantly in the public eye.

As a movie star first, a writer of a best-selling autobiography, volunteer crime fighter, troublemaker, he was always publicized, for better or worse, by the media. 'The most decorated soldier of World War II', as he was invariably described, was still known to the general public when many other heroes had sunk into oblivion.

But the public that idolized Audie Murphy's public image had no idea of the horror and heartache that Murphy suffered during and after the war. Nor did it know anything of the permanent tension between the man and the image; the fact that those twenty-five years in Hollywood, his triumphs, his failures, could never seriously challenge the wartime legend. Even when, in 1970, he was put on trial for attempted murder, the media still focused on the fact that Murphy was 'America's most decorated soldier'. How he must have hated it all in the end!

'War robs you, mentally and physically', Murphy once said. 'It drains you. Things don't thrill you any more. It's a struggle every day to find something interesting to do'.[10] For twenty-five years, Audie Murphy fought valiantly to keep on living in that boring postwar world, going to a garage to watch mechanics work on cars, for example, simply to pass the time. Time and time again, try as he might, he failed to stave off that overwhelming ennui. For after combat, what comparable thrill could civilian life offer him?

Perhaps, in the end, he welcomed that sudden, swift death the air crash offered him on that remote mountain slope in Virginia? Like poor cowardly Eddie Slovik back in 1945, the 'uncertainty' was over. Audie Murphy, the Last Hero, could die.

NOTES
1. W. Huie. The Execution of Private Slovik. New York: Signet, 1953.
2. Ibid.
3. Ibid.
4. The New York Times. June 1945.
5. Letter to author.
6. 'Who Made the Difference', Esquire. December 1983.
7. Ibid.

ONE

THE INITIATION

You watch out, Henry, an' take good care of yerself in this here fighting business… Don't go a-thinkin' you can lick the hull rebel army at the start because yeh can't. Yer one little feller amongst a hull lot of others, and yeh've got to keep quiet an' do what they tell yeh.

- Stephen Crane
- The Red Badge of Courage

1

Now all was silence. In the far distance the heavy guns rumbled. Closer by, the brooding silence was broken by the occasional chatter of a machine gun, the white glowing tracer splitting the inky darkness for a few moments. Now and then flares sailed effortlessly into the night sky on the German side of the river line. But they were routine. It was obvious the enemy suspected nothing this freezing January night.

Crouched in the ankle-deep snow or in the icy drainage ditches, men of the U.S. 3rd Infantry Division's assault regiments, the 7th and the 30th, shivered and waited as the minutes ticked away remorselessly. An icy wind was blowing from the snowy peaks of the Vosges Mountains to the west and was racing straight across the barren Rhine plain. The temperature had now fallen to well below zero. One year before to the day, January 22, 1944, the 3rd had also been waiting to go into the assault: the beach at Anzio in Italy. Back then the doughboys of the Marne Division had quipped, 'See forty-four - and win the war!' Now twelve months later, and after having suffered nearly 30,000 casualties in two years of combat, the weary veterans dolefully maintained, 'See forty-five - and survive!'

This night the veterans, and the green replacements who had been pouring into the division since Christmas to fill the great gaps in its ranks, were going to assault the German held Fecht and Ill rivers. Once that was done, the two attack regiments would push into the so-called 'Colmar Pocket', the German salient on the west bank of the Rhine River, centred on the French town of Colmar. If everything went well, the 3rd would attack Colmar itself or cut off the German line of retreat to the Rhine from there by capturing the fortress town of Neuf-Brisach. But the whole bold plan was predicted on rushing up armour once the bridgehead on the Fecht-Ill rivers had been secured. For without tanks the lightly armed infantrymen would be at the mercy of the German counterattack; and war-weary veterans knew the Krauts always counterattacked.

At ten o'clock that night the leading battalion of the 30th Infantry Regiment, commanded by Col. Lionel C. McCarr, started to cross the Fecht by stealth. With their equipment muffled, all of them clad in their 'spook suits' - white, camouflaged uniforms made from pillows, mattress covers, sheets, anything white - the first infantrymen stole across, stumbling up the muddy banks on the other side without encountering any opposition worthy of mention. Within the hour, two battalions were across and were advancing toward Ill River.

Here and there the Germans were now beginning to react. There was the high pitched hysterical burr of German spandaus, firing a thousand rounds a minute, as the leading men bumped into enemy machine gun nests. One company in the lead stumbled into a German mine field, and the darkness was split by scarlet flame as the deadly mines exploded and hysterical voices screamed for the medics. But, in general, progress was excellent, and already before dawn the leading elements of the 3rd were dug in on the west bank of the Ill River, waiting for bridging equipment to come up.

Some didn't wait. They got into the rubber boats they had dragged with them across the snowfields from the Fecht River and started to paddle across the sixty-foot river. As the winter sky started to flush an ugly gray, heralding another bitter day of war, several companies were over the Ill and straggling forward through the knee-deep snow against sniper fire and those damned mines. The attack was going well and now the order was flashed to the rear, 'Get the armour across - at the double!'

The site selected for throwing across the American armour to support the leading infantry was situated at the small hamlet of La Maison Rouge, 'The Red House', aptly named; for soon what was to happen there was going to result in the spilling of much American blood. While the infantry had been advancing through the night, 1st Lt. Keith Miller and Sergeant Neal Wesson had volunteered to check out the French bridge supposed to be still standing at La Maison Rouge. They had found it intact. Checking for demolition charges with their hands in the freezing darkness, they had discovered to their dismay that it was 'a plain old country bridge that did not even have side railings'[1]. Without being reinforced, they realized, the French bridge wouldn't support amour.

Next, the two bold volunteers had scouted the area. They had come across an abandoned German armoured car, its crew dead. But the three Germans they had found in the farmhouse at La Maison Rouge weren't; they had simply been asleep. Miller, who had honed up a steel file until it was as sharp as a razor, and Wesson, who was armed with a combat knife, swiftly dispatched them as they slept. "It was no time for conversation", Miller said afterward.[2] Then the two of them had settled in to wait for the arrival of the engineers and the American armour.

Now as the 30th Infantry Regiment started to attack toward the fortified villages of Holtzwihr and Riedwihr, the 10th Engineer Battalion, commanded by a Major Hayden, arrived. Miller and Hayden fell into a heated argument almost at once. Miller wanted to have a prefabricated Bailey bridge brought up. Its parts were already loaded on trucks to the rear, waiting to be called up. Hayden, however, insisted on using the old French bridge. He thought he would save precious hours by reinforcing it with treadway. In the end the major won, and immediately his men set to work while Miller fumed in impotent, hot-blooded rage.

By noon, the sound of tank engines and heavy infantry fire could be heard plainly on the other side of the Ill, and thick columns of black smoke started to ascend ominously above the fir forest that fringed the twin villages under assault. A hapless Miller told himself he didn't need a crystal ball to know what was going on. The 30th had run into German tanks!

Now it was of the utmost urgency to get American armour across the damned river to the support of the hard-pressed infantry. But the 10th Engineers had run into a serious problem. They were fifteen feet short of the vital treadway, needed to shore up the rickety French structure! Worse, the roads to the rear were so clogged up with the division's stalled vehicles, all waiting to cross the Ill, that no additional treadway could be brought up in time.

A harassed Major Hayden made his decision, as the Sherman tanks lined up along the riverbank, waiting for their orders, and the sound of the fighting in the forest grew ever louder and more alarming. He ordered the first tank, commanded by 1st Lt. John Harmon, up to the rickety bridge.

Miller yelled, "Get that fuckin' tank off the bridge!" He rushed forward onto the bridge, waving his hands in an attempt to stop the thirty-ton monster advancing any further.

A tank Colonel popped his head out of a second tank, as the turret gun traversed around to point directly at the excited young lieutenant, and snapped coldly, "Get your ass off the bridge, or I'll blow it off!"[3]

Reluctantly Miller moved, and the thirty-ton tank started to edge its way inch by inch, onto the bridge. In the Sherman's lowest gear, the driver crawled across the unreinforced section of the structure. It held! Hayden breathed out with relief. The tank was going to do it. The armour was going to reach the 30th before it was too late. The Sherman moved on, watched by the tense engineers.

Suddenly, startlingly, the vital bridge began to sway and tremble like a live thing. The engineers yelled their urgent warnings. Too late! There was a rending and a twisting. Just as a truck carrying the missing treadway came churning its way through the mud and the slush the bridge gave way altogether. "You're not going over the bridge", an irate Miller had just shouted. *"You're going through it!"*[4] Now he was proved right with a great metallic thump the Sherman dropped to the bed of the Ill River.

The German counterattack, as one officer put it bitterly afterward, 'couldn't have been better timed if they'd had a liaison officer with us!'[5] In the very same moment that the Maison Rouge bridge collapsed and effectively stopped the vital armour from being sent to the aid of the 30th Infantry, things went disastrously wrong. Around the villages of Housen, Riedwihr, and Holtzwihr, a battle developed that the divisional history records, 'as one of the most bitterly fought engagements' in the history of the 3rd. As it started to grow dark, German infantry of the elite 2nd Mountain Division, newly arrived at the front, started to push forward, covered by enormous sixty-ton Tiger tanks. There was absolutely no cover for the men of the 30th. The ground was frozen solid, and it would have taken TNT to blast a foxhole. Moreover, the 30th had still failed to establish radio communication with their artillery on the other side of the Ill. So the scared infantrymen now had to fight off the advancing Germans with what they carried - and their two-inch bazookas were puny, impotent toys, their rockets bouncing off the Tigers' thick hides like glowing Ping-Pong balls.

What happened next was predictable. Attacked on three sides by armour and infantry, the 30th's 3rd Battalion broke and retreated in disorder, some men abandoning their weapons in their flight and swimming the freezing Ill River in their panic.

At five that terrible afternoon it was the turn of the 1st Battalion. Again the Tigers and the Jagdpanthers, with their infantry hugging their tails, rolled up the infantrymen of the 3rd. Here and there brave, obscure men tried to stop them, ineffectual 'Davids' armed with grenades and bazookas, trying to flight off those metallic 'Goliaths'. But there was no halting them. They came on, crushing all opposition in front of them.

Two young officers, Lieutenants Walker and Calvert, tried to make a stand in a wood. But when the enemy tanks entered and the firing ceased, the officers were dead, crushed to death. A Sergeant Murphy attempted to hold them up with his machine gun, ordering his men to withdraw while he fought on. The enemy tanks got within fifty yards of the lone non-com. Then he was cut down by a vicious burst of machine gun fire at point-blank range. Posthumously he would be awarded the DSC. He wouldn't be the only Murphy to win high honours in those bitter woods this last terrible week of January 1945.

Now it was the turn of the 2nd Battalion. It was hit while working its way through some snowbound woods, the men divided up into small groups by the clumps of trees. Confusion broke out immediately. The great lumbering German tanks came crashing through the trees, turret machine guns spitting fire. Men began to surrender on all sides. Others simply broke, flung away their weapons, and raced for the rear, crying out in their overwhelming panic, 'The Krauts are coming… *The Krauts are behind us!*' By nightfall the battalion had lost 350 men, most of them having surrendered to the enemy: half a battalion had vanished in a matter of hours!

By the time the fighting had begun to die out that terrible day, the shattered 30th Infantry Regiment, which had gone into the attack three thousand strong, had been forced back across the Ill River everywhere, save for the handful of brave men still stubbornly holding out near Maison Rouge.

Hurriedly, officers made an attempt to reorganize the badly hit regiment. Food, clothes, and rifles, for those who had flung away their weapons in their panic-stricken flight, were swiftly brought up from the rear. Straggler posts were set up along all possible routes to the rear. Here officers, armed with carbines and 'grease-guns' directed 'stragglers' back into the line, whether they liked the prospect or not. According to the 3rd Division's history, these chilled, shocked men still had enough spirit to tell officers, 'Yes, sir, we can hold. No goddamn Kraut is gonna kick the hell outa us and get by with it. We'll be here in the morning!'[6] The history of the 30th's sister

7th is more down to earth. It records bluntly that 'Between the Fecht and Ill rivers, the 30th Infantry met with a catastrophe and was so badly hurt that it was kept out of offensive action for quite some time thereafter'.[7]

Now General 'Iron Mike' O'Daniel, the tough, scar-faced commander of the 3rd Division, who had lost his only son (a nineteen-year-old paratrooper) in Holland the previous fall and who had now become an embittered man, threw in his final reserve. The pressure was on from above and O'Daniel brooked no failure. *

He ordered the 15th Infantry Regiment to cross the Ill River and seize a bridgehead opposite Maison Rouge. There, covered by the fresh infantry, the engineers would attempt to throw across a new bridge so that this time armour could support the attacking infantry. The attack would commence on the night of January 23/24, and this time the stern divisional commander expected the 'Can Do' Regiment (a pidgin English phrase it adopted during its long service in China at the beginning of the century) to do exactly that.

This time General O'Daniel wanted the Krauts kicked out of the villages that were holding up the whole Corps advance once and for all - or he'd want to know the reason why; and 'Iron Mike' was a dangerous man to tangle with.

Notes
1.   Letter to author.
2.   Ibid.
3.   Ibid.
4.   Ibid.
5.   D. Taggart, History of Third Division. Linz, Austria: Privately printed. 1945.
6.   Ibid.
7.   E. Fellers, ed. From Fedala to Berchtesgaden. Washington, DC: Infantry Press, 1947.

* In later life, Lt. Miller always maintained that O'Daniel tried to get him killed by giving him dangerous assignments because he knew too much about the Maison Rouge bridge fiasco.

2

At three o'clock on the morning of January 23, the 3rd Battalion of the 'Can Do' Regiment, laden down by equipment like pack animals, crossed the Ill River. Luck was on their side - at the start, at least. They made the crossing, without serious opposition, although the Germans must have known own they were coming, and started to make good progress. But as always, the Germans didn't give up that easily. The 3rd had just emerged from some snow-heavy trees when the enemy counterattack struck them in full force - four heavy tanks, scuttling across the snow like evil black beetles, supported by infantry, yelling in wild triumph.

Three American tanks came rumbling up to support the suddenly stalled 3rd. To no avail. They were easy meat for the much superior German panzers, who could knock them out at twice the American tanks' effective range. One by one they were shot into smouldering wrecks by German armour-piercing (AP) shells. It was too much for the 3rd, which already had begun to take serious casualties. The survivors, 'mauled and exhausted', as one observer reported, started to pull back to the Ill once more, leaving the snowfield behind them litter with their dead, sprawled out in the extravagant postures of those done to death violently.

'Iron Mike' flung in his 2nd Battalion. By mid-morning it was engaged in a desperate ding-dong battle with the Germans, taking casualties all the time. Frantically a makeshift bridge was thrown across the Ill for a second time. Two Sherman tanks and a tank destroyer crossed it and rumbled up to the support of the hard-pressed infantry. Still the Germans fought stubbornly. They were going to make the *Amis*, as they called the Americans contemptuously, pay for every inch of ground they gained.

On the morning of January 25, the Germans launched a full-scale counterattack against the Americans. The 2nd reeled under the impact. Reluctantly the 2nd started to give ground. Desperately they fought back. But the Germans exerted ever more pressure, forcing them ever nearer to the Ill.

That day the first member of the 3rd Division to gain the coveted Medal of Honor in the Battle of the Colmar Pocket sacrificed his young life to do so. Pfc. Jose Valdez, again one of those underprivileged young men who so often won the highest awards for bravery, was on outpost duty with five other men, when he spotted a German tank approaching their position. Undaunted by the fact that they possessed no heavy weapons, Valdez managed to drive it off with automatic rifle fire.

Some time passed in nervous anticipation. Valdez and the rest knew that the enemy knew where their position was now. Soon they would attack again. They did. Three of them crawling through the snow, reconnoitring the American position. But not for long. Coolly, Valdez shot the German scouts, one after another.

Now the enraged Germans flung in two full companies against the American position. The patrol leader decided it was high time to pull back as nearly three hundred Germans advanced upon them. Valdez volunteered to cover his comrades. As his comrades sneaked out of their hiding place, one by one scuttling to the rear and safety, Valdez kept up a well-aimed and withering fire on the advancing Germans.

In the end, of course, his luck ran out; the odds against the lone soldier were too great. As the citation for America's highest award for valour read afterward: 'He was struck by a bullet which entered his stomach, passing through his body, and emerged from the back. Overcoming agonizing pain, he regained control of himself and resumed his firing position... By field telephone, he called for artillery and mortar fire on the Germans and corrected the range until he had shells falling within fifty yards of his position. For fifteen minutes he refused to be dislodged by more than two hundred of the enemy, then seeing the barrage had broken the counterattack, he dragged himself back to his own lines'.[1]

Later the brave young man died of his wounds in the hospital, unaware that he had won the Medal of Honor, dead before he had really begun to live. History would soon forget Pfc. Valdez. He would become merely a footnote in a divisional history of a war long past. But time would not forget an equally young and equally brave young man, who was engaged in that desperate battle on that same afternoon of January 25, 1945.

The day before, Murphy's 1st Battalion of the 'Can Do' Regiment had moved through the positions of the 3rd Division. 'It is our turn to move up and take a beating', he wrote about it later. 'As we dogtrot through the snow, no smile appears on a face, no lip murmurs the customary wisecrack. As we move through an area littered with dead men and abandoned equipment, the soldiers mutter curses and speak bitterly of suicide missions'.[2]

That night the young man had attempted to sleep in the woods outside the embattled village of Riedwihr, he and his men taking turns to stay awake; for they expected a counterattack, of the kind that had decimated the 3rd, at any moment. The young man had been unable to keep his eyes open in spite of the freezing cold. A cannon had cracked nearby. Startled, he had raised his head from the ground and had yelped with pain, for his head had been frozen to the grass and now he left 'patches of my hair in the ice'.[3]

Now the first light of a new day of war reluctantly illuminated this cruel lunar landscape, as if God on high hesitated to reveal its awfulness. The young man took his place at the head of Company B as they began to fight their way into Riedwihr. He limped badly, for he still bore a bandage on his hip where in the fall five pounds of rotten flesh had been gouged from the wound he had already suffered in Alsace in the previous October. He was a slight young man, very handsome in a boyish way, with a freckled, open face and a helmet that seemed much too large for him. Indeed, he seemed entirely out of place on this harsh, cruel battlefield. What was this teenage boy doing, masquerading as an infantry officer leading desperate men into battle?

In fact, the young man had been engaged in combat for nearly two years. He had fought in Sicily, Italy, and now for four long months in France. He had been wounded twice already and had been awarded a dozen medals for bravery, being granted a commission in the field for his valour and fighting ability. Only his eyes gave a clue to the real man, as he slogged doggedly toward the village, his men all around him with their skinny bodies bent, as if tensed for a sudden storm. They were sharp, quick, hard, constantly on the move, looking for danger - and for victims - like those of some predatory animal seeking its prey. As one of his closest and oldest friends would say long afterward; 'His appearance is deceptive. Beneath that shy exterior, there is a keg of dynamite - *with the fuse lit!'*[4]

Now, as the 1st Battalion (commanded by Major Potter) advanced ever closer to the fortified village, the German resistance stiffened. As always there were German snipers everywhere, tied to the trees, concealed in ruined barns, taking advantage of what little cover they could find to carryout their deadly handiwork. The Germans had their feared multiple mortars right up front, too, and the gray air was twisted hideously with the obscene howl of their shells. Up front with his Company B, the young man watched in horror as two of the young ex-enlisted men who had been commissioned with him the previous October rushed for cover into a steaming shell hole. It was struck by a mortar bomb the very next moment. Their bodies were ripped to shreds. The two of them had lasted as 'officers and gentlemen' for exactly three months.

But the young man had little time to concern himself with the fate of the other two. A moment later, another mortar shrieked in from the sky. It exploded only yards away. The hot blast flung him from his feet. He yelped with pain, ears ringing. He had been hit yet once again. Hurriedly he rolled into a hole and jerked up the bottom of his ruined trousers. 'From the knees down flesh is peppered with tiny steel fragments. But the luck of the Irish is with me. The wounds are all superficial'.[5] The young man staggered on, dripping blood on the snow.

But now it was growing dark again. The long winter night was beginning to descend upon the battlefield and the 1st Battalion's ammunition was starting to run out. During the day's fighting, the 1st had penetrated six hundred yards into the forest against fanatical resistance. Potter, as weary as his men, decided the battalion had had enough for the day. He ordered his men to take up defensive positions for the night. They would wait for fresh ammunition to be brought up and start to attack again at two in the morning. With luck, they might catch the Germans off guard, but Potter wasn't too confident of that. Still it was a pious hope with which to encourage his hard-pressed GIs.

Gratefully, the survivors of the day's action slumped down in the snow among the shattered firs. Little was said. Each man seemed wrapped in a black cocoon of his own thoughts. Company B had gone into action that morning with 155 men and six officers. Now it had been reduced to two officers and twenty-eight men, plus a handful of bewildered, scared replacements who had suddenly found themselves in the middle of a battlefield in a place whose very name they did not know. They huddled in the snow in silence and dug their spoons into cans of greasy hash.

At one o'clock on that morning in January, a day that would change his life irrevocably, the young man received his orders from the Company Commander. B Company would change direction. It would advance to the edge of some woods facing the Alsatian hamlet of Holtzwihr: the town was no more than a church surrounded by a straggle of unkempt peasant houses running the length of a single road. There, what was left of the company would dig in and wait for a fresh outfit to attack through its positions. As the executive officer of the 15th Infantry, Col. Keith Ware said later: "Control (of the Bois de Riedwihr) had been wrested from the enemy at a heavy cost in blood".[6] Now somebody else was going to continue the fight. Company B would not be expected to pay the butcher's bill any more - or so the young man told himself.

The advance through the freezing, inky forest toward Riedwihr was surprisingly easy. The young man and his weary survivors stumbled from tree to tree in the deep snow, firing occasionally into the darkness, but encountering no real resistance until they reached the position outside Riedwihr allotted to them. Here they tried to dig in. To no avail. 'The efforts are futile', the young man wrote later, 'but the exercise keeps us from freezing. When we finally give up trying to chew holes in the ground, we stamp up and down a narrow road winding through the woods to stir up heat in our bodies'.[7]

Another dawn. The infantrymen had forgotten their weariness, the freezing cold, the lack of hot food. They all know that this is the most critical part of the day. The Germans dearly love to counterattack at first light. They finger their weapons, casting anxious glances to their front. Here and there the younger men urinate, the yellow liquid sending up hot steam in the icy air: a sure sign of extreme nervousness. Others yawn almost continuously, another sign of nerves. A few pray. But not many.

Half an hour later, enemy mortars opened up. With their usual stomach-churning howl, the deadly little eggs began to fall from the gray winter sky, exploding in bursts of angry, ugly red flame, scattering silver-gleaming fragments of lethal metal everywhere. To the young man's front, the Company Commander fell to the ground with a groan. He had been hit by one of the red-hot shards. Hastily he was carried away moaning, leaving the young man in charge. Two years earlier he had joined this same company as a baby-

11

faced rookie. His then Company Commander had been so shocked at his boyish appearance that he had tried to get the young man appointed to the safe job of company clerk; he had seemed too frail for combat. Now he was the new C.O. of Company B, with not one single man left of those who had started out with him in North Africa back in 1942.

Hastily, the young man made his dispositions. He established his command post in a drainage ditch behind one of the two tank destroyers that were supporting the infantry. Then he called the commander of the second tank destroyer and told him he better find some cover - the Krauts could see him plainly from Holtzwihr with their glasses. The tanker refused. He felt safer with the infantry. He didn't like the idea of being alone off the road in the trees, with some Kraut stalking him with his feared panzerfaust. *

The young man accepted his reasons and now settled in to wait. Soon the new battalion would pass through his thin line of defence to attack Holtzwihr, and his task would be completed. Perhaps then, after nearly forty-eight hours in action, he and what was left of Company B would finally be allowed to get some desperately needed sleep?

But that wasn't to be. The morning dragged on, and still the new troops had not appeared. The nervousness of his men increased. The young man could see just how jittery they were and wished fervently they would be relieved. The Krauts would not simply sit tamely in Holtzwihr forever. Surely they knew already just how fragile his perimeter really was?

Sometime that morning, a forward artillery observer, 1st Lt. Walter Weispfennig, made his appearance. He brought with him his own radio, but for some reason Weispfennig was unable to make really good communication with the artillery farther to the rear. So Company B had to rely on the young man's field telephone that linked him to the headquarters of the 1st Battalion.

Time passed leadenly. The sky was gray and overcast and brooding now. The icy branches of the skeletal trees rattled in the cold wind. The very air seemed heavy with tension. The young man decided to contact the battalion CP. 'What orders?' he asked over the field phone. The answer was cold and dogmatic, 'No change… Hold your position!' [8] And that was that. The waiting continued

Midday came and went. Nervously the unshaven, weary, freezing GIs, strung out in a series of shallow depressions or hiding behind trees as best they could, swallowed the cold rations from the olive-drab cans. From the direction of Holtzwihr there came the muted sounds of many voices and the first rusty rattle of tank tracks. The men looked at each other in unspoken alarm. Were the Krauts coming at last?

They were. 'At two o'clock in the afternoon I see the Germans lining up for the attack', the young man wrote of that moment much later. 'Six

*The German bazooka, which was more accurate and had more penetrative power than the U.S. equivalent.

12

tanks rumble to the outskirts of Holtzwihr, split into groups of threes, and fan out toward either side of the clearing. Obviously they intend an encircling movement, using the fingers of trees for cover. I yell to my men to get ready'.[9]

The German tanks were fanning out. The first American tank destroyer took up the challenge. Smoke and fire erupted from its long overhanging cannon. There was the sudden, white blur of an AP shell hurtling toward its target. Later the young man would swear he saw the shell strike one of the enemy tanks and not even 'cause it to falter'.

The German tanks took up the challenge, as the men on the leading TD alternated between firing the cannon and manning the turret machine gun spraying the advancing German infantry with fire. Shells started to land all around the young man's position. The first TD tried to withdraw. The driver must have panicked, for suddenly the steel monster was slipping helplessly into the drainage ditch at the side of the road. In virtually that same moment, the second TD was struck a sickening blow. There was a great echoing boom of metal striking metal, and the TD reeled crazily, its commander and gunner killed outright. The rest of the crew bailed out madly as a fire broke out inside the wrecked vehicle. Thick black smoke began to pour from its open turret.

Abruptly the handful of frightened infantry realized that they were without their armoured protection and over two hundred Germans dressed in 'spook suits' and shrieking like demented men were advancing upon them. But they had not reckoned with their new Company Commander He had been in tight situations like this before. He ordered his men to withdraw to a prearranged position about half a mile to the rear. Next, he commanded Weispfennig to pull back behind him and save the radio while he tried to contact the artillery boys through battalion HQ by means of the field telephone. Later the young man would say, 'The reason he sent his men back was that he couldn't see why all had to get killed when one man could do the job that had to be done. And it was up to him to do it.'[10]

Now the yo ung man was all alone. Afterward he would say, 'He had no idea of how he would ever get out of the spot, but for some reason he didn't care a damn.'[11] So he waited there, armed only with his carbine and the field telephone, watching them come, a baby-faced twenty-year-old boy, who was going to go down in the history of the U.S. Army as its 'greatest fighting soldier'. His hour of destiny had come at last.

His name?

Audie Le on Murphy.

NOTES
1. Taggart, op. cit.
2. A. Murphy. To Hell and Back. New York: Henry Holt, 1949.
3. Ibid.
4. Letter to author.
5. Murphy, op. cit
6. Taggart, op. cit
7. Murphy, op. cit.
8. Ibid.
9. Ibid.
10. Letter to author
11. Ibid.

3

What made Audie Murphy do what he did next?

What had America ever done for the lone twenty-year-old standing there in the snow, armed solely with a carbine, facing up to two hundred-odd Germans and six sixty-ton steel monsters? His native Texas, as Audie Murphy once remarked cynically in later life, had given him nothing but 'free advice - and malnutrition'.[1] His schooling hadn't gone beyond the fifth grade, and no authority had cared one bit when he had finally dropped out. Even now, the newly created 'officer and gentleman' made mistake after mistake in his letters home, spelling 'I' as 'i' and proudly informing his sister Corinne that he had been awarded the 'Distgh ser Cross' (i.e., Distinguished Service Cross).

His family life had been no great shakes either. The son of an Irish-American sharecropper who had abandoned his long-suffering wife and nine children when the boy had been in his teens, he had been 'thrown into the struggle for existence' as soon as he had been old enough 'to handle a plow, an ax, or a hoe'.[2]

The America of the Depression in rural Texas had certainly not heaped her favours on the boyish, freckle-faced second lieutenant. Certainly at that moment of extreme danger, Audie Murphy would have been fully justified in surrendering just as had many more senior and more privileged officers in the face of overwhelming odds in these last few terrible days of the attack into the Colmar Pocket. After all, he had already been wounded once and was still limping from a previously wounded hip that had kept him in the hospital for nearly three months. It would have been easy.

Yet the lone officer didn't. He stayed and fought back, doing what an awed Lt. Walter Weispfennig later reported as being the 'bravest thing that I had ever seen a man do in combat': an action that would gain the twenty-year-old America's highest honour for valour - the Congressional Medal of Honor.[3]

Now Weispfennig to the rear watched as the 'Kraut tanks rumbled past Murphy's position, passing within fifty yards of him and firing at him as they went by. They did not want to close in for the kill because they wanted to give our tank destroyer, which was burning but not in flames, as wide a berth as possible'.[4]

But Murphy was not going to let them pass and strike his men to the rear. Blazing away with his carbine, he called down artillery fire onto the tanks. At first, battalion headquarters did not seem ready to comply with Murphy's request for fire. A lieutenant on the staff asked how close the Germans were. His Irish roused by now, Murphy, as he kept popping off shots at the stalled German infantry, cried above the vicious snap and crackle of small arms fire, '*Just hold the phone and I'll let you talk to one of the bastards!*'[5]

That did it. As the men of Company B to the rear opened up with their bazookas and the first artillery rounds started to fall in the snowy fields all around, digging great, steaming brown holes like the work of giant moles, Murphy decided to take on the advancing German infantry: two companies of them, later calculated to be in full strength of 125 men each!

With his carbine ammunition gone, he retreated to the slowly burning tank destroyer and clambered into the turret. Here he manned the .50 caliber machine gun, spraying his front with bullets. An awed Weispfennig later reported, 'He was completely exposed and silhouetted against the background of bare trees and snow, with a fire under him that threatened to blow the destroyer to bits if it reached the gasoline and ammunition.'[6]

The German infantry could not comprehend where this new hail of fire was coming from. The Americans had abandoned their positions, they knew, and they thought nobody was crazy enough - or brave enough - to be fighting back at them from the powder keg of the burning tank destroyer. So they milled around, taking casualties all the time.

Not the German tanks. They had spotted the source of the deadly fire. Now 'the enemy tanks… returned because Lieutenant Murphy had held up the supporting infantry, and they were apparently loath to advance further without infantry support', as another eyewitness, Sgt. Elmer Brawley, recorded later. 'These tanks added their murderous fire to that of the Kraut artillery and small arms fire that showered the lieutenant's back without stopping'[7]

Back at battalion headquarters, they could now hear the thwack-crack of the German 88mms over the phone, as Murphy telephoned his instructions to the artillery. One excited HQ sergeant cried, in between the boom of the explosions, "Are you still alive, Lieutenant?" Carried away by the crazy illogic and blood lust of combat, Murphy - his clothes already smouldering and smoking - yelled back, "Momentarily, Sergeant… And what are *your* postwar plans?"[8]

Now the infantry, too, had spotted the direction the deadly machine gun fire was coming from. Twelve Germans detached themselves from the main force and tried to out-flank the lone defender by stealing up a snow filled gully to Murphy's right. But the young Texan, who once said that as a kid if he didn't shoot accurately, he 'didn't eat', spotted them - just in time. He swung the .50 caliber around and ripped into them with a vicious burst at fifty yards' range.

Other Germans were pressing home their attack on the lone soldier who, as Weispfennig reported later, 'was now enveloped in clouds of smoke and spurts of flame. His clothing was torn and riddled by flying shell fragments and bits of rock. Bullets ricocheted off the tank destroyer as the enemy concentrated the full fury of his fire on this one-man stronghold.'[9] Other enemy infantrymen started to crawl in on the tank destroyers from three sides, using what cover they could find, in part aided by the fog of war, as shells, American and their own, exploded on all sides.

'The German infantrymen got within ten yards of the lieutenant', Sergeant Brawley recalled afterward, 'who killed them in the draws, in the meadows, in the woods - wherever he saw them. Though wounded and covered with soot and dirt that must have obscured his vision at times, he held the enemy at bay, killing and wounding at least thirty-five during the next hour.'[10]

Now Murphy resorted to one final, desperate measure. He called the American artillery to the rear to bring down a barrage on what was virtually his own position. As he explained later: 'I figured that I could luck out the barrage - if those goddamned Germans could. With those shells bursting all around me, they couldn't even hear the machine gun, much less locate it.'[11] Perhaps that last correction saved his life, for a moment after he had shouted it through frantically above the roar of battle, the phone went dead in his hand. He was cut off from the rear!

One of those inexplicable lulls that happen at the height of the most fierce of battles now occurred. It was as if both sides were winded and needed a few minutes to regain their strength. A good handful of the German infantrymen simply bypassed the lone figure on the burning TD and penetrated as far as the battalion headquarters, where clerks and cooks took up the challenge for a while.

During this time, the gray afternoon cloud parted for a brief period. It was the opportunity the pilots of the American TAC Air Force had been waiting for. They had been buzzing the battlefield all afternoon, flying just above the cloud base, anxiously seeking a break in it. Now they had found it, and they didn't hesitate. The feared American *jabos* *, as the Germans called them, swooped out of the sky screaming, engines going all out.

Immediately they spotted the infantry and tanks milling around on Murphy's extreme left flank. Cannon and machineguns blazing, spitting tracer toward the Germans, they surged into the attack at treetop height.

The sight of the *jabos* tearing in, angry lights crackling the length of their wings, was too much for the German infantry. They started to pull back. The tankers wavered. They knew a direct hit from one of the *Ami* cannon could put *them* out of action, and they were afraid of losing the protection the infantry afforded them. It was slowly getting dark, and without infantry they would be at the mercy of any lurking soldier armed with a bazooka, stalking them at close range. They decided they had had enough. Hesitantly, reluctantly, realizing that they had been held up by one lone *Ami*, they began to withdraw toward Holtzwihr.

It was then that Murphy dropped from the battered TD, its deck and turret gouged silver with the impact of the enemy shells, the holes like the

* Jagdbomber

symptoms of some loathsome skin disease covering its metal hide. It was then that he noticed his field map, which he had been holding in his outstretched hands to direct the artillery fire from the rear. It had been tattered by flying rocks and steel fragments. His raincoat was similarly full of holes. But not one fragment had penetrated his skin. It seemed he had come through that tremendous battle without being hit. Suddenly, he felt a dull throbbing in his right leg. 'Looking down', he wrote much later, 'I see that the trouser leg is bloody. That does not matter.'[12]

'As if under the influence of some drug, I slide off the tank destroyer and, without once looking back, walk down the road through the forest. If the Germans want to shoot me, let them. I am too weak from fear and exhaustion to care'.[13] But Audie Murphy had not quite reached breaking point yet - that would come many years later.

As the tank destroyer finally exploded with a muffled roar, sending a great circle of black smoke out of the turret into the darkening afternoon sky, he limped back to where what was left of Company B was positioned. His bravery in facing the German attack all by himself had inspired even the green replacements. Under his command, they surged back to attack the Germans still remaining in the woods. As Sergeant Brawley reported, Murphy 'refused medical treatment'. Instead, he led his men 'in a strong attack against the enemy, dislodging the Germans from the whole area'.[14]

That evening Company B was dug in, in their old position in the woods just outside Holtzwihr, where it would remain until it was relieved the following day. Thereupon, the 'Can-Do's' 3rd Battalion assaulted the fortified hamlet, taking it with comparative ease, for the Germans had pulled out most of their strength. The great retreat of what was left of the German Nineteenth Army had commenced from the Colmar Pocket.

The enemy was pulling back over the Rhine, their last natural bastion, at last. Soon the soil of France would be cleared of the German occupiers after four years of occupation. *

We know little of Audie Murphy's thoughts and feelings at the end of the action that would make him famous. In his autobiography he wrote: 'Except for a vague pain in my leg, I feel nothing; no sense of triumph, no exhilaration at being alive. Even the weariness seems to have passed. Existence has taken on the quality of a dream in which I am detached from all that is present.'[15]

To his longtime friend David McClure, he confessed later that what surprised him about the Holtzwihr action was that he could 'understand why those German foot soldiers didn't get him', but added that he could 'never forgive those blasted tanks for missing' him. [16] Indeed, in later years, the whole subject of how he won his Medal of Honor seemed to bore Murphy totally, and he appears to have given different accounts of the action to dif-

---

*However, there would be German garrisons at such ports as Dunkirk and Lorient right up to the end of the war.

ferent people just as the mood took him. In the end, the story of the events at Holtzwihr became so fantastic as to be almost unbelievable. Could one lone twenty-year-old have stopped the attack of two whole German companies, supported by six heavy tanks, from the deck of a burning tank destroyer that threatened to explode at any moment?

But four years after the action, that eyewitness who was closest to the scene of the action, former 1st Lt. Walter Weispfennig, the artillery observer, confirmed that they really did take place. Asked after the Ralph Edwards show, 'This Is Your Life!' featuring Audie Murphy, whether the events had really been portrayed accurately, he answered, they were 'as accurate as could be under the circumstances… When a man is figuring on getting his ass shot any minute - and I did - he does not think how the situation is going to look in writing. But Audie Murphy earned the Medal of Honor time and again, and I was only too happy that my testimony finally helped him get it'.[17]

As for the young man who would soon receive the country's most coveted award for valour, he maintained, as he told a Texas historian in 1953, that the 'only thing they (medals) ever meant to me during the war was another five points toward coming home'. [18] By the time the war was over, Murphy had acquired 146 such points, surely a very high score indeed for such a young man who was not even twenty-one in May 1945!

Even to his family, the young officer did not indulge in any boasting, justifiable as it might have been. Writing to his sister Corinne one month after the Holtzwihr battle, he says vaguely, 'I may get some sort of award pretty soon. I don't know what it will be yet. I haven't got my purple yet, it takes quite some time to get them. I have two oak leaf cluster coming also I didn't tell you I got hit again did I? It wasn't bad, it only had me limping around for a week or so, I didn't even go to the hosp. Well sis that's all about for now so be good and write often. Love all, Audie.'[19]

What does one make of such a young man? How could he remain so modest, so seemingly unconcerned about the medal that was to change his whole life? Was Murphy simply just another Texan redneck, lacking in any kind of imagination; just another bar-room brawler to whom fate happened to give a rifle and a war in which he could legitimately kill his fellow human beings?

But if Murphy was that sort of coarse, unfeeling roughneck, would he have written to a friend, Haney Lee, even as far back as early 1944: 'Gen, do you ever go hunting? I guess not, too much walking, huh. Remember how I use to bug you to go with me. Oh well *when* I get home I'll not get out of the house far enough to shoot a squirrill… I've seen so much blood 1 don't think I ever want to shoot anything else.'[20]

Could a 'fighting Texan redneck' have felt, as he states in his autobiography, that 'I may be branded by war, but I will not be defeated by it'?[21]

These are not the thoughts or feelings of some hard hearted glory hunter - and for the rest of his life Murphy remained exceedingly careless about his medals, giving some away, losing others. One visitor to his house in 1967 noted that his second wife, Pamela, had gathered up a selection of her husband's medals and put them in a glass case to preserve them for their two sons. But 'I saw the Medal of Honor was awry and looking tacky. Murphy's premier Purple Heart had slipped down to the bottom of the case and turned over on its face'.[22] For his part, Murphy maintained right to the end of his short life about the medals, 'I feed they belong to a lot of people and not just me.'[23]

So what did motivate him? What made him fight like he did for a country that had given him so little, save hardship, suffering, pain? Why should this semi-illiterate son of Texas sharecroppers become America's most celebrated combat soldier?

Henry James once wrote: 'We are all ready to be savage in some cause. The difference between a good man and a bad one is the choice of the cause.'

What was the course - consciously or unconsciously - that Audie Leon Murphy chose back in those forgotten thirties in the northwestern part of Hunt County, Texas, where, as a boyhood friend, William Bowen, recalled long afterward, Murphy 'never tried to start a fight, but he never ran away from one'.[24]

NOTES
1. Letter to author.
2. Murphy, op. cit.
3. Taggart, op. cit.
4. Ibid.
5. Murphy. op. cit.
6. Taggart, op. cit.
7. Ibid.
8. Murphy, op. cit.
9. Taggart, op. cit.
10. Ibid.
11. Letter to author.
12. Murphy, op. cit.
13. Ibid.
14. Taggart, op. cit.
15. Murphy, op. cit.
16. Letter to author.
17. Ibid.
18. H. Simpson. Audie Murphy. American Soldier. Dallas: Alcor Publishing 1982.
19. Ibid.
20. Ibid.
21. Murphy, op. cit.
22. Esquire, op. cit.
23. Ibid.
24. Simpson, op. cit.

4

In those days, they said, Texas was a place where life was simple and people had not yet developed doubts; it was a place where you needed a mousetrap to catch a mosquito. Texans were so tough and hard-boiled that they slept in sandpaper sheets. Here David Crockett fanned himself with a hurricane. Texas was a place where canaries sang bass; where if you spilled some nails, you'd harvest a crop of crowbars; where houseflies carried dog tags for identification; and where that legendary creature Pecos Bill (the Texan equivalent of Paul Bunyan) could rope and horse-tie a streak of lightning!

Texas was big, loud, virile - and rich. But not where Audie Leon Murphy was born in Hunt County on Boles Farm, near the township of Kingston, on June 20, 1924. Here, fifty miles below the Red River that divides Texas and Oklahoma, the soil was black and fertile. Cotton was the crop, and it was farmed by tenants working by hand on small tracts. It was into such a family of tenant sharecroppers that Murphy was born to Josie Murphy who, before she was deserted by her husband, Emmett, would have eleven children, of which nine grew into adulthood.

Emmett, known as 'Pat' Murphy, was in the year of Audie's birth a tenant father in the employ of W. Foster Boles, and he lived with his ever growing family in a four-room clapboard house, heated by a fireplace on which the cooking was done and lit by coal oil. There was a cistern outside for drinking water. The Murphy family lived and worked in conditions little different from those that their forefathers in Ireland had wanted to get away from when they left the Oud Sod back in the nineteenth century to start a new life in America.

The Murphys were typical sharecroppers of their time, improvident, breeding too many children for their circumstances, scratching a poor living from the soil in an area of backward people like themselves. Here prejudice thrived, as it always does among poor folk who desperately need to have someone *they* can look down upon. They hated Negroes and they hated Mexicans. 'An honest Mexican is one who *stays* bought', they joked cruelly about the Mexican vote. Naturally, religion - the Baptist creed - and a harking back to past 'traditions' and lost glories thrived. On the day Audie Murphy was born, the local newspapers reported that the Federation of Women's Clubs was 'agitating for the suppression of bathing girl revues, beauty contests and similar parades of feminine pulchritude"[1]; and that the local chapter of the Daughters of the Confederacy, named after the Civil War hero General Thomas Green, had raised enough money (*sixty years* after the war had ended) to put a statue to that sad, lost cause on the lawn of the County Courthouse at nearby Greenville.

'We were sharecrop farmers', Murphy wrote many years later, 'and to say the family was poor would be an understatement, poverty dogged our every step. Year after year, the babies would come until there were nine of us children living... Getting food for our stomachs and clothes for our backs was an ever-present problem. As soon as we grew old enough to handle a plow, an ax, or a hoe, we were thrown into the struggle for existence.'[2]

The problem of getting food and clothes for Josie Murphy's ever growing family was not helped by 'Pat'. Throughout the time he lived with his hardworking wife, he was never a good provider. Short, black haired, heavyset, barely literate, he was addicted to those three evils that the 'black Irish' had brought with them when they had emigrated to the United States - drink gambling, and the fostering of too many children without a care about their future. If he had been a Catholic like his forefathers had once been he would have thrown up his big hands in an easy gesture and exclaimed carelessly, 'Och, the Good Lord will provide!' But the 'Good Lord' didn't.

As the twenties gave way to the thirties and the Great Depression started to bite home, the lot of the Murphy family became even worse. In 1933, Pat moved his family to the small town of Celeste, where first they lived in a converted railroad boxcar and then in a run down shack like all the other run down shacks that the Murphys had lived in. For the four years that the family stayed in Celeste, they lived on relief aided by the handouts of food and castoffs given to them by the good ladies of the local Baptist and Methodist churches, who undoubtedly wrinkled their noses and frowned in disapproval at these improvident Irish with 'all those children'.

Thus, for most of the thirties the Murphys lived on monotonous diet of biscuits and gravy, which a growing Audie would demand even for his breakfast, which was usually just corn bread and molasses. Occasionally there would be hogmeat or fish and, naturally, game. For as soon as he was old enough to handle a rifle, Audie went hunting, developing an uncanny knack for killing a bird or animal with the first shot because if 'I missed, *we didn't eat!*'[3]

Pat Murphy, who had been going away for years now on mysterious trips and staying away for weeks, only to return to his long-suffering wife without an explanation, now departed for longer and longer trips, leaving Josie to manage the best she could. The result was that Audie turned more and more to his mother, who at thirty-five looked like fifty. He idolized her and tried to help her out when she was sick. Perhaps that close son and mother relationship was to blight his relationships with other women for the rest of his life; for Audie Murphy, who remained handsome and attractive to women almost to the end of his days, never seemed able to find one who measure up to his mother's standards. It seemed women were to b taken - and then forgotten.

In spite of his hard life, the freckle-faced kid with the infectious smile had his dreams. Hoeing the weeds on one of the farms that his parents and their children laboured, the weeds 'became the enemy and my hoe a myste-rious weapon. I was on a faraway battlefield, where bugles blew, banners streamed and men charged gallantly across flaming hills; where the tem-perature always stood at eighty and our side was always victorious; where the dying were but impersonal shadows and the wounded never cried; where enemy bullets always miraculously missed me, and my trusty rifle forever hit home. ..I was only twelve years old; and the dream was my one escape from a grimly realistic world'.[4]

One day he would realize that boyhood dream of being a hero on the battlefield; though then the wounded would cry and the enemy bullets wouldn't always miss him 'miraculously'. But already his hard life as a young sharecropper was training him for the battlefield to come. He was a born hunter, for example, displaying unusual accuracy with his ancient, small-bore rifle, his reflexes uncannily swift. As his longtime friend David McClure, another American-Irishman from a similar poor, rural background, noted after the war, 'I have never seen a man with such fast reflexes. With him, to think is to act. Audie fires on instinct and is deadly accurate... His vision is fabulous. It must be better than twenty-twenty. He often points out tiny ob-jects to me at night; and even with his help I cannot see them except upon close inspection. His sense of smell is very acute... During the war he was sent out to capture prisoners for intelligence on night patrols and was able to locate the Germans by the smell of the tobacco they smoked and thus gain the advantage of surprise.'[5]

He had developed a hot Irish temper, too, which flared up and van-ished as quickly as it came: a compound of pent-up emotions and a feeling of having been wronged. Perhaps there was also the knowledge that he was smaller and skinnier than most of his fellows and had to compensate by being quicker off the mark with his fists; always ready to see or sense an insult whether it was intended or not. 'God knows where my pride came from', he wrote later. 'But I had it. And it was constantly getting me into trouble. My temper was explosive and my moods, typically Irish, swung from the heights to the depths. At school I fought a great deal. Perhaps I was trying to level with my fists what I assumed fate had put above me.'[6]

One of his teachers in grade school, Ruth Rutherford, who nicknamed Audie 'my Little Pat', also remembers his poverty, pride - and pugnacity. 'He seemed to carry a chip on his shoulder', she recalled many years later. 'I always thought of him as my "Fighting Irishman", and many, many times I had to be referee. After I had learned of his home background, I could more easily understand his feelings and attitude.'[7]

Later, Audie Murphy would say himself, 'I never seek trouble. Trou-ble has a way of looking me up.'[8] But as his friend McClure wrote, 'Audie has a flaring temper, but is incapable of prolonged anger. He has too much humour.'[9]

So as he grew into a wiry, handsome, little teenager, Audie Murphy seemed to be a typical product of his time and background: a semi-illiterate boy, the son of a father who would soon desert the family and an adored mother who was already dying, a child who had learned to take on the responsibility for his own fate early. He had been hungry many a time and demeaned just as often by the attention of the local lady bountifuls whose prissy Baptist morals were accompanied by sanctimonious 'tut-tuttings' is they give handouts to the undeserving poor.

Yet the hardness of his life was animated by his temperament, his moods that swung from the heights to the depths, easily given to laughter and to anger. To it was allied the daydreaming that was an escape from the soulless hardness of his life. As he wrote himself, 'I was never so happy as when alone. In solitude my dreams made sense. Nobody was there to dispute or destroy them.'[10]

And a loner Murphy was going to remain. In the service, after he had some combat experience, he shunned close relationships. All too often they were suddenly and violently destroyed in battle. Once his original buddies of his old platoon had been killed and wounded, he never seemed to make any more. It was the same later when he had become a movie star. More often than once, Lillian Ross, observing him during the making of perhaps his best movie, *The Red Badge of Courage*, noticed just how absent he was, staring out of the window during important discussions with the director, John Huston, eyes far away, having to be dragged back into the conversation by an infinitely patient Huston. It was no different with his own family. Neither of his wives could reach him. A womanizer, a compulsive gambler, he remained apart from them. Just like his father, Pat, going off on those long mysterious trips, he stayed a loner to the very end.

In November 1940, Pat Murphy disappeared for good. Behind him in Farmersville, Texas, where the family was now living, he left Josie and the three children who were still at home. Now Audie's mother became bedridden, her condition weakening rapidly. In the spring of 1941, her serious heart condition was complicated by pneumonia. She was dying, and on the evening of May 23, she passed away in her sleep while Audie sat at her bedside, 'with tears streaming down his cheeks'.

At the age of sixteen, Audie Murphy was on his own, the family broken up, the younger children placed in an orphanage, he himself a fifth-grade dropout earning his keep as a clerk in a combination grocery-store/gasoline-station in Greenville owned by a Mr. Snow Warren. Later, Mrs. Warren would recall the teenager with the ready smile but sad eyes as being 'honest, humble, shy, proud, and neat as a pin He was a good worker and tried on what little he had to keep his family. He was a sad type person, but always wanted to do the best he could. He was also a very sensitive person and could have a temper and he (could be) hurt very easily. We loved him very much'.[11]

And there Audie Murphy could have been fated to remain: an obscure young man in an obscure rural Texas township, destined for an early marriage, a lot of children, and a lifetime of unremitting poverty and menial work until death mercifully put an end to the sheer boredom of it all. But even in that remote Texan township, the far trumpets, sounding the call to war, could be faintly heard. Five thousand miles away in Europe, there had been something called the blitzkrieg. France, which some of the old-timers whom Audie had worked with in the cotton fields still remembered, had fallen. Over Britain, the decisive Battle of Britain had taken place. Already adventurous Texans in their scores, their hundreds, had trekked to Canada to enlist in the RCAF, so that Montreal wags talked of the 'Royal Canadian-Texan Air Force'. The draft had come to the United States, and Sam Rayburn, that veteran Texan, had quipped, 'The real reason Congress passed Selective Service was to get someone in the Army not a Texan!'[12]

We do not know just how much Audie burned to get into the fighting. Even to the semi-illiterate youth who could barely read the newspapers, it was clear from the radio bulletins that the time would not be far off when America would be in what was called then 'the shooting war'. Men were being drafted everywhere. With the new markets being offered by Europe, the Depression was coming to a rapid end, and the home armaments industry was thriving, with new factories, plants, shipyards being opened daily. The isolationists were fighting a losing battle, and the coming war not only threatened death and destruction but also promised profits and excitement. As one female Red Cross worker recorded later: 'The war was fun for Americans. I'm not talking about the poor souls who lost sons and daughters. But for the rest of us, the war was a hell of a good time. Farmers in South Dakota whom I administered relief to and gave bully beef and four dollars a week to feed their families, when I came home were worth a quarter of a million dollars.'[13]

We do know, however, that Murphy 'ate vegetables he didn't like so he could grow big enough to get into the army', and that he would weigh himself every few days, 'to see how close he was to the minimum weight acceptable for military service'.[14]

When Pearl Harbor struck the nation, Murphy 'was half-wild with frustration'. 'Here was a war itself; and I was too young to enlist. I was sure that it would all be over in a few months and I would be robbed of the great adventure that had haunted my imagination.'[15]

His turn would come. For the time being, the skinny, undersized youth, who looked more like thirteen than seventeen, burned with impatience. Like so many other callow, enthusiastic youths all over the world that fateful winter of 1941/42, he fretted at the leash, impatient for some desperate glory, even if it led to death. But then, young bold men never think they will die in battle. How leaden time must have seemed until he reached his eighteenth birthday and he could volunteer for the service legally! What torments he must have suffered as, in the Pacific, America suffered one black defeat after another, her fleet sunk, her prestige in ruins, her garrisons annihilated, kicked off one remote island after another ignominiously!

On his eighteenth birthday, June 20, 1942, with America facing defeat on every front, Audie Murphy hurried to the Army Recruiting Office in the basement of Greenville's local post office. Already the Marines and the Paratroops had turned him down as being underweight and undersized. Now all that remained was the U.S. Army. There the recruiting sergeant was not too keen about this enthusiastic volunteer either. Not only was he a mere 5' 5" and weighed a bare 110 pounds, but he also seemed distinctly under age. The recruiter turned the enraged youth away and told him that before he could be inducted he had to prove that he really was eighteen.

He returned with a certified copy of his birth certificate and a letter from his sister Corinne stating his age. They were accepted. He was told to report back on June 30 for the bus ride to the Federal Building on Dallas's Commerce Street, where his formal induction would take place Previously, he had never been further than a hundred miles from home. Now, 'with a pocket full of holes, a head full of dreams, and an ignorance beyond my years'[16], he boarded the bus that would take him to Dallas.

That afternoon, Audie Leon Murphy was accepted into the infantry. The U.S. Army had just inducted its most famous soldier - ever.

NOTES
1. Simpson, op. cit.
2. Murphy. op. cit.
3. Ibid.
4. Ibid.
5. Letter to author.
6. Murphy, op. cit.
7. Taggart, op. cit.
8. Letter to author.
9. Ibid.
10 Murphy, op. cit.
11. Taggart, op. cit.
12. J. Gunther. Inside the U.S.A.. New York: Harper, 1951.
13. Letter to author.
14. Taggart, op. cit.
15. Murphy, op. cit
16. Ibid.

5

Audie Murphy took to the U.S. Army from the first and that in spite of the fact that his first sergeant at the training camp, Camp Wolters, four miles east of Mineral Wells, Texas, called him 'Baby" on account of his size and looks; and succeeding Company Commanders, taking pity on his puny physique, tried to get him transferred from the rigours of the infantry to the cooks' detail or a service outfit. Murphy persisted in wanting to be a 'fighting' soldier. As he said many years later; "I have to admit I love the damned Army. It was father, mother, brother to me for years. It made me somebody, gave me self-respect" [1] and "I was proud of being a tough soldier."[2]

His start in the infantry was hardly auspicious. One of his fellow rookies at the training camp, Corliss Rowe, remembered he looked 'no bigger than a guinea (hen) and was skinny and pale, like he suffered from malnutrition'.[3]

Nor had he reckoned 'with realistic army training. During my first session of close-order drill', he wrote in his autobiography, 'I, the late candidate for the marines and the paratroops, passed out cold!'[4]

Again a well-meaning officer tried to have him transferred from the infantry to the cooks' and bakers' school. But he would not go. Murphy swore that 'I would take the guardroom first' and thus the army was 'spared the disaster of having another fourth-class cook in its rank'.[5]

But after the initial difficulties, Murphy started to fill out on the good army food, although he was still drilling in shoes several sizes too large for his small feet. In his first letter home to his sister Corinne he informed her that he 'like(d) the army fine so far, they let you sleep till 5:30. On the farm I had to get up at 4'.[6]

After thirteen weeks at Wolters, he was transferred to Fort Meade, Maryland, for advanced infantry training, though as he and many others would discover once they actually got into combat, the U.S. Army's idea of 'advanced infantry training' in the summer of 1942 was hopelessly out of date. In the bitter future ahead, some would die and the others would learn their 'advanced infantry training' from the Germans!

It was at Fort Meade, that 'Baby', as Murphy was still being called by some of his comrades, first 'gave an inkling that he had the makings of a soldier', as Jane Wilkie, a West Coast writer, reported in 1956. According to the story that Audie told her, he was detailed to 'escort two prisoners to the quartermaster to draw shoes'. One man was a murderer and the other a rapist and both dwarfed their puny and nervous escort. Undoubtedly they miscalculated the steely purpose of the eighteen year old, who had absorbed the quite erroneous barrack-room lore that if a guard let a prisoner escape, he, the guard, would have to serve the rest of the escaped prisoner's sentence.

Murphy trailed them with his shotgun at the ready, watching the two hulking, cynical prisoners like a hawk, waiting for the first wrong move. Something told him that they were going to try something, and he swallowed hard and flicked off the shotgun's safety catch.

One of the two heard the sound and turned. "What would you do, if we tried to get away?" he demanded, staring down at the boy.

Audie said quite coolly, "I'd shoot you - *both of you*!"

The prisoner saw the look in those green eyes that had changed from Murphy's usual good-humoured look to a killer's hard, relentless glint and realized the kid was not joking.

Later Audie's C.O. asked him, "What *would* you have done?"

"I told you, sir", Audie drawled in his almost incomprehensible Texan accent, "I'd have killed 'em. I don't cotton to spending the rest of my life in jail for something other guys did!"[7]

Murphy's freckled-faced innocence had again proved deceptive. People who saw him for the first time seldom recognized how he had been shaped by the hardship and bitterness of his youth, and by the knowledge that he was, to all intents and purposes, an orphan who could rely on no one but himself. That innocence fooled not only men. Women fell for it, too, and always would throughout his short life. As his postwar friend David McClure points out: 'There was something about Audie that few women could resist… When Audie relaxed, his facial muscles produced a sad and wistful look. I called it the "little boy lost" look. He might be cursing a blue streak under his breath, but this did not interfere with the "little boy lost" look. He had a voice to go with the look, too. Women wanted to save that little lost boy… Audie seduced more girls than any man I ever knew with the possible exception of Errol Flynn. He might even have topped Flynn'.[8]

A well-meaning officer tried to do Audie a favour and, while his comrades awaited shipment overseas at the end of their training, had Audie transferred to work in Fort Meade's post exchange. Perhaps he thought Audie would remain behind in the permanent cadre and not be subjected to the rigours of combat. Murphy made the most of the opportunities open to him in the PX, staffed mostly by young women recruited locally, and, having struck up a friendship with one of the clerks, seduced her easily as 1942 gave way to 1943. Thus, while many of his comrades went overseas virgins, to die before they ever 'lost their cherry', as the parlance of the time had it, Audie Murphy became a full-grown man.

That didn't change the fact that he didn't want to stay behind in the permanent cadre, however alluring that prospect might have seemed to some of his less martial comrades. He harassed the overworked clerks and officers in the company office, *demanding* to be sent overseas! In the end, the persistence of this youth, who actually *wanted* to go over there and have his head blown off, paid off. On January 23, 1943, he was posted with the men who had trained with him to Camp Kilmer.

Now Audie Murphy, no longer called 'Baby' by his comrades but 'Murph', had two more weeks left in the United States. Soon he would be leaving a land that had remained and would remain virtually untouched by the total war that had been raging elsewhere since 1939.

Behind him Murphy left a cosy, comfortable America, whose concept of the war was so fashioned by the media that the men and women who stayed behind would never even begin to comprehend what Audie Murphy and his comrades went through. Much of it was the patriotic, small-town America that responded so naturally to Kate Smith singing 'God Bless America' on the radio; where Andy Hardy still reigned, as did Dagwood, Blondie, and Baby Dumpling; a land that was all sweetness and light and happy endings; where Norman Rockwell still interpreted America to itself on the front cover of the *Saturday Evening Post*.

For Hollywood, which would one day mean so much to the young man now locked in his camp under armed guard (for the authorities did not allow any word of their sailing to be mentioned - the German U-boats were still very active off America's eastern seaboard), the war was a simple matter of black and white. The old prewar formulas were applied to the new sensations. Uncle Sam was now engaged in a straight forward melodrama made up of heroes and villains, and Uncle Sam was the knight in shining armour, mounted on a white charger, come to save the fair damsel of democracy.

About the only thing we know of Audie Murphy's activities while he was waiting for shipment overseas at Camp Kilmer was that he saw Humphrey Bogart and Ingrid Bergman in *Casablanca*. With perfect timing, it had been released the previous November to coincide with the Allied landings in North Africa.

It was ironic, in view of what the young man was going to experience in Europe in the years to come, that his last real contact with America should be this celluloid dream of patriotism, liberal idealism, and heady, unashamed romanticism. How could Murphy, with his head full of heroics, resist Humphrey Bogart as the embittered introvert changed by the European Ilsa (Bergman) and her love into a champion of democracy? Bogart's brand of self-sacrificial heroism, crackling with hard-bitten dialogue - 'What's your nationality? I'm a drunkard' - must have appealed totally, epitomizing for the callow, semi-illiterate youth, the dreams, the ideals, the style of wartime America.

The reality was to be very different...

On February 8, 1943, Private (Acting Corporal) Audie Leon Murphy staggered up the gangplank of his troop transport, together with hundreds of other young men. They were laden like pack animals with their weapons and rifles and each man was marked with a number chalked on his helmet. The troop transport was the *Hawaiian Skipper*, a 7,000-ton cargo steamer that had crossed the Atlantic many times already in the employ of the British

Ministry of War Transport. There were the usual jeers, wolf whistles and calls of 'you'll be sorry'. But down below, the military policemen in their white-painted helmets, swinging their billy sticks, and the port officials, with their check boards, remained unmoved. They had seen it all before -and they weren't going. The war 'over there' would soon take the piss and vinegar out of these cocky young men.

Silently that evening the transport slipped out past the Statue of Liberty into the Atlantic. For security, it is likely that the young men were kept below deck and were not even able to wave farewell to the statue. The convoy for the long, dangerous voyage ahead had already begun to form up. Slowly, America became a dark smudge on the horizon; then it vanished altogether and they were alone, dark specks on the tossing green sea, heading into the unknown.

All we know of Audie Murphy's long voyage to war was that he was constantly seasick, as were many of his comrades. Most of them had never been on the sea before, and the North Atlantic in winter is not the calmest of oceans. For eleven days the convoy battled the waves, the destroyers zigzagging busily to port and starboard, always on the lookout for a German periscope. But there was none. At this time of the year the rough weather made it hard for the German wolf packs to find their prey.

On Saturday, February 20, 1943, they sighted land, and for the first time the young soldiers learned that they were sailing for Casablanca in French North Africa. Here on November 11, 1942, General Patton's Seventh Army had come ashore, hoping to be greeted with flags and flowers by the oppressed French -they had even brought their regimental bands ashore with them in the first wave. Instead the French had stubbornly resisted the Americans and British who had come to 'liberate' them and had succeeded in killing and wounding a thousand of their liberators before the cease-fire was sounded. The first American casualties suffered by the U.S. Army in the European theatre in World War II were inflicted by an erstwhile ally.

That was three months before. Now Murphy and the rest of his unit disembarked into a strange and - for them - exotic world. A world of 'A-rabs' in what looked like mattress-covers, riding barefoot on skinny ribbed donkeys while their black clad, veiled wives walked behind them, carrying heavy loads, watched by French colonial officers who wore their kepis tilted to one side at a jaunty angle. Cigarettes glued to the corner of their cynical mouths, looking just like Claude Rains in Casablanca. Gawping like country yokels, sweating in the unaccustomed heat, pestered by dark skinned, fresh, little kids begging for 'cigarettes for papa' and 'chewings-gum' and making obscene gestures that promised other, less innocuous, pleasures, the young soldiers staggered to the gleaming white railroad station.

Here they boarded what they later called 'cattle cars', the same kind of primitive rolling stock that had taken their fathers to the front in France back in 1918. Hanging out of the open door, they watched as the fertile littoral swung by, crying out with excitement at their first sight of a camel, or shouting at the barefoot kids goading blind donkeys around and around in an endless circle to draw water from the primitive wells needed to irrigate the fields.

Theirs was not a long journey, which was fortunate for there was neither water nor sanitation in the cattle cars and some of them were already beginning to suffer from the 'squitters'. It was going to be the lot of most of them soon. Sixty miles up the line, the train stopped at Rabat. They were hauled out of the train by the waiting non-coms and officers and marched to the new replacement centre, recently set up just outside the Arab town.

Here they spent a few days finding their bearings before being allotted to their new units. Murphy was delighted to be made an infantryman. He was to be assigned to Company B, the U.S. 3rd Infantry Division, located at Port Lyautey, named after the great French soldier of the previous century who had made Morocco French. It would be some twenty-eight months later, his skinny chest adorned with twenty-five awards, before First Lieutenant Audie Murphy, the only surviving member of that original Company B. 15th Infantry Regiment, 3rd Division, would return to the United States.

NOTES
1. Letter to author.
2. Ibid.
3. Taggart, op. cit.
4. Murphy, op. cit.
5. Ibid.
6. Taggart, op. cit.
7. Ibid.
8. Letter to author.

6

The 3rd Infantry Division had first gone into action in World War II on November 11, 1942. Under the command of General George S. Patton's Seventh Army, which had sailed for North Africa directly from the States, the leading battalions had hit the beach at Fedala. It had been dark and the landing had been a hopeless shambles.

Landing a little after the first assault wave, Major General Lucien K. Truscott, a dashing ex-cavalryman in the Patton mould, who affected riding breeches, a leather jacket, and a jaunty silk scarf, found himself in the midst of total confusion.

In the darkness, stabbed here and there by the scarlet spurts of French artillery, for the French were resisting their would-be liberators manfully, he found soldiers burrowing into the wet sand on all sides. They neither knew nor cared what their next objective was supposed to be. They had done their bit; they had 'hit the beach'. Now let the war take care of itself.

In disgust, Truscott who had been empowered by Patton himself to supervise the initial advance inland, decided to ride to the sound of the guns, as every self-respecting cavalry general should. He commandeered the beachmaster's personal half-track and set off into the darkness to find the front. Hardly had he started when the nervous soldier manning the half-inch machine gun behind him loosed off a sudden burst and nearly took his head off. Grimly Truscott told himself it had been a long time since 1918. He had forgotten that more soldiers were killed by battlefield accidents than by the enemy.

Later he recalled his attempt to find out what was going on at Fedala: 'As far as I could see along the beach, there was chaos. Landing craft were beaching in the pounding surf, broaching to the waves and spilling men and equipment into the water. Men wandered around aimlessly, hopelessly lost, calling to each other and for their units, swearing at each other and nothing.'[1]

Truscott decided he couldn't do much till dawn. Moodily he squatted in the wet sand, dearly wishing he could light a cigarette. Patton had forbidden any lights to be struck in the hours of darkness. Finally the temptation was too great and he succumbed. Immediately all around him in the darkness other soldiers lit up.

Squatting there moodily, feeling very lonely and wondering what to do next with the totally disorganized 3rd Division, Truscott was suddenly startled by a strange lumbering figure who cried in an alien accent, "Heyyuh, gimme a cigarette."

Dutifully Truscott held out a cigarette, as out of the darkness one of his staff loomed up and thrust a tommy gun into the stranger's stomach yelling the password for the assault, "*George!*"

But he didn't receive the expected answer, which was "Patton".

"*George?*" came the indignant answer in a strange singsong. "George, hell! Me no George. My name Lee... cook, Company C, 540th Engineers!" The stranger was a Chinese-American who had lost his outfit. *

Squatting in the sand, Truscott didn't know whether to laugh or cry. The U.S. 3rd Infantry Division's first taste of combat in World War II had not been an overwhelming success.

The 3rd Division, made up of the 7th, 15th, and 30th Regiments (of which the 7th could trace its history back to the War of 1812) and which had had in its ranks no less a person than the Chief of the Army General Marshall, had gained an outstanding record in its short fighting career in World War I. Formed in Texas in 1917, it had been assaulted one year later by *three* German divisions. Under the German pressure, it had been forced to retire, and its Commander, General Dickman, had declared fervently, 'The American flag has been forced to retire. This is unendurable... We are going to attack!'[2]

Attack they did with 1st Lt. George Price winning the division's first Medal of Honor. For its steadfast stand on the Marne River the outfit gained the nickname 'the Rock of Marne'. Thereafter the men of the division would call themselves the 'Marnemen' and their division 'the Rock'.

When the new replacements arrived at 3rd Division, there was little of 'the Rock' about it, and its new Commander, General Lucien Truscott (its first Commander, General Jonathan Anderson, had been relieved after the poor showing at Fedala), was determined to retrain his division before it went into action again. Thus, while the fighting in North Africa raged hundreds of miles away in Tunisia, where the Afrika Korps was fighting its last desperate battles, Audie Murphy found to his disgust that instead of the combat he dreamed of, 'we were given another long, monotonous period of training.'[3]

Ahead of the 3rd would be over five hundred days in combat, which would gain it a *staggering* forty-six Medals of Honor - more than any other outfit in the whole of the U.S. Armed Services - at a cost of over 30,000 casualties (again more than any other unit in the American service), i.e., three hundred percent casualties. But the eighteen year old replacement posted to the 15th 'Can Do' Regiment, chafed at the bit. He had not come all this way to start training again. However he did not let his chagrin show through in his first letter home to his sister Corinne. Dated February 26, 1943, and headed 'Somewhere in Africa', it states baldly, 'Will write you a few lines to let you know that I am OK. It is nice here in Africa. Am glad to be here. How are all the folks? Hope they are well. I never felt better in my life. Well there isn't much to write at this time. I hope to see a little action soon... Well I had

---

* Lee became General Truscott's Cook then later served General Patton.

better sign 30* for now. Love all. Leon'[4]

For a boy who up to his induction into the service had never been farther than a hundred miles from the small town that he called home, the fact that he was now serving in an exotic country, some five thousand miles away, seemed to have registered not at all. 'It is nice here in Africa' did little justice even for a person with Audie Murphy's lack of formal education, to the new surroundings in which he now found himself.

Still, General Truscott, undoubtedly, did not give his men such time for sightseeing and reflecting on the new country in which they were located. Truscott was one of the few American generals (most of whom had last experienced combat as junior grade officers in the trenches back in 1918) who had studied the British Army's more realistic training methods. The year before he had spent four months in that country, where he had conceived the idea of a Ranger battalion, based on the British commandos. Now he introduced the British idea of the 'battle school' to the 3rd. His predecessor, General Anderson, had not trained his men hard enough, and, as a result, they had gone to ground far too early in their first experience of combat. Truscott wanted his men to 'train hard and fight soft'.

So Audie Murphy, together with the rest of his new buddies of the 15th Infantry Regiment, was now introduced to the 'Truscott Trot'. This entailed marching five mph for one hour, four mph the next two hours, and then marching the rest of the thirty-mile hike at three and a half miles per hour - that under a blazing hot African sun!

At the end of that ordeal, the Marnemen were required to crawl under a field of barbed wire on their bellies while live ammunition fired by the regiment's sharpshooters cut the air above their helmeted heads. At the time Murphy and the rest roundly cursed Truscott. Later, however, in the rugged mountainous terrain of Sicily and Italy, they would come to appreciate the hardening that their Commander had inflicted upon them.

Truscott knew what faced his division soon. Under the command of General Patton, the 3rd would be one of the U.S. Seventh Army's assault divisions attacking the mainland of *Festung Europa* on the coast of Sicily. Most of Patton's Intelligence staff were confident (perhaps too confident, Truscott thought) that the Italians defending the coast of the island would fold up easily. But in Truscott's opinion, the staff had not taken into consideration the Germans in Sicily. Just as they were currently doing in Tunisia, they might well fight to the bitter end. Truscott wanted *his* division to be prepared to take up the German challenge.

While General Fredendall's U.S. II Corps was smashed and routed at the Kasserine Pass by Rommel, the men of the 3rd Division enjoyed the off-duty pleasures that Morocco offered. There was plenty of potent local red wine at five cents a glass, and in the cities there were eager, adoring

* Murphy would often end his letters with this phrase, which was the sign-off trademark of a popular prewar news commentator. Earl Garner.

Frenchwomen, the wives and daughters of the *colons*. Soon GIs, armed with the olive-drab coloured Army phrase book, were out everywhere, trying out the same old weary phrases their fathers had used in France. And so much in a hurry were the young soldiers that soon *'voulez-vous promener avec moi?'* was being replaced by the more basic, *'voulez-vous coucher avec moi?'*

Arab women, however, had to be treated with respect. The GI Guide that had been handed to every soldier on-board ship made it quite clear that the soldier should 'Never stare at one. Never jostle her in a crowd. Never speak to her in public. Never try to remove her veil'.[5]

A few of the bolder soldiers, who ignored that advice, found out what it meant to offend the local women. Their dead bodies would be discovered in alleyways with their testicles sewn into their mouths.

The wine meant nothing to Audie; he did not drink. As for the local women, we know nothing of his dealings with them. He seemed to have confined himself to gambling during his off-duty time, both with cards and dice. One of his comrades recalls him 'cleaning out everyone in the game'. Like his father with whom he had now had no contact for over three years, Audie Murphy had a passion for games of chance. In combat, that gambler's instinct of his paid off many times; in civilian life it would become something that was a serious problem, one that Audie would never be able quite to cope with.

In early May the hard training was interrupted for the 3rd Division. Truscott was alerted for action in Tunisia. Murphy was overjoyed. 'Finally the great news came', he would write in his autobiography. 'We were to go into action in the Tunis area. We oiled our guns, double checked our gear; and prayed or cursed according to our natures. But before we could move out, the order was cancelled. The Germans in the area had surrendered'[6] Audie recorded, 'I took no part in the general sigh of relief.'

Now it was back to training. By June 21, 1943, the day after Murphy's nineteenth birthday, the training program for the amphibious landing in Sicily was complete. On the following day a full-scale rehearsal was held. It was so realistic that some of the men taking part in the trial landing thought it was the real thing. Senior observers stated later, with the confidence born of inexperience, that 'never, anywhere, was a combat division more fit for combat... more in readiness to close with the enemy than the 3rd Infantry Division'.[7]

But the 3rd had not met the Germans yet.

One month later, only a few days before Operation Husky, as the assault on Sicily was code-named, was launched, the 3rd Division passed in review before its commanding general. It was July 4, 1943.

Back home it was a public holiday. There would be fireworks, plenty of drinking, picnics, and all the rest of the easygoing, mindless celebrations that went with the country's most important holiday. But here the mood was sombre and grave. Soon these sweating young men parading under the harsh

North African sun, their red faces glazed as if with grease, their uniforms already black with perspiration, would be among the first American troops to land on the mainland of Europe. The British had been waiting for this moment for over three bitter years. The 'new boys' had not had such a long wait, but they had not gained the combat experience the British had during those long months since the Germans had thrown them out of Europe at Dunkirk. Admittedly some of the 3rd had had three days of combat back in November fighting against the French. But the latter's resistance had been half-hearted and the French weapons had been out of date.

Now they were going to attack the first team, for although most of the defenders of the island were Italian, there were among their ranks the soldiers of two crack, full-strength, experienced German divisions: the 15th Panzer, which had fought all throughout the Desert Campaign, and the Hermann Goering Panzer, recently returned from Russia. The latter division was named after the flamboyant, roly-poly head of the Luftwaffe, Hermann Goering, who was known jokingly behind his back as 'Fat Hermann". But, Truscott knew, there would be nothing to joke about the way *they* would fight once the Allies had landed.

Now Lucien Truscott stared down at his young soldiers under the burning sun of Africa. He knew full well his responsibilities to them. Soon he would order them into battle, and undoubtedly before this month of July 1943 was over, some of these earnest young men blinking up at him would be dead - at his orders. But he was a general, cut in the Patton mould, given to bold, dashing phrases. So he kept his doubts to himself and kept his speech short and spirited. "You are going to meet the Boche", he rasped in that throaty voice of his that would gain him the nickname of 'Old Gravelmouth' with his British colleagues later in the campaign in Italy; "Carve your name on his face!"[8]

NOTES
1. L. Truscott. Command Missions. New York: Scribner's, 1953.
2. E. Rickman. Soldier. New York: Harper and Row, 1953.
3. Murphy, op. cit.
4. Simpson, op. cit
5. North Africa. Washington, DC: Department of the Army, 1942
6. Murphy, op. cit.
7. Simpson, op. cit
8. Ibid.

7

Friday, July 9, 1943.

The great wind struck the largest seaborne assault force the world had ever seen till then with savage fury. In an instant the ugly, awkward landing craft rode up and down the white capped waves, as if they were on a giant roller coaster. For their part, the bigger ships in the great armada strained to keep the timetable. Desperately, they punched their way through the vicious, howling storm, shipping tons of cold, green water.

Now the storm rose steadily, as the 2,500 transports, merchantmen, liners, oilers, battleships, and other vessels grew ever closer to the enemy coast. It shrieked and roared to an earsplitting crescendo. Force four... force five... force six... Would it never stop? Within the hour, the convoys that had converged here in this wild, angry sea, from North Africa, Britain, the United States, were being tossed and buffeted by a force seven gale! It looked as if God himself were conspiring to stop this Allied invasion of Hitler's vaunted *Festung Europa*.

Now the huge invasion fleet was racked by a terrible stomach churning, nauseating outbreak of seasickness. Even some of the sailors were green and hanging onto stanchions, unable to carry out their duties, as the Sirocco flung the sea at the ships, and swept their decks so that they looked like half-awash submarines. Soldiers lay helpless in their own vomit everywhere. The heads were clogged and the decks between the roof-high bunks were awash with puke. Even the rumour that the whole operation had been ordered cancelled by no less a person than Supreme Commander Eisenhower, if the weather did not improve soon, had no effect. All the green soldiers wanted to do was to die - and have done with the whole miserable business.

Audie Murphy was no exception. After the war he admitted that he, like the rest of his company, had been 'green to the gills' that terrible Friday as the invasion fleet (and with it the plan of attack) was put in jeopardy by the storm.

Then, as a worried Eisenhower in nearby Malta really began to seriously consider what to do about Operation Husky, the luck of the Allies changed. As abruptly as the storm had blown up, it began to calm down in the strange manner of the Sirocco. There was a sudden transformation. The hot fierce wind that had started hundreds of miles away to the south in the Sahara Desert ceased with startling suddenness. Instead of the great raging, whitecapped waves, there was a calm sea, gentle ruffled by a fatigued breeze, under a heaven full of silver stars. The invasion was on!

Now the soldiers began to move across the deck in an awkward, stiff-legged gait to the waiting boats, each man's fingers hooked under the belt of the man in front, platoon linked to platoon, until a whole company coiled in and out across the wet deck like a human snake.

Laden like pack animals with rifles, automatics, picks, shovels, packs - almost one hundred pounds of equipment - the men clambered down the swaying rope ladders and cargo nets to the wildly bobbing landing craft.

Among the Americans of Patton's two assault divisions, the 3rd and 45th Infantry, was Audie Murphy, feeling 'scared and seasick'. Now, at five o'clock on the morning of Saturday July 10, he climbed out of the landing craft and began to wade ashore at Yellow Beach, just east of the Sicilian town of Licata. Both divisions landed with little opposition. After firing a few shells, the Italian coastal artillerymen fled into the interior leaving the *Americanos* to stumble up the sand virtual unopposed. Indeed, so easy was the landing that the beach engineers, supposedly preparing the beaches for the second wave, forgot their duties altogether and set about looting the personal effects of the men of the 45th ('Thunderbird') Division, which didn't endear the rear echelon men to the infantry.

Audie Murphy had no time to concern himself with the inequities of the 'canteen commandos' of the rear echelon. His B Company had just lost one man to shellfire. Now they were being hurried inland by their officers, with Murphy grudgingly carrying out an assignment he bitterly disliked. Just prior to the invasion he had been given the job of company runner - again his youthful looks had caught up with him - and now he felt himself little better than an officer's dogsbody.

Not for long, however. Driving from the coastal township of Licata toward the bigger town of Canicatti, Murphy came under enemy fire for the first time. The youngster who had declared a few days before that he had felt 'scared and seasick' suddenly forgot all his fears. According to his first platoon Commander, Lt. W. H. Reeves, just as the platoon was 'pinned down on a hillside Murphy jumped up, started firing from the hip and yelling for the rest of us to follow. He was that kind of soldier'.[1]

Soon after Murphy was promoted to corporal and put back on combat duty. Now he would never leave frontline action until he finally won his Medal of Honor in 1945 and the top brass decided he had had enough. (Even then they would find it exceedingly difficult to keep him out of the firing line.)

It was at about this time that the nineteen-year-old killed his first men. He was ahead of Company B together with the scouts, when two Italian officers tried to make a break for it to their front. 'They should have surrendered', he wrote in his autobiography. Unfortunately - for them - they didn't! Instead 'they mount two magnificent white horses and gallop madly away. My act is instinctive. Dropping to one knee, I fire twice. The men tumble from the horses, roll over and lie still'.[2]

The young officer in charge of the patrol was horrified. "Now why did you do that?" he demanded.

"What should I have done", Audie countered, seemingly unmoved by the fact that he had just killed two fellow human beings. "Stood there with egg on my face waving them good-bye?"

"You shouldn't have fired", the officer persisted.

"That's our job", Audie said hotly. "They would have killed us if they'd had the chance. That's their job. Or have I been wrongly informed?"

The officer gave up. He shrugged and said, "To hell with it. I guess you did the right thing."[3]

Later Audie would write: 'Now I have shed my first blood, I feel no qualms; no pride; no remorse. There is only a weary indifference that will follow me throughout the war.'[4]

A quarter of a century afterward, he would tell an interviewer, "The way I remember it, the first shock of combat numbs your senses. That's a good thing because numbness keeps you from running away. The shock in combat is a little like the shock after a wound. You don't feel the pain right away. Then after another little while you sit down and appreciate the situation. You realize you are going to do what you have to do. Once you accept the fact that you are going to get it, if you are going to get it, your mind clears up. You become decisive. That is important because indecision kills people in war more often than anything else."[5]

Indecisive, Audie Murphy would never be - perhaps that is why he survived so long. Still, he paid a terrible price for that survival. While those who hesitated died, Audie Murphy would live on to be tormented to the end of his days, always sleeping with a loaded pistol beneath his pillow, tortured by nightmares of the war. "There was the nightmare, the recurrent nightmare", he would tell the same interviewer five years before his death. "I would dream I am on a hill and all these faceless people are charging up at me. I am holding a Garand rifle, the kind of rifle that I used to take apart blindfolded. And in the dream, every time I shoot one of these people, a piece of the rifle flies off until all I have left is the trigger guard."[6]

In all the long months of planning for the invasion of Sicily, the planners had basically concentrated on landing the troops. Little consideration had been given to the future strategy once that objective had been obtained. Now the Italo-German defences on the coast had been overcome with surprising speed, especially on the American front. What were the Allies going to do next? With the Supreme Commander far away in Algiers in North Africa, the man on the spot knew what he was going to do. General Patton, the Commander of the U.S. Seventh Army, decided he wanted the headlines; he would capture Palermo, a major city, but with no strategic importance.

To do this, Patton formed a provisional Corps, consisting of the U.S. 82nd Airborne Division, the 2nd Armored Division (nicknamed the 'Hell on Wheels'), and Truscott's 3rd Infantry Division. Under the command of General Keyes, this Corps was to race northwest - well away from the real strategic target, the city of Messina, through which the Germans could escape to the mainland across the Straits, once they started to withdraw in earnest - and capture Palermo. As Patton radioed to Truscott, 'I want you to capture Palermo in five days!'[7]

It was a tall order; Truscott's men and the paratroopers of the 82nd were going to have to hike the whole way - and it was one hundred miles under the burning hot sun of midsummer Sicily!

Although later the official U.S. history of the war characterized the march as 'little more than a road march', Col. 'Slim Jim' Gavin of the 82nd Airborne thought, 'it was a strange business unlike anything else I encountered during the war. Suddenly a machine gun or antitank weapon would open up and then the white flags would appear. A shot had been fired for 'honour', but it was just as likely to cause casualties as a shot fired in anger.'[8]

A very sick Audie Murphy toiled up the dusty roads under the burning sun, trying all the time not to vomit, but not succeeding. 'The march toward Palermo became virtually a foot race', he wrote later. 'We had to average twenty-five to thirty miles a day over rugged terrain. Dust lay over the highways like a smoke screen; not a cloud appeared in the sky. Often we could not stop even to eat. We gulped our rations as we walked.'[9]

The dust stained infantrymen, their shirts wet with sweat, plodded on. Patton, living off his nerves and now in a state almost bordering on hysteria (soon he would strike the first of the two soldiers he would assault during the Sicilian campaign), was always urging them forward, harassing their commanders, and threatening courts-martial if his orders were not carried out.

Audie knew nothing of Patton's ambitions. All he was concerned with was his frail body, which was now giving him serious trouble. 'My brain swam; and my internal organs rumbled. Finally I could take it no longer. I fell out of the ranks, lay down on the roadside and heaved until I thought I would lose my stomach.'[10]

At that moment a jeep halted near him and a major called out, "What's wrong? Are you sick, soldier?"

According to Murphy in his autobiography, he answered, "No sir, I'm just spilling my guts for the hell of it!"

The major wasn't offended. "Maybe you'd better report to the medics", he said.

"Yes sir", Murphy answered.

'But I did not. I rose to my feet and staggered up the road, cursing the war in detail.'[11]

Next day he blacked out completely.

One day before the commanding general's deadline, the provisional Corps took Palermo and Patton made his triumphal entrance, to be greeted by the wildly enthusiastic *Sicilianos*, who had long experience in changing sides swiftly. But the flowers and the cheers didn't elate Patton. The Sicilians went to the bottom of his 'personal shit-list' even below the hated 'A-rabs'.

Audie Murphy knew nothing of Patton's triumph. For he was in hospital suffering from what he later reported to be 'malaria', lathered in sweat. In fact, he had been taken to the Palermo military hospital suffering from 'nasopharynitis'. The would-be hero had been struck down by the kiddies' complaint - *inflammation of the nose and throat!*

For five days Audie languished in the hospital, while the wards started to fill up with real casualties. For the first time Patton's army had met the A-team - the Germans - and they were hitting back hard, unlike their erstwhile ally, the Italians.

After a week, Audie Murphy was again passed fit for duty and was on his way back to a hard-pressed 3rd Division. 'As we pass through Palermo', he recorded later, 'on the way to the front, the streets swarm with our men. The natives gape, and supply trucks speed through the town. Lines of soldiers, with their weapons slung on their shoulders, stand before brothels, patiently awaiting their turn. Individual dignity has been transformed to fit the nature of war.'[12]

The young soldier had no time for the dubious pleasures of the Sicilian city, with its truculent, fawning men, ancient crones, big-bosomed, dark-haired *ragazze*, and the children, flashing their winning, dark-eyed smiles at the American innocents, hands out for *'caramelli'* and gum, offering under their voice to sell their sisters the next moment, 'good girl... nice jig-jig' - naturally for an appropriate fee.

For General Patton had decided he would indulge himself in another race against Montgomery, the British general whom he was wont to call, 'the little limey fart'. Disgruntled by the fact that General Bernard Montgomery's Eighth Army seemed to be making all the headlines and that the BBC had reported the British were doing most of the fighting while his men rested 'in the shade of the olive trees', Patton now wanted to win what he considered was a race for the last major objective in Sicily, Messina. Montgomery's, Chief of Staff, Freddie de Guingand protested there was 'no such thing as a fucking race', but Patton thought otherwise. In his opinion, Montgomery was going all out to beat him to the city. He ordered Truscott's 3rd Division, which had been resting for a week, into action. It would relieve the weary GIs of the 45th Division and capture Messina first.

NOTES
1. Simpson, op. cit.
2. Murphy, op. cit.
3. Ibid.
4. Ibid.
5. Esquire, op. cit.
6. Ibid.
7. L. Faxago. Patton. New York: Dell, 1970.
8. J. Gavin. On to Berlin. New York: Viking, 1978.
9. Murphy, op. cit
10. Ibid.
11. Ibid.
12. Ibid.

8

On August 1, the regrouped 3rd Division was concentrated, ready for the final attack on Messina. With the 30th Infantry in the lead, the division attacked across a river position that had previously held up the men of the 'Thunderbird' Division. By the afternoon of the second day of the assault they were across. Now it was the turn of the 'Can Do' Regiment. They advanced up to the bank of the Furiano River, where, as Audie Murphy described it later, 'we are caught in a concentration of artillery and mortar fire. The earth shudders; and the screaming of shells intermingles with the screaming of men. We fall back, reorganize and again storm forward.'[1]

Again the German barrage descended upon the assault infantry, and once again the disorganized 15th pulled back. In spite of Truscott's urging, pressured as he was by an increasingly impatient Patton, his men were forced to dig in. The Germans were determined to hold the Furiano line as long as possible. Behind it they were swiftly withdrawing the rest of their men from Messina across the Straits to the mainland. In Sicily there was not going to be the same kind of mass surrender that had taken place in North Africa only three months before; German public opinion would not tolerate yet another Stalingrad.

So the men of the 3rd Division and elements of two German panzer divisions slogged it out for five long, bloody days on the Furiano.

On the fourth day of the desperate American attempts to cross the river, Audie was pulled out of the fighting to guard a machine gun post, while the rest of the regiment attacked under the cover of a smoke screen. 'The assignment suits me', he wrote later. 'I now see that the fighting will not run out.'[2] So while his comrades struggled desperately to turn the German flank, the young infantryman sat out the battle, viewing the fighting beyond as if he were in a movie theatre watching a newsreel, whiling away the time eating the plump black grapes that he had found growing on some abandoned vines near the machine gun post. Then as his comrades battled and died, Audie began to suffer too. He had stuffed himself with too many of the juicy grapes and he was attacked by 'a bad case of diarrhea'. First the kiddies' complaint and now 'the squitters'. For a future hero, this was a poor initiation into the glory of the battlefield!

But then the whole Sicilian campaign was now turning into something of a farce. On August 16, after successfully breaking through the Germans, the leading elements of the 3rd started to enter the suburbs of Messina. Hurriedly, the nervous local dignitaries offered to surrender the city to General Truscott.

The 3rd's Commander was forced to decline, although he would have dearly loved to accept. But that wasn't to be. Patton had ordered that there would be a parade and *then* a formal surrender; and the 3rd Division would be led in by no less a person than the Seventh Army Commander himself! Patton was not about to let the newspaper headlines back in the States escape him. *The glory of capturing Messina was going to be George S. Patton's!*

Angrily, the men of the 3rd Division did as ordered, waiting on the outskirts, watching in helpless rage as the Germans ferried ever more troops across the Straits of Messina to Italy, where they would fight another day. Bradley, one of Patton's Corps Commanders, was 'so angry', he wrote later, 'at Patton's megalomania that I was half tempted to enter the city myself and greet him on a street corner when he arrived.'[3]

At ten o'clock on August 17, 1943, Patton drove up in his command car, sirens shrieking as usual, and demanded of the waiting Marnemen, "What in hell are you all standing around for?"[4] He waved his swagger stick at the dusty, shabby infantrymen. The men of the 3rd started to move into the seaport.

'Messina no longer had anything worth bombing', one eyewitness reported later. 'It was just a pile of rubble where people used to live. But as we came in, life had come back to the rubble. The people were streaming out of their caves, marching through the streets, yelling and cheering, drowning out their small bands whose members were playing on their battered instruments. In the back streets we could see old people and kids and pregnant women loaded down with sacks of flour and boxes of canned goods. Too long starved, they had broken into an Italian warehouse, almost rioting, grabbing as much as they could carry.'[5]

Patton, every inch the conqueror, did not seem to notice either the fact that the enemy civilians were cheering him as a 'liberator' or that behind the scene in this military farce, mass looting was taking place unhindered. Standing upright in his command car, as immaculate as ever, he wore his 'war face number one', a stern, imperious look, which he practised assiduously in front of the mirror in the privacy of his own quarters.

By now a token British force had arrived at the other end of the city, for as Truscott remarked maliciously, "General Montgomery had no doubt been anxious to beat General Patton into Messina for he had landed a patrol a few miles down the coast for the purpose of being here before us."[6]

Well, if the 'little limey fart' had, he had failed. Now the British officer in charge, Brigadier D. V. Currie of the 4th Armoured Brigade, treated his 'defeat' gallantly. He saluted, extended his hand, and said, "I congratulate you, sir... It was a jolly good race."[7]

Thus the campaign in Sicily ended on a note of farce. 'The jolly good race' had cost the Allies in thirty days of combat, 22,000 young men, British, Canadian, and American, in dead and wounded. Already the 3rd Infantry Division had begun to live up to its mournful record. For of those 22,000 casualties, *five thousand* of them came from that one division alone (and over a quarter of a million Allied soldiers had been involved in the campaign). And for what? Admittedly the Allies now had a toehold in *Festung Europa*. But the great majority of the German enemy had escaped. Forty thousand of the Führer's most experienced troops had now decamped to the mainland where they would continue to fight the 3rd for many a month to come.

A few days later, Audie Murphy missed the opportunity of listening to 'Ol Blood and Guts' give his celebrated, blistering, fighting speech to the officers and sergeants of the victorious 3rd Division; he was still a corporal and lacked the necessary stripes. Not that the matter bothered him greatly. In that strange, apathetic limbo that afflicts a fighting man after combat ceases and he slowly begins to come out of the nightmare of the most recent battle, he was starting to assess himself.

He had survived his first campaign without a scratch, although it was clear that he was not as physically tough as he should be. Within the month he had fallen sick twice.

He had seen his first men killed violently and he, too, had killed men. He had been involved in several firefights and an amphibious landing. In a way, he was already a veteran, in comparison with the pale-faced 'wet noses', coming to Sicily straight from the States to fill up the gaping holes in the ranks of the 3rd Division.

But already his first campaign had begun to take its toll on the nineteen-year-old. 'The Sicilian campaign has taken the vinegar out of my spirit', he wrote later. 'I have seen war as it actually is and I do not like it.'[8] 'Now it seemed', as one biographer put it, 'once he had killed, Murphy's spirit seemed to fade. He fell into a kind of existential void'.[9]

That void would become a kind of protective armour for Audie Murphy for the rest of the war. His naturally quick reflexes, his gambler's luck and love of risk, both bred in the black dirt of his native Texas, would not have been enough. He had to possess something else. In Murphy's case it was not that cynical hardening, that shell that the average infantryman acquires. He was not one who *appears* to become accustomed to the horrendous noise, the danger, the hardship, and who then abruptly, startlingly, is one day completely out of control. He weeps, he vomits, he shakes, unable to hold his rifle or make his legs move another step. Combat fatigue! Or he reaches that state where he simply no longer cares whether he lives or dies. He becomes slow and careless under fire, exposing himself recklessly, almost as if he is glad to have it done with, and be finished with the whole damned noisy, miserable business of combat.

Murphy had to possess something different, which saw him through those weeks, months, years of constant combat. Over the next two years, Audie Murphy would be in combat virtually all of the time in a division that was always in the forefront of the fighting; hence the 3rd Division's tremendous, appalling casualties. In Italy, southern France, Alsace, Germany, Austria. He would be wounded three times and each time he would return to the front, his nerve unbroken. Once a mortar shell landed at his feet and the two men on either side of him were killed, yet he remained unscathed physically and, so far as anyone could see, emotionally as well. Never once did he crack. Never once did his great spirit let him down.

Even when his best friend, Lattie Tipton*, was killed at his side in southern France, after his initial rage and feeling of loss, he could tell himself, 'Again I look at the Germans to be hated only impersonally. Again I see war as it is: an endless series of problems involving the blood and guts of men... I do not want to think beyond this. I need to march, to shoot, to destroy.' [10]

For all the terrible bloody months to come, Audie Murphy would be constantly on his toes, reflexes hyperactive, skinny little body always tensed for action and the next potentially lethal move. Where tougher and older men cracked, broke down and wept, refused to fight any longer, he would keep going to the bitter end. 1943 - 1944 - 1945 - the years would slip by - and not one single time did Audie Murphy fail. In the four decades that have passed since the end of World War II when Audie Murphy became a public figure, and thus a legitimate target for sceptical questioning about his conduct as a soldier and his official record as America's most heroic soldier, not one of his former comrades or those who served under him as a platoon leader ever came forward to accuse him of unworthy conduct of any kind.

Not that he was without fear as a soldier. Once he told his friend David McClure that 'when moving into a fight, he had the feeling that somebody had stuck a cold hand in the middle of his intestines and was twisting them into knots. But the feeling went away usually once he got into action'.[11] He also told McClure 'that it seemed that he had been grappling with fear all his life. He and fear had each other by the throat, and he never knew which was going to conquer'.[12] In the event, Audie Murphy constantly conquered that fear.

But what was the price? Of his original 235-man company, which set off for Sicily in July 1943, only one other man besides Murphy was going to survive the whole war - all the others were killed or invalided home. What effect did the killing in combat of an estimated *240* Germans have on the young Texan? The years to come were to show that, whatever his conduct under fire, the war did not leave him unscathed.

NOTES

1. Murphy, op. cit.	7. Farago, op. cit
2. Ibid.	8. Murphy, op. cit.
3. O. Bradley. Bradley: A Soldier's Story. New York: Random House, 1978	9. Esquire, op. cit.
	10. Murphy, op. cit.
4. Ibid.	11. McClure to author
5. Letter to author	12. Ibid.
6. Truscott, op. cit.	13. Ibid.

*In his autobiography, To Hell and Back, Murphy uses pseudonyms for Tipton and the other men who served with him in the war, but in this book I use their real names.

TWO

TOUGH OLD GUT

You've got to believe you are right to be a good soldier. That's why mercenaries are no good. It's emotion that makes a good fighting man and knowing you are fighting for a good cause.

Audie Murphy

9

'My American Eagle', Churchill called him jovially the first time they had met in England, drinking brandy into the small hours, happy that the Americans were finally going to get into the war. It was on account of his huge beak of a nose that dominated the craggy face set on a long, lean, rangy body. Now after thirty years or more in the U.S. Army, the 'American Eagle' had achieved a combat command at last.

His experience was very limited, his sum total of combat being one afternoon back in France in 1917. He had been feeding his company of the U.S. 11th Infantry into the trenches when the new boys had been hit by a 'Fritz' barrage. He was struck by a shell fragment before he fired a single shot in anger and was evacuated immediately. Thereafter, he spent the rest of World War I in supply.

At the beginning of World War II he had been an obscure lieutenant colonel, but after Pearl Harbor, his rise had been meteoric, easily overtaking that of officers much older and more senior than himself, including Patton. Patton, five years older than he, hated him with a passion. For 'Ol Blood and Guts', the 'American Eagle' was a 'no-good, unreliable sonuvabitch!'

Now this general, who was vain, ambitious, and totally devoted to furthering his own career, was to be the arbiter of Audie Murphy's fate for the rest of the time the latter spent in Italy. His name was Mark Clark; his command was the newly formed Fifth Army, which, together with Montgomery's Eighth Army, was going to slice its way up the 'soft underbelly', as Churchill called Italy with unwarranted optimism. Soon that 'soft underbelly' was going to be transformed into a 'tough old gut'.

As August gave way to September 1943, it became clear that, after the downfall of Mussolini, Italy would get out of the way. As a result, the Allied Commanders agreed that a mere landing in the toe of Italy would be too tame a response to the opportunity now offered them. In addition to Montgomery's routine crossing of the Straits of Messina in the extreme south of Italy, a much more daring operation was needed.

Thus it was decided to land three divisions, two of them British, under the command of General Clark, at the pretty Italian coastal resort of Salerno. Once ashore, this force would strike north for Naples. Naples would then become the Allies' most important supply port in southern Italy, from which they would supply the whole 'lightning' campaign.

Montgomery didn't like the idea. He thought it too risky. With eighteen German divisions still in Italy, all of which could be speedily rushed south, what chance did a mere three Allied divisions stand? But after the Eighth Army's own successful landing on September 3, when the most serious opposition to the Canadian 1st Division had come from a puma and a monkey that had escaped from the zoo at Reggio and had bitten a Canadian infantryman, the sole casualty, Montgomery's doubts vanished. It was decided to go ahead with the bold operation, in spite of the fact that Montgomery's army would be separated from the landing site at Salerno by three hundred miles of very rugged terrain. Thus if Clark's Fifth Army ran into trouble, Montgomery's Eighth Army would find it very difficult to go to the aid of the mixed Anglo-American force.

Clark was unconcerned. After a lifetime waiting for this chance, he was not going to be put off by any risk, imagined or otherwise. That night, September 8, 1943, as the convoy carrying his army approached the Italian mainland, he read a prayer, as was his custom, just before he went to bed. It read: "With Thee I am unafraid for on Thee my mind is stayed. Though a thousand foes surround, safe in Thee I shall be found… In the air, on sea, or land. Thy sure protection is at hand."[1] It is recorded that the commanding general slept soundly.

At the start everything seemed to be going well, perhaps *too well*. The 100,000 British and 69,000 Americans, some ten miles off the Italian shore, were mostly in a state of high elation. The BBC from London had just announced some tremendous news. Italy had surrendered. Moments later the news had been followed by an extract from a speech made by Eisenhower from Radio Algiers. In it, he stated, 'The Italian government has surrendered its armed forces unconditionally… Hostilities will cease at once and the Italians can now have the assistance and support of the United Nations to expel the German oppressors from Italian soil.'[2]

For several seconds the infantrymen had simply stood there stunned, unable to comprehend the news. Then it had registered. Now spontaneous cheering broke out. Beer and bottles of Algerian red wine passed from hand to hand. Officers consumed their monthly drink allowance in one go. Sing-songs were organized. On the American ships, some of the jubilant troops asked their padres for impromptu services of thanksgiving. Everywhere there was laughter and happiness. The faces that had been tense and strained were now smooth and relaxed. *The war was over!*

Their optimism was misplaced. Already the day before, 'Smiling Albert', as Field Marshal Kesselring, the German Commander in Italy, was known to his troops, due to the fact that his broad, ugly face always seemed set in a smile, had issued two orders: one, to disarm the treacherous Italian Army; two, to prepare to repel an Allied landing in the area around Naples.

It had not taken his Intelligence men long to discover Clark's intentions. The Luftwaffe had already spotted the invasion fleet in its North African harbour of Bizerte; lax Allied security had aided the Germans. It was recorded that onlookers and well-wishers seeing the invaders off had called jokingly, 'See Naples - *and live*, boys!' Indeed one British Major General was sent home in disgrace just before the fleet departed because the censor caught him writing to his wife that he would be celebrating their wedding anniversary in Italy.

As for the local Italians around Naples, it was too obvious where the *Americanos* were going to land. For nearly a week their bombers had been dropping their deadly little eggs all over the area, including the town of Salerno itself. But the place's docks had been left untouched. Wasn't that indication enough that the *Americanos* were going to land there? In that first week of September 1943, the question asked by the locals was not 'where?' but simply *'when?'*

Now as Clark's men prepared to land - unopposed - the German 16th Panzer Division received the code word *'Orkan'* (hurricane), from Kesselring's HQ. Immediately the plan worked out days before went into operation. The tanker's reconnaissance unit, under the command of Major von Alvensleben, drove to the coast and disarmed the staff of the Italian 22nd Coastal Division. Its Commander refused to hand over his pistol to the hard-faced German aristocrat, crying "A Conzaga never lays down his arms!"[3] It was a dramatic nineteenth-century gesture. But von Alvensleben's troopers had no sense of occasion. One of them jerked up his Schmeisser machine gun pistol and ripped the old Italian general's chest apart with a cruel burst.

Almost immediately the advanced elements of the 16th Panzer began to take over the demoralized Italians' positions, as down below in the beautiful bay, the unsuspecting, jubilant Allies sailed straight into the trap.

For nearly two weeks the 16th Panzer Division held the thirty-six miles of the Salerno Gulf against the whole weight of nearly five Anglo-American divisions, while 'Smiling Albert' poured more and more men southward. 'See Naples - *and die!*' had now become more than a tired wisecrack for most of the hard-pressed infantrymen edging their way up the beach at Salerno.

A desperate Clark, panicking as he often did when things began to go wrong, as always putting the blame on the failings of other generals, started to bring up more reserves, as the British grew closer to Naples, the vital supply port. On September 17, Audie Murphy's 3rd Division was alerted for action. Truscott sailed with his 30th Regiment on the night of September 17/18, followed two days later by the 7th Regiment. Then on September 21, Colonel Ritter's 15th Regiment, including Corporal Audie Murphy, waded ashore at Battipaglia, a few miles south of Salerno. Here the 15th went into action immediately, being sent into the mountains that overlooked the gulf to protect the 3rd's left flank.

Murphy, like the rest of his buddies of Company B, had thought that now that Italy had surrendered it was going to be easy. He recorded later: 'We land with undue optimism... We are prepared for a quick dash to Rome.'[4] Almost immediately the 3rd ran into the enemy, some of the best troops that 'Smiling Albert' had under command, including his feared elite paratroopers - 'the Green Devils'. Now for fifty long days (a staggering *seven weeks*), the Marnemen would be in constant action. The 'quick dash' would 'soon slow to a walk... and the walk to a push'.[5]

Finally, as far as Company B was concerned, it stopped altogether. For to their immediate front there was a German machine gun nest hidden in some reeds near the bank of a stream. Here for the first time Murphy engaged in what was virtually hand-to-hand combat, a foretaste of what was to come.

Together with his best friend 'Lattie' Tipton 'a skinny, long-necked, homely man with a Tennessee ring to his voice'[6], as Murphy described him after the war, he decided to knock out the German post. The rains of the winter had not come yet and the stream was virtually dried out so the two of them, supported by other members of Company B, advanced along it toward the waiting Germans

Murphy's nerves were tense as they crept through the brittle, dusty reeds, which seemed to make a hellish racket. But Tipton, married and much older, seemed quite calm. As he often proclaimed in his plaintive accent, "Come on - they can kill us, but they can't eat us. It's agen the law!"[7] He pushed forward almost eagerly.

Suddenly - startlingly - a helmeted head popped up from a hole to Murphy's front. There was no mistaking that helmet. He dropped to his knees in the dust and fired in the same instant. Tipton reacted equally quickly. Ripping out the pin of his grenade, he hurled it toward the German position. It exploded in a flash of ugly yellow flame and smoke. Even before the smoke had cleared, he had thrown two more.

Now Tipton, carried away by the crazy blood lust of battle, decided to go it alone. Lanky body crouched, his last grenade clutched in his dirty hand, he walked along the bank, while behind him Murphy shouted urgently, "Keep down! Keep down! Are you nuts?"[8]

But Tipton didn't seem to hear. Suddenly he wheeled around, lobbed the grenade expertly to the other side of the road and dropped swiftly. There was the familiar muffled sound of a grenade exploding - then silence.

Hastily Murphy scrambled to his feet and dashed forward. Tipton had risen too and was staring down at the men he had killed. Five of them, sprawled out in the violent extravagant posture of those killed in battle.

Tipton's bold one-man attack on the German machine gun nest that day confirmed Murphy's admiration for the older soldier who he said 'taught me the meaning of courage' and who he thought 'the bravest man I ever knew'.[9] He began to develop a very close friendship with Tipton, who was married and had a nine-year-old daughter, whose photograph in pigtails he was never tired of showing to any one who was remotely interested. After the war, Murphy would tell a magazine correspondent that "I guess I was closer to Tipton than anyone else - with a friendship that you usually tried to avoid because most likely it was going to end tomorrow".[10]

It was the kind of friendship that two buddies could only develop in combat. If, as the wartime cliche had it, 'there are no atheists in a foxhole', there are no heroes either. The men of Murphy's platoon who were going to share the next miserable months together in the Italian campaign had no secrets from each other. Under the daily strains, stresses, and dangers of combat, a man's true personality *had* to emerge.

Perhaps it is significant that it was to be *after* Tipton was killed in action at Murphy's side, tricked into being shot by a German offering to surrender, that old, old trick in combat that Tipton should not have fallen for, that Murphy turned into a fighting demon. Thereafter, when 'the death (of Tipton) made the war more real to, me'[11], Audie Murphy would win all his major medals for bravery in the short space of five months.

But for now, Tipton remained alive and the war in Southern Italy developed into a hard, slogging match. 'Smiling Albert' retreated admittedly, but he made the Anglo-Americans pay dearly for every yard of ground they gained. As one weary Intelligence officer put it, 'Every five hundred yards, there is a new defensive position for a company; every five miles a new line for a division'.[12] So after the capture of Naples by the British, the 'Battle for the Boot' became one more river to assault and one more mountain peak to be captured. Murphy remembered later, 'As we plod through the country, seeking contact with the enemy, the rain slashes down, wetting us to the skin'.[13]

In the first days of October, with the thin, bitter rain still falling, Murphy's 15th regiment reached the first great river line, one of the many that 'Smiling Albert' was going to use so expertly during the long campaign in Italy. Here, while General Truscott decided how he was going to attack the swollen river, Murphy, Tipton, and three other members of his platoon were ordered to set up a forward observation post in an abandoned German dugout.

With the Germans dug in within hailing distance on the other side of the Volturno, the five of them spent a miserable and interminable five days. They had nothing to do save 'to pull our shifts and fight insects'.[14] After three days of this clandestine underground existence, their spirits were low, even those of Tipton. Water was short, in spite of the river being close by, 'and we dare not eat lest the food increase our thirst. Nerves stand on edge. We growl at one another and quarrel over trifles red eyes gleam like the eyes of caged animals.'[15]

In the end, one of the little group could not stand the strain. In spite of the protests of the others, he determined that they would have water from the river. He didn't get far. The enemy on the other side of the Volturno spotted him almost immediately, and he was shot dead before he had gone more than a few yards, clutching the empty canteen to his ruined body as if it were the Holy Grail.

A few hours later, the exhausted forward patrol was relieved. The 3rd was crossing the Volturno in force. But already another natural barrier, the Rapido River and the surrounding mountain peaks, was awaiting the weary dogfaces. It seemed there was no end to them; and Audie Murphy was be-ginning to learn that war was not a place where 'bugles blew, banners streamed and men charged gallantly across flaming hills'. [16] The youth des-perate for glory was now realizing that battle was a dirty, hard, unrelenting slog, where men die obscurely, for 'no apparent purpose and no apparent reason'.

NOTES
1. M. Blumenson. Mark Clark. New York: Congdon and Weed, 1984
2. Daily Express. July 1943.
3. R Trevalyn. Rome '44. London: Collins, 1984
4. Murphy, op. cit.
5. Ibid.
6. Saturday Evening Post, The. September 1955.
7. Ibid.
8. Murphy, op. cit.
9. Saturday Evening Post, The. Op. cit.
10. Ibid.
11. Murphy, op. cit.
12. BBC War Report. London, 1945
13. Murphy, op. cit.
14. Ibid.
15. Ibid.
16. Ibid.

10

Winter came with extraordinary abruptness. One moment all had been bright sunshine and brilliant white dust, next the showers fell, and then suddenly everything was mud and snow. With the winter there came the pitched battles - no longer the skirmishes of the road north. Hundreds died daily and the corroding, bitter cold made it hellish for those who clung to life. That winter an American Corps Commander wrote: 'It has rained for two days and is due to rain two more... It is as cold as hell I don't see how our men stand what they do.'[1]

Their life became more primitive and less satisfying than that of prehistoric man. One officer recalled: 'After the first couple of days we had to stretch groundsheets to catch rainwater for drinking. No chance of shaving as any cut would have become infected. But I had a good wash in a shellhole. Men's feet and hands were swollen after rain and exposure... Had only one blanket each... and had to sleep two or three together to keep warm.'[2]

Chest and lung complaints became epidemic. Trench foot was a major problem. This type of foot rot that older officers remembered from the trenches in the Old War could immobilize a man for days, or for good. In the Fifth Army it became the major source of casualties; too many of the dogfaces kept their shoes on for weeks. Tissue died, sores broke out, and then the gangrene set in. It was not uncommon in the forward dressing stations to see long lines of men spread out on stretchers, with wads of purple-tinged cotton stuck between their toes, while harassed doctors went down the rows smelling each man's feet for the sweet stench of putrefaction. Shoes had to be cut off swollen feet and sometimes the feet themselves were cut off, too.

As the American war correspondent Ernie Pyle, who would be killed by a sniper's bullet in the Pacific before the war was over, noted at the time: 'Our troops were living in almost inconceivable misery. The fertile black valleys were knee-deep in mud. Thousands of men had not been dry for weeks. Others lay at night in the high mountains with the temperatures below freezing and the thin snow sifting over them. They dug into the stones and slept in little chasms and behind rocks and in half-caves. They lived like men of prehistoric times... How they survived the dreadful winter was beyond us.'[3]

Naturally, Murphy and the men of the 3rd Division were, as usual, in the thick of it. Fighting in the mountains against fresh German troops, the division battled its way toward the Rapido River, yet another of Kesselring's natural defensive positions. It was a struggle that the divisional history characterized as 'the most bitter and heartbreaking the division had ever undertaken... The enemy was dug in on solid rock, the only approaches to his strongholds being over heavily mined, narrow, slippery roads, deep gorges, and along sheer precipices'.[4]

In his autobiography, Murphy makes more of the difficulties of the ground than the opposition, writing, 'The terrain over which we advance is a nightmare for offensive troops. The narrow trails over which we advance are so treacherous that pack mules often lose their footing and tumble to their death. Sometimes the mules cannot make it at all. Supplies have to be dragged up the slope by men inching their way on all fours… The Germans holed up among the rocks are difficult to locate until we are upon them. The ground is slippery with mud; and visibility is cut drastically by a heavy autumn mist that lies over the land.'[5]

Slowly, as if pushing a gigantic boulder up a steep mountainside, the 3rd, in conjunction with the rest of the Allied armies, ground its way up the boot of Italy. Mount Lungo… Hill 193… Mount Rotunda… Mount de la Defensa - remote grim mountains where scores of men died daily to gain a handful of ground, dying before they even knew the name of the place where fate overtook them.

During that period, Murphy wrote only one letter home that survived. It was scrawled on a V-mail form in a laboured hand in pencil, reading, 'Just a line to let you know I am fine and hope you are the same. I am in Italy and it is simalor (sic) to Sicily. I really don't know of what to write at the present but intend to write you a longer letter soon. So I am going to close for now saying good-bye & good luck'.[6]

It gave no indication of the kind of life the nineteen-year-old was living so far away from the black dirt of Texas. Men were being killed all around him, and he was doing his share of killing, too. But all he could say was, 'I really don't know of what to write', as if he were deliberately bottling it all up within himself; or as if he could not find the words to depict the immensity of the horror through which he was going. No doubt he paid later for this deliberate suppression of what was happening to him. As he would confess to a reporter after the conflict was over: "War robs you, mentally and physically, it drains you. Things don't thrill you anymore. It's a struggle every day to find something interesting to do… It made me grow up too fast. You live so much on nervous excitement that when it is over you fall apart."[7]

By now the 3rd had lost 683 men killed, 2,412 wounded, and 170 missing in action, nearly one-fifth of its original strength. Again the 'Rock of the Marne' Division had paid a heavy price for a few score square miles of barren real estate. Suddenly, without any real explanation, Truscott was ordered to pull his outfit out of the line. The Rapido River, overshadowed by Cassino, was still not crossed. The 3rd was relieved by the 36th Infantry Division, a National Guard unit from Texas, to which Murphy would belong after the war. In due course the 36th would be decimated in the crossing of the Rapido and a secret coven of its officers, embittered by what they thought of 'Butcher' Clark's strategy, swore they would bring the commanding general to trial after the war.*

But all that lay ahead. Meanwhile the survivors of the 3rd Division's Salerno campaign were trucked to a swampy area outside Naples, where they were told they would undergo a period of rigorous training. Why, neither they nor their commanding general knew. They settled into their tented camp, wondering what it was all about. 'Twice daily we have hot chow', Murphy wrote after the war, 'and we sleep on cots in pyramidal tents. Weariness drains from our flesh', and 'the mystery deepens'.[8]

The truth was that the first invasion of the European mainland, which had started with such high hopes, had bogged down and become a liability, eating up battalions, regiments, even whole divisions. Soon Clark would have a dozen different nationalities from Brazilians to New Zealanders fighting under his command. The front urgently needed new 'bodies'. One day, in the strictly segregated U.S. Army of the time, there would be a whole black U.S. infantry division fighting in his Army: something that would have been absolutely unthinkable only a year before.

Now the top brass who would command the invasion of France were leaving the theatre, Eisenhower first, then Bradley and the disgraced Patton, finally Montgomery himself. Behind them they left the second-rater Clark. But the campaign in Italy still had one very important and enthusiastic supporter, Winston Churchill.

As he lay ill in North Africa that winter and the 'fever flickered in and out', the problem of Italy was very much on his mind. He was the one who had campaigned most strongly for the attack on the 'soft underbelly ' that had turned out to be such a tough old gut. He wondered, as he fought gamely to live, 'Were we to leave it a stagnant pool from which we had drawn every fish we wanted?'[9]

He felt not. All the 'fish' had not yet been caught. Churchill, sick as he was, wanted a great new offensive to bring new life to the static Italian campaign. He wanted Rome itself captured, for he felt that the taking of the Italian capital would be a natural curtain raiser to the invasion of France. Churchill did not want any more of the hard, bitter, costly slogging up both coasts of the 'boot'. He saw the stagnation of the campaign in Italy as 'scandalous '. One decisive blow was needed to break the German hold on the country for good.

Churchill had long been an advocate of naval landings. Back in 1915 he had been the prime mover in the disastrous Gallipoli landing that had cost him his ministry and sent him out into the wilderness for the first time. Now he wanted to use sea power once more to turn the campaign in Italy in the Allies' favour.

Soon, he knew, nine-tenths of the existing Allied landing craft currently in the Mediterranean would be diverted to the Pacific and Far East, and to England for the coming invasion of France. Now, sick as he was,

* They attempted to do so, but the Supreme Court turned them down.

Churchill advocated that these craft assigned to Britain should be kept a few weeks longer in their African and Italian harbors for one last great seaborne operation.

The plan was simple. While Clark's Fifth Army assaulted the current German frontline positions, known as the 'Gustav Line', another Anglo-American force, under the command of American Corps Commander General John Lucas, would turn Kesselring's right flank by an amphibious landing to its rear.

Two divisions, the British 1st and the American 3rd, would land at a spot only thirty-five miles from Rome itself. Once the landing had been successfully completed, the assault force would head for Rome and at the same time cut off Kesselring's German Tenth Army holding the Gustav Line It was a bold, daring plan and the code name for this rapier like thrust was apt enough - Operation Shingle. Later the Tommies and the dogfaces who would carry it out would have another name for it. They called it *bloody Anzio!*

For the time being, Murphy and his comrades of the 3rd were being trained for the slaughter to come. The young soldiers knew that they were being prepared for something unpleasant; the infantry always knew. 'The men are in a dark mood', he wrote after the war. 'They are certain we are being prepared for slaughter. We pick fights with rear echelon troops. Tempers snap; and fists fly among old comrades at little provocation'.[10]

Rumours buzzed throughout the 3rd's tented camps, of course. 'We are to spearhead an assault on a new beachhead. We are to invade southern France. We are to be sent to England for a cross-channel D-Day'.[11] And some of the depressed dogfaces even got perilously close to the truth. 'And despite the amphibious training, some say we are to lead an all-out drive on Rome'.[12]

In the end, the young infantrymen of Murphy's Company B forgot their fears of the future - briefly at least - in the usual anodyne of the combat soldier: drink and women. Like the rest of his buddies, Murphy went to Naples during his off-duty hours, trying desperately to find some solace and to escape the ever-present company of males.

At the San Carlo Opera' House, untouched by the bombs and delayed action mines the retreating Germans had left behind (some went off months after they had left), a good company was playing *The Barber of Seville* and *Lucia di Lammermoor*. In the quays below the Excelsior Hotel, exclusive little black market restaurants served the kind of food most other European cities had not seen for years. There were even musicians in evening dress strolling from table to table, serenading the Allied officers and their plump dark-eyed Italian mistresses.

For while typhus raged in the back streets and the majority of Neapoltans eked out a miserable existence on potatoes, chestnuts, and figs. Corruption among the base troops and the black market in American goods flourished. 'The canteen commandos', as the frontline troops called the men of the rear echelon contemptuously, waxed fat and prosperous. One correspondent, Australian Alan Moorehead, thought 'the whole motif was that of a gaudy tropical flower that springs out of decay and smells rotten to the heart'.[13]

But not for Murphy and his comrades. Together with his friend Kelly, he strolled down the darkening streets, listening idly to the hawkers offering their wares with Italian persistence, "Hey, Joe, you wanta fried eggs? You wanna scramble eggs? You wanna beefsteck?"[14]

But it wasn't food that the young soldiers sought that evening. Many years later Murphy's ghostwriter, David McClure, made up a bittersweet Hollywood-type story about his subject's leave in Naples for his autobiography *To Hell and Back*. There was a sweet little Italian girl. Naturally she was called Maria. 'La guerra male', she told Murphy plaintively, as they held hands at the humble kitchen table under the suspicious gaze of her parents. Fortunately, just before he was supposed to go the air-raid sirens sounded and he stayed the night. What happened next we never learn, because in the fifties the Great American Public was not allowed to believe that its heroes went to bed to fornicate with members of the opposite sex. Thus it ended in the purple dawn with Murphy protesting that 'I'll write. I swear I'll write'. But of course, she didn't believe him, his Maria. She had seen it all before. "A soldier never writes; never come back. Eet ees not the first time", she told him sadly.[15] Thus they parted, star-crossed lovers.

The truth was, however, that for Murphy and his kind there were only the paid fleshpots. 'Good' girls were not interested in young American infantrymen. Murphy and his comrades took their pleasures in the manner of the usual combat soldier, brutalized by the life he was forced to lead and knowing that he was tolerated only for what he could pay, not for himself. Then drunk, sober, maudlin or happy, desperate or relaxed, they staggered back to the 'deuce-and-a-half', which would take them back to the war and the bloody battle to come.

Once again the newly promoted Staff Sergeant Murphy's frail body caught up with him. One day after the 3rd Division was alerted for the great attack on Anzio, Murphy fell ill yet once more. Desperately he tried to conceal his illness, as he tossed and turned on his cot in a high fever. 'The malarial attack puts me in an embarrassing situation. If I go to the infirmary, I think that it will seem I am deliberately trying to avoid the coming action. I lack the guts to take being thought a coward'.[16]

In the end his good friend Sergeant Kelly reported Murphy's illness to the Battalion Commander. The latter ordered Murphy to report sick. Thus while the 3rd's ships stole out into the January darkness for the landing at Anzio, Murphy, the would-be hero, was left behind in Naples in the hospital, with a raging fever and a temperature of 105°

NOTES

1. Blumenson, op. cit.
2. Trevalyn, op. cit.
3. Stars & Stripes. October 2, 1943
4. Taggart, op. cit.
5. Murphy, op. cit.
6. Simpson, op. cit.
7. Esquire, op. cit.
8. Murphy, op. cit.
9. Trevalyn, op. cit.
10. Murphy, op. cit.
11. Ibid.
12. Ibid.
13. A Moorehead. Eclipse. London: Collins, 1952
14. Murphy, op. cit
15. Ibid.
16. Ibid.

11

A thin slice of moon took the edge off the January darkness, as the great invasion came to anchor. It was now one o'clock on the morning of January 22, 1944. The Anglo-American force was less than a mile off the Italian shore. At two, the British 1st Infantry Division would land between Anzio and Nettuno. To the south of them, the American 3rd Division would do the same. First, however, the American Rangers would storm Anzio itself. Suicidal, was the opinion of most of those waiting to land.

Indeed most of those who had been through Salerno four months before thought the whole business would be a blood-bath. This included their commander, U.S. General Lucas - 'Old Corncob', as he was known to some of his officers due to the corncob pipe that he affected.

Now the invaders waited tensely. Any moment they could be discovered. In a flash the shore, dark, brooding and sinister, could well explode into flame. Here out in the bay, packed together like sardines in their ships, they would be sitting ducks. Each man was wrapped up in a cocoon of his own anxious thoughts. What in God's name was going to happen?

Suddenly, the heavy stillness was broken by a tremendous, earsplitting burst of fire. The British rocket ships had opened up. In less than ten minutes they fired 780 rockets, which blasted away the mines, the barbed wire, and any other obstacle facing the Rangers on the beaches. For those minutes all was noise, fiery flame, confusion. Then, as abruptly as it had commenced, the barrage stopped, leaving behind a loud, echoing silence. Again the waiting infantry tensed. It was going to happen now. *It had to!*

Nothing, absolutely nothing happened. The shore and the town beyond remained totally silent. Not a single shot was fired at the invasion fleet, not one. Slowly it dawned on the watchers. This was not going to be another Salerno. 'Smiling Albert' had been caught out. The Germans had been taken by surprise.

The first of the British started to land. Again no opposition, save that here and there the remaining mines, untouched by the rockets, exploded. Hastily the combat engineers were whistled up. They went to work at once, clearing a path for the stalled infantrymen. But that was about all the opposition the British met - a few odd mines. Even the pillboxes built by the Italians were unmanned by the enemy.

It was no different on the American beach. Truscott's 3rd landed according to plan. Its *War Journal* for that dawn reads like the account of some peacetime manoeuver:

0145. Rocket ships fired.

0220. Second Wave hit Red Beach. Landed dry.

61

0229. No opposition met by first and second waves.

0335. 1st Battalion, 7th Infantry reports: All Companies now fairly well together. No opposition.

The *Journal's* last entry reads simply: '0450: Congratulatory message from Commanding General VI Corps.'

Above the Americans of the 3rd, as the light grew ever brighter that January morning, the sky began to fill with more and more Allied fighters, forming an umbrella over the invaders. The only sign of German resistance was one lone cannon, sited further inland, firing at the beaches at regular intervals, but it was already being engaged by a British destroyer. Even the slaughter of Colonel Darby's Rangers did not take place as they advanced inland. Back at Clark's headquarters in the great echoing palace at Caserta, Darby had told the planners that his only hope of capturing his objectives would be to go in quick and fast: 'When I run out of the landing craft, I don't want to have to look right or left. I'll be moving too fast'.[1]

Now, however, the burly colonel of the Rangers, who would be dead before the year was out, advancing at the head of his men into Anzio, found there was no opposition. The only Germans he found there were dead, sprawled out in the dirt or were ashen-faced and terrified from the rocket bombardment, only too eager to throw up their hands and yell *"Kamerad!"* Within the hour all three Ranger battalions were passing through Anzio without a single casualty. It was all just too easy.

Indeed Truscott felt there was no need to go to the front to visit his forward elements. He decided to enjoy a good breakfast on the eggs that his cook, Private Lee Hang, had hoarded so zealously for him. Hardly had the general started to at his eggs and bacon on the hood of a jeep, watching his troops pouring ashore, when the top brass in the shape of General Clark and staff arrived. Hong was ordered to rustle up more eggs and bacon, and he went on his way grumbling, 'Goddamn, general's fresh eggs all gone to hell!'[2] But what did matter this fine January morning with victory in the air? Rome was just over the hills and there would be eggs aplenty for the victorious Anglo-Americans in the Italian capital soon.

Back in Africa, Field Marshal Harold Alexander, the British overall commander, told Churchill who was the father of Operation Shingle, 'We appear to have got almost complete surprise. I have stressed the importance of string-hitting mobile patrols being boldly pushed out to gain contact with the enemy, but so far have not received reports of their activities'. Delighted that the operation was not going to turn out to be another Salerno, Churchill replied, 'Thank you for your messages. Am very glad you are pegging out claims rather than digging in beachheads.'[3]

Meanwhile, Colonel Darby told his opposite number, Colonel Churchill of the British commandos, who had also landed unopposed, 'They (the brass) seem to think it will all be free love and nickel beer… I'm not so optimistic'.[4]

British war correspondent Wynford Vaughan-Thomas was also uneasy. He wrote to a colleague with the Eighth Army, 'It's just the normal military fuck-up with an American accent. We are commanded by a dear old pussy-cat, who purrs away, that we are all happy on the Beachhead, and in a sense we are'.[5]

That 'dear old pussy-cat' was the VI Corps Commander Gen. John Lucas, who was now fifty-four. On the day of his birthday he wrote in his diary, 'I am afraid I feel every year of it'[6] The following day he confided to the diary, 'I must keep from thinking of the fact that my order will send these men into desperate attack'.[7]

For Lucas had no confidence in the success of the Anzio landings. The shadow of Salerno hung heavily over him. Indeed, as he had embarked for Anzio, Clark had told him, "Don't stick your neck out, Johnny. I did at Salerno and got into trouble."[8] Now as his patrols started to probe inland, Lucas decided he was not about to 'stick his neck out'. Having gained surprise at the landing, he completely disregarded the advantage it gave him. Instead he dug his feet in. *Two* days after the landing he was still *thinking* of pushing out of the beachhead. 'I must keep in motion if my first success is to be of any value', he noted in his journal.[9]

Meanwhile, Kesselring was frantically summoning up reinforcements and fresh troops from all over Italy; and not only from his own command, but also from France and the Reich itself. Hitler personally ordered him to wipe out the 'sore of Anzio' and that he was determined to do, cost what it may. All this time, 'Old Corncob' continued to consolidate his beachhead, personally supervising the construction of the airfield and the air raid and antiaircraft systems. He was greatly concerned that his sea route and connection with Naples should not be cut off.

Another day passed. The British played cards and brewed up endless cups of 'char' on their little gasoline cookers. The Guards, in particular, had hoped for a bold dash to the Italian capital. The Irish Guards had declared happily, 'We'll give the Holy Father a holiday and make Father Brookes (the Catholic chaplain) acting unpaid Pope!'[10] Now they squatted on the beach and waited.

It was little different on the American front. Truscott sent out a reconaissance patrol, which prepared the bridges over the Mussolini Canal to the division's front for demolition. But that was all. They, too, waited impatiently for what was to come.

On the fourth day Lucas decided at last it was time to move. He ordered his mixed force of Rangers, paratroopers, and infantrymen, British and American, to start pushing inland. Here the advancing troops noticed that the hastily abandoned farmhouses and barns, 'would have made excellent defensive positions for the Germans, if they had been there waiting for the invaders. Even the outside bakehouses that most farms possessed, with their stout stone walls and roofs, would have made cannonproof pillboxes. But there were no Germans.

Another day passed in 'manoeuvring and displacing', as the history of the 3rd Division put it. There were occasional, small patrol actions, but that was all. Darby's Rangers hardly saw a German.

Then, at the end of the fifth day, the full force of the Luftwaffe fell on the beachhead. As fighters swept across the sands dragging their evil shadows behind them, going all out, cannon chattering, the dive-bombers arrived above the invasion fleet. The first into action were the antiquated Stukas. They fell out of the hard blue sky at a tremendous rate, sirens howling hideously, hurtling down vertically, as if hell-bent on destruction. Only at the very last moment did their pilots pull out of that death-defying dive to release a straggle of bombs at the fleet anchored virtually powerless below

But while the ships threw up a tremendous barrage at the Stukas, so that the sky was peppered with drifting blobs of black smoke, other German planes circled the fleet warily like wolves looking for a stray sheep. When they found one - some unfortunate vessel unprotected by the flak - they went into action. The pilots released the glider bomb that was slung under their wings and steered it unerringly toward the intended victim by radio beam. There was little that the fleet gunners could do against this new secret weapon that they had first experienced at Salerno; the German pilots kept well out of range and the flying bomb was much too small a target to hit, unless by sheer luck.

First the Germans struck the British destroyer *HMS Janus*. She went under within twenty minutes taking with her the skipper and 150 men of her crew. The rest were picked up singing the popular marching song of that sad year 'Roll Out the Barrel'... for 'the gang's all here'.

Their next victim was the fully illuminated, white-painted British hospital ship, *St. David*. She took a direct hit and began to sink immediately. Next the *Leinster* was hit as she was loading wounded, both Allied and German. A fire started but the crew went into action immediately, calmed the terrified patients and controlled the fire as the ship limped into the bay.

Meanwhile, the *St. David* was sinking rapidly, with only six minutes left before she went under for good. The harassed British nursing sisters and the doctors hurried back and forth, fitting their wounded patients into life preservers and convincing them to jump from the tilting deck into the freezing water below. One with both eyes bandaged was fitted with a preserver and *thrown* into the sea. He survived. Another who had just received major abdominal surgery to rectify a wounded stomach somehow managed to haul himself onto a raft. He also survived.

"Wait for the sisters!" the captain of the stricken ship yelled urgently, as the *St. David's* bows rose dramatically and frighteningly out of the water, for she was going down stern first. But there was no further waiting. The boats began to pull away quickly before they, too, were submerged by the rapidly sinking hospital ship. She went down, taking with her the captain, several nurses, and the senior doctors, plus most of the medical staff.

Bobbing up and down in the freezing water, an American soldier, who was wounded in the arm, noted the Red Cross brassards worn by the nurses floating next to him, and gasped, "I guess you're the only ones who believe in God here today!"[11]

The battle of Anzio had begun. The Germans were bombing and bombarding the beachhead with artillery, and they could hardly miss. There were 18,000 vehicles and 70,000 men packed in a tight area with little cover. Radio Berlin called it, 'a prison camp where the inmates feed themselves'. At Anzio there was no rear echelon. Everyone, including the nurses, was in the front line. Both General Truscott and General Penney of the British 1st Infantry were hit and wounded.

On January 30, the Germans launched their first counterattack. They killed both Battalion Commanders of the Rangers and decimated their ranks. Desperately Darby flung in his reserve battalion. It had no better luck, although Truscott, who had raised and trained the Rangers, tried to help. They, too, ran right into a trap and either surrendered, died, or fled. By the end of the day, Darby's Rangers no longer existed. From the 1st and 3rd battalions only six men came back. It was recorded that Darby, who had commanded them through North Africa, Sicily, and now Italy, and who was now without a command went into a farmhouse and wept.

This was the state of the beach at 'Bloody Anzio' when Audie Murphy arrived there one week after the landing to rejoin his battalion.

NOTES
1. Trevalyn, op. cit.
2. Truscott, op. cit.
3. E. Linklater. The Campaign in Italy. London: HMSO, 1951
4. Trevalyn, op. cit.
5. W. Vaughan-Thomas. Anzio. New York: Holt, Rinehardt & Winston, 1955
6. Trevalyn, op. cit.
7. Ibid.
8. Ibid.
9. J. Gavin, op. cit.
10. Vaughan-Thomas, op. cit.
11. Daily Telegraph Diary of the War: The First Quarter. London: 1944.

12

Audie Murphy arrived at Anzio with a boatload of anxious replacements, some of whom had been just released from hospital like himself. One man complained that he had not been cured of his 'dose', i.e., of gonorrhea, and that he still had a 'run'.

"That's the only kind of discharge you'll get in this army', someone commented unfeelingly.[1]

To Murphy, the beachhead seemed calm enough. Trucks moved back and forth. Boats came sailing in, bringing fresh supplies. But the calm was deceptive. Hardly had he stepped ashore when five German dive-bombers came zooming in low. The new men scattered like frightened chickens. But he kept on plodding up the beach. 'An experienced eye can see that the Krauts are after the boats'.[2] Murphy was right. Within five minutes the German dive-bombers had dropped their load on the boats and had vanished back to their own lines.

As they moved further inland, Murphy came across the true face of war once again. 'Jeeps drawing trailer loads of corpses pass us. The bodies, stacked like wood, are covered with shelter-halves, but arms and legs bobble grotesquely over the sides of the vehicles. Evidently graves registration lacks either time or mattress covers in which to stack the bodies.'[3]

What the young staff sergeant was viewing was the daily transport of bodies to the huge, sprawling cemetery close to the place where replacements always landed. It was not a very encouraging sight for the 'wetnoses'. Nor for Murphy. 'My step quickens. I have an urgent need to learn how my comrades have fared'.[4] Behind him Murphy left the cemetery, and 'Hell's Half Acre': the evacuation hospital that was constantly bombed and shelled. Some GIs would conceal their wounds rather than be sent to the most hazardous spot on the beach.

The 'Old Heads' - Tipton, Kelly and the rest - were still in the line. Veterans that they were, they had learned how to survive and look after each other. But virtually the rest of Company B was made up of replacements. It was with these new men that Murphy now went into action in the 3rd's abortive attempt to capture the key township of Cisterna. The attack failed and Murphy retained bitter memories of the German defenders turning their multiple 20mm flak cannon on the attackers, and firing a steady stream of white tracer that made it look as if they were advancing into a brilliant white, lethal fog.

After that first failure, Murphy was assigned as platoon sergeant to take over Company B's 3rd Platoon, a post usually held by a second lieutenant.

Now, at the age of nineteen, still looking like an undernourished six-teen year old, he was in charge of nearly forty men (when the company was up to full strength, which was not often) divided into four squads, each commanded by a sergeant. It was a tough assignment, especially since most of the men under his command were older than he. But he managed it well and continued to command a platoon for another nine months until he was finally commissioned in the field as a second lieutenant.

His senior officers knew they could rely on the freckle-faced kid. Already his conduct at Cisterna had been noted by his CO, Lieutenant Colonel Paulick, who told a reporter ten years after the war: 'It was (at Cisterna) that I came upon Audie's company with the Company Commander wounded, and only two inexperienced lieutenants left. I took command of the company and we continued to attack for three days, fewer than thirty men survived. Audie was the only noncommissioned officer left, and there were no officers except myself. If I had never seen Audie Murphy again, I would remember him from that action. He was a soldier, a born leader, potentially a fine officer'.[5]

The whole terrible month of February, Murphy, in company with the rest of the 3rd, went on the defence, dug in along the Mussolini Canal, which could have been taken easily if Lucas (who was soon to be relieved by a wounded Truscott) had moved swiftly on that first day. Time and time again the Germans attacked the 3rd's positions. Covered by massive artillery bombardments, including the much feared 'Anzio Annie', which fired a tremendous shell from somewhere miles to the German rear, the German soldiers raced forward behind their tanks, trying to overcome the Americans' resistance. To no avail. Although the 3rd suffered awesome casualties, they held their positions. But by the time February came to an end and the German attack faltered, the average strength of a company in the 15th Infantry Regiment had been reduced from over a hundred men to a pitiful twenty-five. Murphy's platoon alone lost twelve men, a frightful toll.

And it was not only the Germans who turned that February 1944 into a living hell. Living conditions were execrable. For days on end, the dogfaces crouched ankle-deep in freezing rainwater in their muddy foxholes, not daring to move during daylight hours for fear of snipers, moodily eating cold C rations flung into their holes at night by frightened supply sergeants. If they were hit they were forced to lie there where they had been struck down, for the medics were often unable to reach wounded men until nightfall. Trench foot, as at Salerno, became epidemic, and after the war Murphy told his elder sister Corinne that he had avoided the complaint, which was now the biggest source of casualties in the American army, by constantly wringing out his soaking socks.

Unlike the British Army, where at the day's end it was the platoon officer's duty to have his men bare their feet so he could inspect them for signs that the wrinkled flesh was beginning to turn blue, the American army took no precautions. It was left to the men to find their own salvation. Murphy was outraged by the treatment the men of his platoon received when he sent them to the rear, suffering from trench foot. 'The men are given cans of foot powder and promptly returned to the lines, still shivering and hobbling'.[6]

He called the aid station on his field phone and complained to the medical officer. "Goddammit", he shouted, "don't shove them back up here with a couple of aspirins and a pack of foot powder!"

The MO asked him angrily whether he realized he was talking to an officer and concluded with the ominous words, "Remember that you may be through here yourself."

"God spare me!" Murphy yelled. The receiver went dead in his hand.

Murphy not only led from the front during combat, but he also took good care of his soldiers, trying to ensure they received the best possible rations and medical treatment. Indeed for a nineteen-year-old he was extraordinarily adult.

On March 2, after he had been on 'Bloody Anzio' for just over a month, Murphy won the first of his many decorations for valour - the Bronze Star. That day he spotted a German tank from the top floor of a ruined Italian cottage that Company B was using as an observation post. In all, there were twenty tanks advancing on the 1st Battalion's positions. With hands that trembled, Murphy lowered his binoculars and yelled back the coordinates to the waiting divisional gunners.

A minute later the 105mm - 'the long Toms', as they were called - thundered into action. The sky flared bright red. The shells hissed above the crouching men of Company B and came smacking down just short of the advancing German armour. Great, steaming, brown holes appeared in the soil. But the German Mark IVs still rumbled forward, turrets moving like the heads of primeval monsters sniffing out their prey.

Frantically Murphy, in the cottage, corrected the gunners' aim. The tanks were almost on him now. Then the first enemy tank was hit. With smoke pouring, thick and black, from its ruptured engine, it squealed to a stop. Almost immediately its black-clad crew began to bail out.

Murphy went into action. He squinted along his sights and pressed the trigger. The first German faltered in flight, throwing up his hands, as if he were climbing the rungs of an invisible ladder, and flopped down - dead. Another was hit. Then Murphy stopped firing, not out of compassion, but because he didn't want to give his advanced position away. Moments later, as the artillery continued to fire, the other tanks started to withdraw, leaving the young platoon sergeant still at his post, trembling with relief.

As the day dragged on, the crippled German tank began to worry him. During the night a German tank retriever might sneak up, as they often did, hitch the crippled Mark IV to its tail, and tow it away to fight another day. Colonel Edson, now commanding the 1st Battalion, thought the same. He ordered Murphy to take out a patrol and finish off the German tank.

In spite of the butterflies in his stomach that the young platoon Commander always experienced before action, he was eager enough to carry out his CO's order. He picked a small patrol, which included his best friend, Lattie Tipton, and they armed themselves with homemade Molotov cocktails - wine bottles filled with gasoline - and set off on their mission.

The crippled tank was not hard to find in the inky March darkness, for the crew, believing that the Mark IV would be towed away later, had placed some kind of lantern in the turret. It could now be seen quite clearly by the Americans advancing along the ditch.

When Murphy was within fifteen yards of the tank, he flung one Molotov cocktail and then the other. Both crashed against the turret, but failed to ignite. Perhaps the homemade fuses were at fault.

In that same instant, the little group of GIs were startled by the sound of gruff voices speaking German nearby. Murphy knew he had to work fast. He pulled out a grenade and ripped out the pin. In one and the same movement, he flung up his right arm and hurtled the grenade at the tank. It landed squarely on the turret and fell inside.

Next moment it exploded with a muffled crump. Still the damned lantern inside didn't go out, and already the alerted Germans were coming closer. Murphy dropped to one knee, heart beating frantically, and started to blast away at the tank's tracks with rifle grenades.

White tracer cut the darkness. There was the familiar high-speed burr of a spandau. It was time to retreat. Hastily he ordered the little patrol to fall back. They needed no urging. As Murphy confessed after the war, in overtaking them, he did the 'fastest two hundred yards' sprint in history'. The next morning the ruined tank was still visible, but evidently it was no longer worth repairing. The Germans never retrieved it. Audie Murphy had won his Bronze Star complete with the 'V' for valour.[8]

It was just after the episode with the tank that Murphy's frail constitution, which seemed so strangely indestructible in battle, let him down again.

On the evening of March 13, Murphy was checking a forward gun position near the ruined farmhouse, when 'not far from the ruins, my knees give way. I collapse in the mud; and darkness blots out the mind'.[9] Later he learned that two members of his platoon had carried him to the aid station on a door. There he came to. 'A face floats over me. I argue with it that my feet are bursting out of my shoes. Then I faint again'.[10]

When he came to, Murphy found himself in 'Hell's Half Acre'. But since he was not sufficiently ill to be evacuated to Naples, he was soon moved from the evacuation hospital to one of the tented hospitals on the beach, where the American nurses tended the wounded wearing steel helmets on their heads and slept at night in foxholes, with their hair in curlers, and their cold-creamed faces peppered with sand from the recurrent explosions.

After nightfall no one left his or her foxhole for any purpose whatsoever. Not only was the beach being bombarded, but the sentries, who were everywhere, were mostly trigger-happy. Thus the cold light of dawn would reveal lines of nurses advancing on the open latrines, carrying cans that they had used during the night to carry out their natural functions.

Here Murphy remained for a week, tormented by high fever. All the time the shells came thumping down with predictable regularity, turning those who were already suffering from combat fatigue into babbling, trembling wrecks who were sometimes gagged by the medics so they would not panic the others.

Every night at precisely eleven o'clock, those who were on duty tuned into *Radio Roma*. Over the airwaves the fat, ugly woman from Brooklyn, already six months pregnant by her married Italian lover, whom they knew as 'Axis Sally' would breathe in that husky, seductive voice of hers that so belied her real appearance, "Beachhead... *deathshead*".

There would be a slight pause while she reached for the record. A scratch of the needle as she placed it on the phonograph and then it would come, the record that they had all been expecting: the catchy little foxhole number of the year... '*Between the Devil and the Deep Blue Sea*'.

NOTES
1. Murphy, op. cit.
2. Ibid.
3. Ibid.
4. Ibid.
5. Simpson, op. cit.
6. Murphy, op. cit.
7. Ibid.
8. Ibid.
9. Ibid.
10. Ibid.

13

"I had hoped", Churchill lamented that March, "that we were hurling a wild cat onto the shore, but all we had got was a stranded whale".[1]

The British Prime Minister was right. Now the stalemate had been reached. The Anglo-Americans could not break out of the Anzio beachhead, and the Germans could not drive them off it. So the latter contented themselves with cutting their enemies off, their only connection with the Allied rear the sea-route to Naples. Thus from the middle of March until the final breakout in May, conditions at Anzio strongly resembled the trenches in World War I. Forward positions were stabilized and remained practically unchanged for three months. The only activity was in the air and in aggressive fighting patrols.

The troops made themselves as comfortable as they could in the sprawling mess of trenches, caves, ruins, dugouts, barbed wire, and barricades. They lived underground for the most part, for protection from the German shellfire was more important than light and comfort. Some of the troops even sank enormous Italian wine barrels that they had looted into the earth and lived in them. The American tankers dug in their Shermans and then hollowed under them to form caves in which they lived. Above them only the turrets of their tanks showed.

As their fathers had done in the trenches in the Old War, the infantry tried to create the illusion of normalcy in this crazy world in which they lived. In the British sector it was beetle racing, which spread like wildfire. Large sums changed hands on favourite beetles, and a champion might fetch as much as three thousand lire - the equivalent to a month's pay for a private soldier in His Majesty's Army in those days.

The 'racing' was simple. Colours were painted on the beetles' backs, and the 'runners' were paraded around the 'enclosure' in jam jars while bets were made. Then all of them were put under one jar in the centre of the 'course' - a circle six feet in diameter. At the 'go' the jar was raised, and the first beetle out of the circle was the winner.

Naturally the Yanks went one better. An American engineer, Sgt. Bill Harr, laid out a 'racecourse', using the white tape the engineers employed to mark paths through mine fields, collected enough horses and mules for a race, and set up a public address system. He even recruited some pretty nurses to give away the prizes to the winners. The odd part of it was that the 'Derby' was in plain view of the German gunners, and they never fired a single shell at the tempting target. Perhaps they were betting too!

Generals had barbecues, with GI magicians performing. One such was Pvt. Roland Ormsby. Known on the stage as the 'Baron', who had brought his own tuxedo with him to the beachhead. When the armoured commander, General E. Harmon, gave such a party, his guests were entertained by a full pipe band borrowed from the British. Afterward, the general turned to the pipe major who was 'a great tall Scotsman' and handed him, as was the custom, a huge glass of whisky. The Scot swallowed 'the not very good whisky' in one gulp, without batting an eyelid. Many years later the general commented, 'The British seemed to have a lot of old customs. This was one of which I thoroughly approved'.[2]

All over the beachhead there was signs announcing '42nd Street and Broadway'... 'The Good Eats Café'... 'Beachhead Hotel - Special Rates to New Arrivals'. In such places crude 'dago red' manufactured in some underground still, was sold, or a potent kind of black market brandy manufactured in a sill made with copper tubing taken from a shot down German plane.

Meals were also served in these places, mostly hamburgers made from Italian cattle that 'just happened to trip over a mine'. In the American sector of the beach, sheep seemed rarely to 'trip over a mine', mainly because the Americans didn't seem to like lamb.

The authorities did not inquire too closely about the source of the wine or the meat. It was hard enough to keep the men in the line under the terrible conditions existing at the front, and if a slug of illegal '*vino*' helped the men to go to sleep or gave the people on the beach enough 'catacomb courage' to face the anguish waiting for them the next morning, well that was all right with the brass. Indeed, some soldiers walked around in an alcoholic daze for days on end. It was recorded that one GI got so drunk on 'dago red' that he staggered, watched by his awed, apprehensive comrades, right into the German front line. Instead of shooting the GI, the German *landsers* laughed, dusted him off, and obligingly pointed him in the direction of his own line.

There were women, too. Some men were bold or sex-starved enough to sneak through the German lines to the Italian farmhouses and hamlets beyond where there were willing peasant girls or farmers' wives who were prepared to oblige them for a can of Spam or a couple of Hershey bars. Indeed, there was an outbreak of VD on the beachhead and the hard-pressed medical authorities, who had their hands full with the daily intake of wounded, had to provide a prophylactic station on the beach to keep the VD rate down. In the end, the Germans solved the problem for the medics. They sowed all the gaps in their line with antipersonnel mines and 'debollockers'.* And that was that.

However, all was not lost. One enterprising sergeant of the 1st Special Service Force, a mixed Canadian and American commando outfit that liked to believe it was called the 'Black Devils' by the Germans, landed on the beach accompanied by some professional 'ladies' from Naples. The brigade

---

* A primitive, homemade mine that when stepped on triggered off a bullet that rose to about the height of a man's crotch.

was shifted to a remote section of the front where the sergeant, Staff Sergeant Walkmeister, pimped for his girls from an ambulance known throughout Anzio as 'Walkmeister's Portable Whorehouse'.

Later, when he was really established, il Sargente, as he was known to his 'young ladies' arranged that his girls would be available 'for parties, festivals or anything needed to take the minds of the Big Brass off their duties for a few hours'.[3] For a small monetary consideration, naturally...

For Audie Murphy, now back in the line, the drinking dens, the black market restaurants, the generals' parties, the duck shoots organized by the top brass, the whorehouses, were a matter of hearsay, a tall tale to wile away the long dreary hours in the foxholes. Immediately after his return to the front, the young Texan got his first mention in the media. Some enterprising PR man made up a story for the benefit of Murphy's local paper, which stated that 'a 48-hour rest was recently given to Staff Sergeant Audie L. Murphy, Route 2, Greenville, Texas, a platoon guide who had spent three weeks almost motionless in a wet slit trench 200 yards from German positions in the Allied Fifth Army Anzio-Nettuno beachhead in Italy'.[4]

It is doubtful whether Murphy ever saw the little article. But his response to the PR's statement that he and his comrades could enjoy, out of the line, such comforts as 'hot meals, movies and morning religious services' would certainly have been unprintable. He had developed a vitriolic tongue and could curse with the best of the veterans by now.

Although the Anzio front had quieted down now, the 3rd Division still had to undergo long, comfortless, and sometimes dangerous spells in the line, and everyone knew that one day they would have to break out of the Anzio beachhead and that that would mean the infantry would pay the butcher's bill yet again.

The weather began to grow warmer and the rains ceased. 'Spring comes to the beachhead', Murphy wrote after the war, 'and on the ruined land new green glistens in the sunlight. When the guns are quiet, we can hear the song of birds; mate calls to mate, their voices swelling uncertainly'.[5]

In the spring Murphy's platoon was brought up to strength. Everyone knew that the great breakout was not far away and Murphy recorded, 'No longer do we feel like orphaned underdogs. Our forces are driving up from the south (to link up with the beachhead) and the beachhead bristles with accumulated power'.[6] Murphy for one was anxious to get on with it, counting the days until the all-out attack commenced. 'We are eager for it to begin. Our every thought and action is concentrated on getting the war over before another winter comes'.[7]

April gave way to May. The 3rd Division was pulled out of the line for training near the township of Torre Austara. Now the Marnemen knew the day of the breakout was growing closer. The division was training all-out, particularly in methods of attacking a pillbox and in house-to-house fighting. The new commander of the 3rd Division, General 'Iron Mike' O'Daniel, a scarfaced, tough-looking soldier who would be Murphy's commanding general till the end of the war, had been ordered to prepare for the offensive that would break the beachhead stalemate.

In the third week of May Clark came to Anzio. There he gave a press conference at Truscott's Corps HQ. The Army Commander let the assembled correspondents into a secret. There was going to be an offensive and it would be under his 'personal command'. He gave them a few details, stating that the 3rd Division was to be given the task of capturing Cisterna, from which it had been driven in what now seemed another age. He also remarked that he would remain 'flexible' during the coming battle.

The correspondents, who had been at Anzio for four months and knew the battle situation extremely well, concluded that after Cisterna was captured. The Fifth Army would be ordered into the Valmontone Gap, thus cutting off the German Tenth Army. Clark had other plans. He knew that within a couple of weeks Eisenhower would launch his great cross-channel Normandy invasion, and Clark didn't want his new campaign to be upstaged by Bradley and Montgomery, the generals who would be commanding the ground forces on D-Day.

On the evening of May 21, the 3rd Division received the command they had been waiting for: 'Move up tonight'. This they did, marching off into the dark, serenaded on their way to battle by the divisional brass band of the 3rd. Whether it encouraged the heavily laden soldiers, many of them replacements going into battle for the first time, is not recorded. Doggedly they slogged on.

Soon the infantry was in position and there was nothing to do but wait. A strange silence fell over Anzio, disturbed only by the muted thunder of the guns on the Gustav Line where their comrades were trying to break through. Tanks and trucks were crammed into farmyards and orchards on all sides. The gunners tensed behind their cannon, huge piles of shells to left and right. Further back the ambulance drivers smoked moodily waiting for it all to begin: and in their tented hospitals, the nurses and surgeons laid out the instruments, preparing for the broken, bloody bodies that would soon be flooding in to them.

Even the top brass came up front, talking in whispers as if afraid to break the brooding silence. Dawn approached with a threat of rain in the air. Even Clark was up, having risen at four thirty, and now he squatted in a forward command post, waiting for the great attack to commence.

He wore his steel helmet, but this morning he did not remove it and replace it with his overseas cap as he did when he posed for the photographers in order to show just how contemptuous he was of danger. This dawn there was danger in the very air and he was taking no chances.

Over 160,000 men, British and American, were crammed behind the line, watching, waiting, wondering, some of them wishing desperately that the hands of their watches would reach zero hour so that they could finally be released from the awesome tension.

At fourteen minutes to six that morning the beachhead artillery thundered. It was a tremendous bombardment with five thousand guns pouring shells down upon the surprised Germans. BBC, correspondent Vaughan-Thomas thought it 'awe-inspiring'. American journalist Eric Severeid felt the earth 'begin to tremble'. Shells 'poured over our heads and our jackets flipped from concussions'.[8]

Next the dive bombers joined in. Dazzling silver streaks, they hurtled down as if intent on suicide, shrieking toward the German positions, and then levelling out at the very last moment. In crazy profusion, their deadly, black eggs fell from their blue bellies.

The armour - Harmon's 1st Armored Division - went in. 'The tanks came clanking up the highway, moving very slowly and well apart', Eric Severeid recorded, 'their radio antennae nodding behind like drooping pennants of armoured horses and knights, jolting slowly to take the field. In and out of their ranks courier jeeps scuttled like agitated beetles'.[9]

It was the turn of the 3rd. The grinning infantrymen thought it was going to be a walkover. 'Our final barrage is so intense', Murphy wrote after the war, 'that it seems nothing could be left of the German lines... We turn from the holes in which we have cowered for nearly four months and march toward the enemy'.[10]

The breakout had commenced.

NOTES
1. N. Nicolosn. Alex. London: Pan, 1974
2. E. Harmon. Combat Commander. New York: Prentice Hall, 1970
3. C. Whiting. The Long March on Rome. London: Century-Hutchinson, 1987
4. Simpson, op. cit.
5. Murphy, op. cit.
6. Ibid.
7. Ibid.
8. D. Congdon, ed. Combat. New York: Dell Books, 1955
9. Ibid.
10. Murphy, op. cit.

14

The task set Audie Murphy's Company B was to cut the railroad south of Cisterna and isolate the town. Here the German defences were the strongest, for they knew that Cisterna was the key to their whole position. Every house and every barn had been turned into a strongpoint. There were mine fields and machine guns firing along fixed sights on all sides.

Murphy's company was the first to cross the railroad tracks, firing from the hip as they advanced and taking intense fire in return, not only from German machine guns but from the self-propelled guns the Germans had brought up. These were now blasting away with their 75mm cannon.

At the railroad tracks, it had developed into a nasty firefight, but Tipton, Kelly, and their sections managed to cross the embankment safely. They turned and gave a waiting Murphy the thumbs-up signal. It was his turn to take the rest of the platoon across the tracks and down the embankment on the other side.

"Let's go!" Murphy ordered.

They surged forward. One of his young soldiers hesitated and was mowed down by a machine gun.

Murphy came last. 'Scanning the banks, I pick my path, draw a deep breath, and start sliding. The handle of a trench shovel fastened to my back wedges between two protruding rocks; and I hang like a pigeon upon the bank with lead splattering all about me. Rock dust from the bullets fills my nostrils. My throbbing temples seem ready to burst'.[1]

The trapped sergeant looked up and saw his friend Kelly preparing to jump down and rescue him, and at that moment he managed to shake free. Yelling to Kelly to stay where he was, he bolted across the tracks to safety.

Not all of Company B got through unharmed. That day, the only other member of the company to win the coveted Medal of Honor besides Murphy, Sgt. Sylvester Antolak, single-handedly silenced several German machine gun posts so that his platoon could get across the tracks. He was not so lucky as his fellow platoon leader. As he silenced the last of the enemy machine guns, he was riddled with German bullets, and not knowing he would win America's highest decoration, died and lies forgotten these forty years or more.

Murphy's 15th Infantry Regiment began to advance up Highway 15 beyond Cisterna. The young platoon leader abandoned his favourite carbine for a tommy gun, which he preferred for house-to-house fighting, as Company B cleared up the straggle of dirty white houses that lined both sides of the highway.

The battalions of the 3rd were radioing back the details of their success to an anxious General Clark, but they were paying a heavy price for reducing the defences around Cisterna. Private Guensberg, an eighteen-year-old replacement to the 15th, recalled later that 'while we waited to advance down the ditch the first wounded came filing past in the opposite direction. Those with light wounds seemed to have a silly smirk on their faces, as if they had won their tickets back to the U.S.'.[2]

However, once they got to the scene of battle, Guensberg saw the casualties who had not received that desirable 'million dollar wound' that would take them out of action. Now 'I had to make my way gingerly between remains of corpses, dismembered limbs, scraps of bodies. A shell must have dropped short. We were too numb to give this any thought. We climbed out of a ditch and crossed a field. A few German soldiers began running toward us, waving their hands high in the air and calling out "Kamerad!" They were terrified'.[3]

But in spite of the casualties, Corps Commander Truscott urged the 3rd on, knowing that if the Marnemen progressed at this rate he stood a good chance of cutting off the whole German Army in Italy. The end of the war in the 'boot' was within grasping distance.

Yet another member of the 3rd won honours in the engagement. A Pvt. John Burko charged a group of German machine gun positions, telling his sergeant he was going to use his 'heater' (his BAR automatic rifle) on the enemy. He did so very successfully, advancing on a dug-in German 88mm cannon. Luck was with him and he knocked it out too. The young soldier, wounded now, was so caught up in the fury of battle that he charged yet another enemy machine gun post. He killed the crew but fell dead across a German gunner. Again the Medal of Honor - posthumously.

Still, the new offensive was going exceedingly well. After thirty-six hours, the Americans had taken one thousand prisoners, Cisterna had almost fallen, and the shaken Germans were beginning their retreat northward. As Murphy wrote after the war, 'With the hard crust of his defences broken, the enemy begins a withdrawal. Though reeling like a punch-drunk fighter, he pounds us with cannon and harasses us with small arms. We are deathly tired, but we must keep hitting the Germans while they are still off balance'.[4]

The threat of sudden death came not only from the enemy. On the afternoon of May 25, as the 15th Infantry Regiment was advancing along the Cori-Giuglianello road, its verges littered with abandoned German equipment and what looked like dirty bundles of gray rags, which had once been soldiers, 'five planes dive at us. They strafe and bomb our ranks fiercely. We spurt for cover, leaping over the soft shoulders of the road to avoid possible mines'.[5] Trembling and shaken, the men of Company B pressed their bodies to the warm Italian earth as if it were a lover. Then the victorious planes zoomed up into the sky and for the first time the decimated infantry could see the white stars that marked them as their own. The column had been attacked by planes of the U.S. Army Air Corps. The cost was high. More than one hundred dead and wounded. Several jeeps carrying 57mm antitank shells and small arms ammunition had blown up, adding to the casualties. 'The highway is strewn with the dead and wounded'.[6]

It was one of those purposeless mistakes that happen in the confusion of battle. 'Exasperated beyond speech', Murphy wrote later, 'the unharmed men stare blankly at the destruction. Occasionally one gets control of his tongue and sputters a volley of oaths against the air Corps'.[7] That was about all the cynical, war-weary grunts could do.

The actual linkup between the men making the breakout from Anzio and those fighting their war from the south caught everybody by surprise. At a small bridge that had been blown up by the retreating Germans, Capt. Ben Souza of Truscott's VI Corps encountered a Lt. Francis Buckley strolling casually up a road. "Where the hell do you think you're going?" Souza cried.

Buckley looked at the captain. "I've come to make contact with the Anzio forces", Buckley declared.

"Well", Souza snarled, "*you've made it*".[8]

Clark's publicity machine sprang into action. This was tremendous news: an event for which they had been waiting for four months. Clark was hurried to the bridgehead by his PR men and the whole business was re-enacted with due formality for the benefit of the correspondents and photographers.

Eric Severeid, the American correspondent and Clark's most bitter critic, was there that 'historic day" and recorded, 'The Fifth Army publicity machine promptly issued a statement saying that Anzio was now justified, and broadly implying that the commanders responsible for the landing there had been right all along, always knew they were, and that, in fact, the whole operation proved the wisdom of the high command, whose subtle methods were frequently misunderstood by grosser minds'.[9] Cynically, Severeid added, 'If any correspondents sent off the statement, I did not observe them'.[10]

On the evening of that 'historic' linkup, which meant now that there was a unified Allied front in Italy at long last, Clark, in high good humour, asked Truscott, "Have you considered changing the direction of your attack toward Rome?"[11]

Truscott was puzzled by the Army Commander's question. His attack was going exceedingly well. Why not continue the drive toward Valmontone? Elements of General Harmon's 1st Armored Division were only ten miles away from the Italian town, and resistance to their front was crumbling fast. Meanwhile the British of the Eighth Army were forty miles off. If the two forces could link up, the German Tenth Army would be cut off, which was the original strategy. Why now this talk of diverting the attack away from Valmontone in the direction of Rome? What use was the Italian capital?

But that evening the 'American Eagle' did not enlighten his Corps Commander. Instead he left for his HQ at Caserta and let Truscott ponder this strange question.

Meanwhile the battered 3rd Division had been relieved in the line by the U.S. 85th Division and was now trucked forward to attack Valmontone and Highway 6. Both were defended by the fresh Hermann Goering Panzer Division, which the 3rd had first encountered in Sicily.

On June 1, Audie Murphy's 1st Battalion attacked on both sides of the road leading to a railroad station just south of Valmontone. The station was defended by infantry and five German tanks, and it took two full companies, including Murphy's B, to finally capture the place, leaving their dead scattered on the road behind. By nightfall the 15th Infantry had pushed on and taken up defensive positions to the north of Highway 6 and just east of the key town of Valmontone.

The news made Truscott 'feel rather jubilant'. But not for long. Back at his headquarters he was met by Col. Dan Brunn of the Fifth Army's staff. Brunn said, "The Boss wants you to mount the assault you discussed with him to the northwest (i.e., toward Rome), as soon as you can".[12]

Truscott was 'dumbfounded'. 'This was not time to drive to the northwest', he wrote after the war, 'where the enemy was still strong... We should pour our maximum power into the Valmontone Gap to insure the destruction of the retreating German Army'.[13]

Brunn was adamant. Truscott told the colonel he couldn't comply with the order. He would have to talk to General Clark first. Clark was not available, Brunn answered smugly. He was neither on the beachhead nor could he be reached by radio. Truscott, angry and impotent, understood. Clark was ducking out of sight in order to avoid awkward questions.

Reluctantly Truscott gave in. Leaving the weakened 3rd to continue the Valmontone attack to no real purpose, he turned the bulk of his Corps in the direction of the Italian capital. Sadly he called together his senior commanders and, feigning enthusiasm, told them that the new direction of attack would bring them easy gains.

They weren't convinced. 'Iron Mike' O'Daniel, commanding the 3rd, was particularly bitter, while Colonel Howze of the 1st Armored called it, 'one of the worst decisions I ever knew'.[14]

Truscott hoped that Supreme Land Commander Field Marshal Alexander might in the end overrule Clark. The urbane elegant ex-Guardsman, who was basically a very brave, but lazy, man, allowed the Clark decision to stand, perhaps not realizing that the Fifth Army Commander was not concerned with cutting off the retreating German Army. Victory in Italy, after so much bitter fighting and so many deaths, was going to be sacrificed for personal prestige.

After the war, when he had more freedom to speak and write openly, General Truscott wrote: 'There has never been any doubt in my mind that had General Clark held loyally to Field Marshal Alexander's instructions, had he not changed the direction of my attack to the northwest... the strategic objective of Anzio would have been accomplished in full. To be first in Rome was poor compensation for this lost opportunity'.[15]

On June 2, 1944, Valmontone fell to the 3rd. Immediately, according to the new directive from Clark, the direction of the division's attack was changed. Now Murphy's 15th Regiment was sent against Rome, motoring along the hotly fought for Highway 6 by truck. But not for long. 'Smiling Albert' Kesselring had already decided to withdraw, hardly believing the good fortune that made it possible to escape the trap set for his Tenth Army. But he still greatly feared a mass rising by the Roman population before he cleared the Eternal City. So Kesselring ordered that the bridges across the Tiber River should be manned in force by his troops to convince the Romans that he was going to make a fight for it; at the same time he commanded his rear guard to hold up the *Amis* for as long as they could.

Dutifully the mixed group of paratroopers and German 'stubble hoppers', as the weary infantrymen called themselves cynically, did just that, making the Americans pay for whatever gains they made. Later Murphy recorded: 'As we approach Rome, the enemy rear guard stiffens its defence. Our route is punctuated by merciless firefights'. [16]

Clark, who was coolly throwing away the fruits of victory, gained at the cost of so many young men's lives, was frantic. Back in the States his ancient, doting mother wrote to her son, 'Please take Rome soon. I can't stand the wait much longer. I'm all frazzled out'.[17]

NOTES
1. Murphy, op. cit.
2. Trevalyn, op. cit.
3. Ibid.
4. Murphy, op. cit.
5. Ibid.
6. Ibid.
7. Ibid.
8. Vaughan-Thomas, op. cit.
9. Congdon, op. cit.
10. Ibid.
11. Nicolson, op. cit.
12. Truscott, op. cit.
13. Ibid.
14. Harmon, op. cit.
15. Truscott, op. cit.
16. Murphy, op. cit.
17. Blumenson, op. cit.

15

The great advance on the Italian capital was in trouble. By now Clark knew Eisenhower's cross-channel assault was scheduled for June 6. He had only a matter of days left if he were going to beat Ike. Yet his attack was being held up all along the line outside Rome. He ordered Truscott up to put some steam into the stalled attack.

As Truscott was discussing the situation with barrel-chested General Harmon, commander of the 1st Armored, a German machine gunner opened up close by and sprayed the area with slugs. The two old campaigners, who had been in the fight together since North Africa, hit the dirt. Later Harmon reflected ruefully, 'This I thought was the ultimate anticlimax. The two of us who had gone through so much together were to be killed by fire from an Italian privy'.[1]

The battered 3rd was once again in the van of the attack. As they slogged it out ever closer to Rome's Tiber River, the division came under repeated attack. On June 3, while Clark sweated it out, yet another two young men of the 3rd won their country's highest award. With his leg shattered, Pfc. Christian and Pvt. Elden Johnson saved a trapped patrol of the 15th Regiment by attacking the Germans while the rest of their comrades withdrew. They saved the patrol and were awarded the Medal of Honor for their bravery in doing so, but, again, it was awarded to them posthumously.

As they dragged back the two soldiers' shattered bodies, Clark was more concerned that no other troops than his should enter Rome first. For he had just heard that the Poles had asked to be allowed to send a detachment into the capital once it had been captured. He signalled Alexander, his chief. 'Please politely tell everybody, including the Swedes if necessary, that I am not framing the tactical entrance of troops into Rome. God and the Boche are dictating that'.[2]

One day later, Rome was still not captured. Clark now had only forty-eight hours left. That day he flew with his personal pilot to a factory some rive miles from the city's centre. Here he met tough old General Keyes, another of his Corps Commanders, cut in the Patton mould, and General Frederick, head of the 1st Special Service Force. Together they walked to the top of a hill where there was a huge blue-and-white sign announcing 'ROMA'.

Before Clark's arrival, Keyes had demanded of Frederick, "What is holding you up here?"

"The Germans, sir", Frederick had replied.

"How long will it take you to get across the city limits?"

"The rest of the day", Frederick said. He explained he was being held up by several self-propelled guns that he wanted to out-flank to save casualties.

"That won't do", Keyes snapped, "General Clark has to be in the city by four o'clock".

"Why?" the veteran officer, who had been wounded four times, asked.

"Because he wants to have his photograph taken", Keyes said solemnly. Frederick stared at him, wondering if Keyes were serious. Finally he said, "Give me an hour".[3]

Clark, Keyes, and Frederick had their photograph taken by the newspaper correspondents posing in front of the *Roma*, till as Clark wrote later, a German sniper put a 'bullet through the sign with a bang'.

The trio of generals fled.

Afterward, General Frederick and a soldier returned at Clark's orders to retrieve the road sign. Clark shipped it home to the States, where it remained as a precious reminder of his 'combat' career.

But if Clark obtained his souvenir that day, he still had not won the capital. The resistance along Highway 6 to Rome was too intense for Frederick's men to take the city 'within the hour'. A frustrated Clark departed for Naples.

But it wouldn't take much longer now. Kesselring was pulling his troops back through Rome ever more rapidly, intent on setting up yet another defensive line in the mountains to the north of the capital. Now, after being ambushed twice, the 3rd's 7th Regiment, 'the Cotton Balers', penetrated the city limits by nightfall on June 4. They set up their command post at the San Lorenzo railroad yards and established a perimeter around the station located there.

That same night, the three battalions of their sister regiment, the 30th, started to push into the city heading for the Tiber River, where it was thought the Germans had set up a last-ditch defensive position. They were ordered to use nothing but small arms. Clark had issued the order himself. There would be no second Cassino here. The Eternal City's monuments would not be damaged; the bad Cassino publicity, after the bombing of the famous Abbey by Allied planes a few months before, had done the commanding general's reputation little good in the States, especially among Catholics.

The 30th Infantry's progress was slow. They were held up well into the next day by a handful of defenders, a few German tanks and self-propelled guns and, if rumours were to be believed, by some well-intentioned and generous *signorinas*, eager to show their appreciation to their 'liberators'. Finally, the thin crust of the German resistance was broken and engineers were hurried forward in front of the infantry. The top brass was frightened that the retreating Germans would do what they had done in Naples the previous fall: plant delayed-action bombs and mines that would explode weeks later.

There were none. Not a single mine was discovered. 'Smiling Albert', too, was conscious of his publicity. He didn't want to go down in history as the member of a '*Kulturvolk*' who had helped to destroy one of Europe's most ancient cities.

More and more Americans began to pour into the city after the 3rd Division's entry. Upon seeing the Colosseum for the first time, a GI was quoted as having said, 'Gee, I didn't know how bombers had done *that* much damage to Rome!' But that was the kind of story that newspapermen were always making up.

In truth, in four years of total war, Rome had suffered little damage. Now there were girls and wine aplenty for the taking. American dollars brought vino at five cents a bottle; and a prostitute for twelve cents. A whole night cost a dollar. It was a soldier's paradise!

The restaurants opened up and started serving wine and prime cuts of horsemeat to the weary GIs who were sick of C rations. They had been doing the same the previous week for the *landsers* of the Greater German *Wehrmacht*. After all, business was business.

As 'Iron Mike' O'Daniel set up his command post in the University of Rome and the city was divided into three zones of occupation, with Murphy's 15th Regiment taking over the western part of the capital and Audie Murphy's Company B taking up their position in a public park, the question arose - where is Clark? He had laboured so long to take Rome and had, indeed, changed the whole direction of Allied strategy to get there. Now why wasn't he in Rome enjoying his moment of triumph?

In fact, General Clark and his small jeep party were lost! For over one hour they had been wandering about the capital, trying to find their way to City Hall. Finally they came across a priest in St. Peter's Square, who asked in English, "Is there any way I can help you?"

"Well", Clark ventured, "we'd like to get to the Capitoline Hill."

The priest, who was an Irishman and a leading light in the Allied POW organization that was based in Vatican City, gave the commanding general the instructions he required and then said, "May I introduce myself?" He gave his name and then asked that of the lanky American with the great beak of a nose.

With undue modesty for him, the commanding general answered simply, "My name is Clark."[4]

The priest knew who Clark was. He shouted to the group of Italians who were beginning to assemble to tell them the exciting news.

Dutifully they cheered, and a small boy in short pants, who was the only one in the crowd to possess a bicycle, volunteered to lead the jeep convoy to the Capitoline Hill. Thus the comic procession reached the place where, when Clark had been an obscure middle-aged major of infantry, the Italian dictator had thundered to his 'sons of the wolf' from the celebrated balcony, which had featured in so many newsreels in the thirties.

Here Clark pounded on the door of the City Hall. Perhaps he anticipated that some Roman mayor in striped pants and frock coat, with the colourful sash of his office across his portly chest, would open the door. Thereupon he would ceremonially hand over the golden key of the city to the conqueror with a dignified bow and a few appropriate words of welcome. After all, Rome had been conquered enough in the last two thousand years, and the Romans should have been used to doing the appropriate thing.

Nothing of the kind took place. The door was locked and no responsible official could be found to open it. Fascisti to a man, they had fled with the Germans, they knew all too well the temper of the 'Romans'.

Clark and his party set off for the *Stampa Estera* Building where the Fifth Army Commander gave an impromptu press conference for the eager correspondents, and posed for the press photographers and for those of the U.S. Signal Corps who had been given strict instructions on how to photograph General Clark on this, his great day of triumph.

Eric Severeid, Clark's arch critic, watched the conquering hero pose in front of his map for the benefit of the newsreel men, and, turning to a colleague, whispered sourly, "On this historic day, I feel like vomiting!"[5]

Audie Murphy's mood now that the 3rd had finally reached Rome, seemed little different. He knew just how much the Marnemen had suffered to get there. There had been 18,000 Americans killed and wounded, plus another 15,000 British and Poles and 11,000 French. And for what'? They had captured the strategically useless capital, and the Germans had retreated in good order, while the Allies stood by helpless to stop them. It would take another year before the war in Italy would be over, and the men who would fight their way doggedly up the rest of the 'Boot' into the Alps would feel themselves a forgotten army. D-Day and the battle for France grabbed the headlines, and Italy was no longer of any interest. 'We're the D-Day dodgers', they would sing bitterly, 'out in Italy, always drinking vino, always on the spree in sunny Italy.'

Murphy wrote, 'Rome is but another objective on an endless road called war. During the bitter months on Anzio, we dreamed of a triumphal entry into the great city. There were plans, promises, and threats of wholesale drinking and fornication. Now that our dream is an actuality, a vast indifference seizes us. Pitching our tents in a public park, we sleep until our brains grow soggy and life oozes back into our spirits'.[6]

Afflicted, seemingly, by the same malaise that had overcome the correspondent Severeid Murphy recorded, 'We prowl through Rome like ghosts, finding no satisfaction in anything we see or do. I feel like a man briefly reprieved from death; and there is no joy within me. We can have no hope until the war is ended. Thinking of the men on the fighting fronts, I grow lonely on the streets of Rome'.[7]

Twelve days after the capital had fallen he wrote to a friend in Texas in that sloping, childlike, semi-illiterate scrawl of his: 'It isn't so bad here now. I have had two passes to Rome but was disgusted with the place. It's nothing like I expected. I wonder if Paris will be a disappointment to (sic). Hope I get to go to France since I came this far I may as well see them all'.[8]

His letters, like all his letters from the front, revealed little of what had happened to him in Italy. His correspondence with his family and friends back home in Texas mostly consisted of requests for 'cheese, candy, crackers and canned meat'.

Five years later in his autobiography he records a different version of the time he spent in that Rome which 'disgusted' him. He sits with his buddies in the twilight over their 'dago red' in the park and sings 'Swanee'.

'Sitting at night in a foreign land, we are strangely moved by those songs that are so much a part of our background. They call up long-buried memories and a tenderness of spirit that has no place in war. But we sing each night until the order comes to buckle on our gear and move'.[9]

> Way down upon the Swanee River, far, far, away,
> That's where my heart is turning ever,
> That's where the old folks stay.

But could that young man of that summer so long ago really have been affected by the sugar-sweet sentimentality of the nineteenth-century song? After what he had just been through as an infantry platoon leader for the last four months, when most of his men had vanished in the holocaust of total war? Was Rome simply a staging post for him to hurry back to Texas, back to the hard grind of a poverty-stricken sharecropper? His early background showed no bourgeois tolerance for the middle-class sentiments of such songs. What did the land and Texas - 'good advice and malnutrition' - mean to him?

What was the truth of Audie Murphy in that Roman summer of 1944? Whatever innocence remained to him, it was unlikely to have been of the kind his autobiography reported.

Notes
1. Harmon, op. cit.
2. Blumenson, op. cit.
3. Trevalyn, op. cit.
4. Blumenson, op. cit.
5. Congdon, op. cit.
6. Murphy, op. cit.
7. Ibid.
8. Simpson, op. cit.
9. Murphy, op. cit.

16

In the late forties when David McClure, Murphy's longtime friend, was ghosting Murphy's memoirs, the writer started to become angry with his subject. McClure found Murphy a very difficult person to handle. 'He was extremely moody, depressed and nervous. Sometimes he would come to my apartment, stretch out on my bed and lie there for long periods. He would just stare at the ceiling with haunted eyes and say very little, if anything… Audie made me nervous because he seemed to transfer his condition to me'.[1]

But that wasn't the only problem for the ghostwriter. Time was running out for their book, the publishers in New York were pressing him to meet the deadline, and though he believed fervently in the book, Audie wasn't co-operating. McClure had come out of the service after two and a half years in Europe, possessed by 'an irrational rage which lasted for a long time. I also suffered from acute depression'.[2] He felt a victorious America had not understood anything of the suffering of the average infantryman in the faraway battle for Europe. Now he had the ideal subject, a man who had been through it all and had proved himself the bravest of the brave. But he had to coax every single word out of him. The handsome, young, would-be movie star seemed to have forgotten most of what had happened to him over there. He'd say a word or two, then relapse into a moody silence, leaving McClure to use his imagination.

One day McClure had had enough. He put down his pen and cried in exasperation, "Audie, this thing is becoming too damned grim. We've got to find some way to lighten it up!" He frowned over his glasses, which gave him his nickname 'Spec' in Hollywood, and asked, "How about girls? Didn't you meet any girls along the way?"[3]

Murphy hesitated and then told McClure a story about the time he spent in Rome in the summer of 1944.

During the ten days the 3rd Division garrisoned the newly captured capital, before being shipped out of the city for the new battles to come, 'Audie, in his usual charming way, got invited to a dinner by a mother with two daughters'.[4] Murphy didn't say how, with his very basic Italian, he managed this, but according to the story he told his ghostwriter, he 'seduced both daughters before dinner and, being very democratic, he seduced the mother after dinner'.[5] Naturally the episode did *not* appear in *To Hell and Back*.

Audie Murphy wasn't simply an innocent, of course. How could he be, after what he had just gone through? The wartime Army was a great forcing school, turning boys into men overnight. Waiting that dawn to go into action for the first time at the Anzio breakout, eighteen-year-old replacement Pvt. Guensberg heard the older men talking about the foreign women they had 'had'; how the English women preferred it standing up 'a knee-trembler', they called it - while the Italians preferred it from behind. Then he had wished fervently he wouldn't be killed before he 'became a man'.[6] His case was typical. In war, death, sex and procreation go hand-in-hand.

Audie Murphy not only became advanced for his years, but he also had heavy responsibilities placed on his skinny young shoulders. He had been in charge of the fate of a score or more young men, who during those four bloody months at Anzio, came and disappeared in combat with depressing regularity. They came up into the line as replacements still clad in clean uniforms with creases in the pants, and then they were gone, dead or wounded, as if they had hardly existed, even before Murphy had really gotten to know their names. *Yet he had always survived!*

So what did he do in such circumstances? His youth and native Texan bravado could not quite hide the fact that he was a sensitive youth. His few letters home, as pathetic and semi-illiterate as they are, reveal that he was a generous boy, concerned about his family and friends, who sent money regularly to his older sister; worried about his ten thousand dollar 'GI insurance' so that 'sis' would not lose out if he were killed in action; interested in the fates of his friends who had been hit in other theatres of the war or were missing. To whom could he talk?

Could he reveal his fears and doubts to the surviving 'old heads', older men in Company B like Sergeants Tipton and Kelly? After the war Kelly, who was invalided home after being wounded in France, never made any mention of such confidences. Besides, what would these basically simple, direct men have made of Murphy's doubts? Was he going 'chicken', they might have thought, and no young man wants to be thought of as a coward. Or was 'Murph' heading for a 'section eight', another one of the many who cracked up under the intolerable strain of constant combat? And there were many of them at every level from Regimental Commanders down to simple buck privates.

In the end, it seemed Audie Murphy had to acquire a thick skin and blinkers so that he could shrug off or simply not see the misery, the squalor, the tragedy that was taking place around him day after day. He had to sublimate his fears and doubts, telling himself that this was the kind of life that he had always wanted ever since he had been a little barefoot kid working with the veterans of World War I in the cotton fields.

Like the 'Young Soldier' from Stephen Crane's *The Red Badge of Courage*, whom he would play one day in a Hollywood movie, 'his eyes seemed to open to some new ways. He found that he could look back on the brass and bombast of his earlier gospels and see them truly... With this conviction came a store of assurance He felt a quiet manhood, non-assertive, but of sturdy and strong blood. He knew that he would no more quail before his guides wherever they should point. He had been to touch the great death and found that, after all, it was but the great death. He was a man'.[7]

Many years later Murphy told a writer, "I remember we came under artillery fire my very first day in action. That was in Sicily. And I saw a couple of guys I knew get blown up. I was very serious after that. Very serious'.[8] Of course he was. Like the 'Youth' at the end of the novel, Murphy had thrown off his early romantic notions of war as being some gallant nineteenth-century cavalry skirmish with wind-tossed banners in the background.

"Mostly", he related to the writer, "your thoughts are elsewhere. I mean the training - the brainwashing - makes you go ahead and you react against the enemy, even though you have so much fear. You become an effective soldier when you get over this fear and you use your training and you try to think ahead. It's a game of chance for a while, but after two or three firefights, you begin to improve your odds by taking advantage of the terrain and your weapons. You get more polished. Your attitude changes. You get a more professional outlook?"[9]

"Losses are inevitable", he told the writer. "So you learn not to get too friendly with anybody. Combat is not like the movies or what you read in books, even my book. Every action is new people. One way or another, people come and go. Your side is just like the other side - people in uniform trained to do what they have to do. There are only fleeting moments of the kind where a unit has the drama of a war movie. Battlefields are empty places. You don't remember the guys' names. You remember that one-one-zero-eight-seven-eight-three is the number of your rifle, * but names are too personal. That's really how it is".[10]

Later, as we shall see, the price Audie Murphy paid for this unconscious act of youthful sublimation would be high. Already in the wartime summer of 1944 he was overcome by a sense of loneliness. He felt that he and his handful of remaining buddies were 'like fugitives from the law of averages. Loosely we cluster together, bound by a common memory and loneliness. The need for reinforcements is desperate. But we are suspicious and resentful of the new men that join us'. [11]

As June gave way to July in that hot summer of 1944, the Western Allies finally started to break out of their Normandy bridgehead, while in the east the victorious Russians surged forward across eastern Poland. By day, the U.S. Eighth Air Force plastered Germany's crumbling cities, and at night the RAF did the same, turning them into stony ruins. Victory was in the very air, and men were wagering that it would be all over by Christmas. 'See Forty-Four and end the war', the Marnemen's fellow veterans of the 45th Infantry Division proclaimed bravely.

It was time for the new and reorganized Seventh Army under General Alexander Patch (who had taken over from the disgraced Patton after

---

*It's interesting that in 1967, twenty-two years after the war was over, Murphy should still remember the number of his M-1.

seeing service in the Pacific) to add another nail to Hitler's coffin.

Operation Anvil was the code name given to the new plan, which envisaged an assault landing by the Seventh, plus a French Corps under General de Lattre de Tassigny (who urged his officers to take 'great care of the vines' during the landing) on the southern French beaches around the prewar tourist paradise of St. Tropez.

Here, preceded by the landing of a provisional airborne division, composed of British and American paratroopers, and a naval bombardment, they would attack German General Friedrich Wiese's Nineteenth Army. It was generally regarded as a weak force, made up of one good division, the 11th Panzer, and seven second-rate infantry divisions, many of whose members were not even German, but recruited from former members of the Red Army, taken prisoner by the Wehrmacht. Allied Intelligence had not reckoned with Wiese, however, who would manage his second-rate troops very effectively against superior odds from now till almost the end of the war.

The aim of the operation, whose code name was now changed to Operation Dragoon, was to stage a linkup with the forces surging out of Normandy and protect their southern flank; and at the same time, capture a major supply port in France, Marseille. For as yet supplies for the Allied armies in France were still being brought across the beaches, and no major port, capable of being worked, had been taken by Eisenhower's forces.

Thus it was that for the fourth time Audie Murphy would take part in an amphibious landing. This time the assault on an enemy shore would take place in daylight. The 15th Infantry Regiment and its sister outfit, the 7th, would spearhead the 3rd's attack. The 15th would land at Yellow Beach, just east of the small town of Ramatuelle and south of the coastal resort of St. Tropez. The 7th, for its part, would assault at Red Beach near the small towns of Calvaire and La Croix.

On a balmy evening, August 12, 1944, Audie Murphy sailed from Naples for the last time. But he had learned a lot in Italy. There he had grown up rapidly and become a man. His youthful illusions about war, women, and the American way of life had, in great part, vanished. The Texas farm boy, who on the day of Pearl Harbor had been double-dating with another boy at a drive-in movie theatre, now three years later had slept with three women in one evening. Italy had taught him a lot and would - indirectly - affect the course of his future life until the day he died.

Now he was on his way to France. Here, in a period of less than five months, Audie Murphy would be wounded three times, be promoted to an officer on the battlefield, and win the United States' highest decorations for valour, one of them, the Silver Star, twice. In the history of the U.S. Army, no one had ever matched that record, nor in the fifty years since then has anyone come close. Murphy was heading straight for the history books.

NOTES
1. Letter to the author.
2. Letter to the author.
3. Letter to the author.
4. Ibid.
5. Ibid.
6. Trevalyn, op. cit.
7. S. Crane. The Red Badge of Courage. New York: New American Library, 1952.
8. Esquire, op. cit.
9. Ibid.
10. Ibid.
11. Murphy, op. cit.

THREE

THE HERO

A man never travels so far as when he does not know whither he is going.

Oliver Cromwell

17

One hour before dawn, the fog started to roll in from inland. It rolled on down the craggy, barren valleys toward the sea like wood smoke.

Suddenly, startlingly, the naval guns thundered into action off the coast of southern France. It was the preliminary bombardment to soften up the German beach defences and destroy their minefields. Twin-engined Mitchell bombers, flight after flight of them in hard silver V's, zoomed in low over the anchored invasion fleet to drop their bombs on Wiese's forts and strong points further inland. The only reply was a few desultory shells from the interior.

It was just as easy when the eleven assault battalions of the three veteran divisions of the Italian campaign - the 45th, the 36th, and, naturally, the 3rd - started to streak toward the beaches in their landing craft. They had caught the defenders of the Nineteenth German Army by complete surprise. As 1st Sgt. Robert Elliott of the 3rd commented afterward: 'It just didn't seem right. It was like somebody giving us something for nothing. It was just too goddamn good to be true. The trouble was we were too busy and too scared to be happy. We never knew when they would start opening up on us from somewhere. So even though it was easy, you still sweat it out. One thing about war is that as long as you live, you're always sweating it out'.[1]

Murphy felt the same as he landed with the first wave of the 15th Infantry Regiment at Yellow Beach, known to holidaymakers before the war as 'Plage de Pampelonne'. 'Under the rocket barrage, scores of landing boats churn toward the shore. I stand in one; and the old fear that always precedes action grapples with my guts'.[2]

But as the landing craft hit the beach of the sandy, curved bay, dominated by the heights beyond that were covered with stunted pines, nothing happened. Here and there a mine exploded and some young man fell screaming to the scuffed sand and stared in disbelief at what had happened to his legs. That was all. The 15th began to push inland at full speed.

German shells began to range in on the invasion fleet, but that didn't worry the infantry. General Patch had commanded that they should advance rapidly regardless of fatigue or shortages because the 'enemy is perplexed and stunned and the opportunity for decisive results is ahead of us'.[3]

For Audie Murphy's Company B, the only opposition that they knew about was an enemy strong point located in the centre hill of the three hills to their right. Here there was a gun emplacement and some machine gun nests. Now, as the hot Mediterranean sun began to burn the dawn mist away, the khaki-clad figures swarming up from the beaches felt themselves abruptly naked. They began to sweat - and it was not just the heat that made them do so. Bodies tensed. They advanced crouched, weapons clutched to their hips, as if moving forward against a strong wind. The veterans and the green-horns waited for the first shot that would signal the battle had commenced.

The platoon Commander was, for once, bringing up the rear of his platoon. He had already 'lost' his rifle squad and machine gun crew in the confusion of the landings. He didn't want to lose any more of his small force.

By this time the leading elements of his platoon had reached the edge of the pinewoods. Beyond it lay a stretch of vineyards thirty-foot wide, flanked on the right by a deep drainage ditch, with directly in front of the vineyard a wooded ridge that rose steeply at a slope of sixty-five degrees. To Murphy's trained eye, it looked like a perfect position for the Germans to have sited a machine gun nest.

Sergeant Murphy was right.

Suddenly, the tense stillness of the advance up the height, broken only by muffled curses and the laboured breathing of the sweat-soaked men, was shattered by the first, frightening high-pitched burr of a German machine gun. Tracer started to spit toward the platoon. Murphy paused. He cocked his head to one side to hear better. He was listening for the slower response of an American BAR.

There was none.

Murphy cursed. His platoon had obviously walked straight into a trap. They had been pinned down and were unable to return the enemy fire. He was needed up there - fast. Clutching his favourite carbine in his right hand, he doubled forward. Above him the German machine gun fired a wild burst at him and missed as he skidded to a stop in a shower of white dust among his terrified men.

He cursed at them to start moving once more, but they hugged the ground and refused. The machine gun that dominated the whole slope had petrified them. They weren't going to risk it.

Frustrated and angry, Murphy dropped back a little into the woods where - in the confusion of battle, he never knew where - he obtained a light machine gun. Soaked with sweat, he went up the hill again, dragging the weapon with him up the drainage ditch till he reached the side of the vine-yard, where he set it up and prepared to fire.

He pressed the trigger. Tracer winged its way angrily toward the German MG nest. But it was no use. The angle was wrong, and his slugs flew harmlessly over the helmeted heads of the German gunners. From his present position in the ditch he hadn't a hope of knocking out the German position.

Dashing forward again, Murphy crossed the length of the vineyard under fire, and with the machine gun in his arms, flung himself down, gasp-ing for breath. Now he was in a position directly in front of the enemy strong-hold, and the advantage was his. He had turned the table on them. In order to fire at the bold, lone intruder, the Germans would have to expose their bodies, and that was exactly what Audie Murphy was waiting for.

He went into action. 'I judge the range, press the trigger, and turn the stream of lead on anything that remotely resembles a Kraut'.[4]

The screams of pain that followed the first burst told a triumphant Murphy that he was hitting the target. Yet still the counterfire did not cease. These were brave men - a handful of last-ditch defenders holding up a whole company.

Abruptly the chatter of the light machine gun ceased. Murphy slammed his clenched fist against the butt. A stoppage'? No, the gun hadn't jammed, he had run out of ammunition!

Murphy ran back under German fire to where he had left his carbine. Hastily he checked its magazine and prepared for yet another crack at the enemy strongpoint.

He heard a movement close by in the undergrowth and swung around, carbine at the ready, murder in his eyes. It was his old friend Tipton. "What you trying to do?" he breathed in relief, "buy yourself a wooden cross?"

The older man was bleeding badly. After nearly two years in combat, Tipton had been hit for the first time. He had had most of his ear shot off.

Murphy urged his buddy to go back to the beach and have the wound dressed. But Tipton refused. "Come on, Murph", he said with a wry grin, "let's move up". And then for the last time he used that old, old phrase he had used so often before, "They can kill us, but they can't eat us. It's against the law".[5]

The two men crawled down from the drainage ditch. Slugs cut the air just above their heads. Straight ahead of them in the ditch a German rifleman was stationed. Hardly daring to breathe they crept closer and closer.

Now they could see there was not just one German rifleman, but *two*. They seemed to be sleeping in the middle of battle, feet drawn up, heads bent upon their chests. They might well have been dead and perhaps they were, but Murphy and Tipton didn't give them the chance to wake up if they weren't. They aimed as one. Each German was struck in the head and reeled back. Next moment a salvo of angry slugs ripped past the two Americans.

Judging the intervals correctly between the bursts of German machine gun fire, they raced for a strip of grassland at the base of the German-held ridge. Now the machine gun was a mere ten yards to their left. Firing as fast as they could to keep the other Germans down, Tipton and Murphy charged the machine gun post yelling crazily, carried away by the totally unreasoning frenzy of combat. In a matter of seconds they had slaughter the two German machine gunners. The hot morning air was full of the pitiful, frightened cries of other Germans hidden in their foxholes. "*Kamerad... Kamerad!*" they wailed in an ecstasy of terror. They were giving up.

Tipton peered over the edge of the hole the two of them found themselves in. He saw the remaining Germans waving something white, and he told Murphy he was going to go across and get them. Murphy was not sanguine. He had seen this sort of game before... one German promising to surrender while behind him his comrade crouched with a stick grenade or a pistol. "Goddamn, Lattie", he said, "keep down! You can't trust them!"[6]

Tipton wasn't listening. Perhaps he had grown overconfident. He had seen so many other men killed, but he had survived. He stood up and in that very instant a German opened fire at close range. Tipton yelled in agony and reeled back, shot through the heart. Falling into the foxhole, he choked out the one word, "Murph". The next moment he was dead. Murphy rolled him over 'gently and held him'. 'There was a strange little smile'[7] on his lips, which were 'choked with froth'.

Something snapped in Murphy. For the only time in his long combat career the young sergeant lost complete control of himself. Half crazed with rage and grief, he picked up the German machine gun, and, flinging two grenades to keep the heads of the surviving Germans down, rushed forward firing from the hip.

Five minutes later he had taken the ridge and shot down all the Germans dug in there without mercy.

The official citation for his Distinguished Service Cross would read, 'Closing in, he wounded two Germans with carbine fire, killed two more in a fierce, brief firefight, and forced the remainder to surrender'.[8]

In truth, Audie Murphy took no prisoners that hot August morning. 'I remember the experience as I do a nightmare', he recalled later. 'A demon seems to have entered my body. My whole being is concentrated on killing as the lacerated bodies flop and squirm, I rake them again; and I do not stop firing while there is a quiver left in them'.[9]

The German resistance on the ridge line was broken. It had taken two hours. As Company B re-formed before continuing its drive inland, Murphy, suddenly drained as if an invisible tap had been opened, staggered back to where Tipton lay dead. He took off the dead man's pack and pillowed Tipton's head upon it. Then he flopped down on his heels and 'bawled like a baby.'[10]

Afterward, when he was informed that he was to receive the Distinguished Service Cross for his valour that August morning, he stated: "I won the medal, but Lattie, who was the bravest man I ever knew won only death for himself"[11] Indeed, after the war Murphy gave the precious decoration away to Tipton's daughter, who, as a nine year old, had seen her father march away to war in 1942 never to return. Now nearly half a century later, a middle-aged woman herself, she still treasures that medal.

Murphy was not ashamed of either his grief or his blind rage. He *could* break down and weep, cradling his dead comrade's head in his arms, although when it came to make the movie of his life, the director refused to allow him to go through the scene exactly as it happened with the tough actor who played Tipton. He said that the viewing public might think it 'too corny'. For the young platoon leader at the time there had been nothing corny about it. He had simply revealed his true self at that moment. Beneath the tough veneer and hard shell that combat had forced upon him, there was still a sensitive person.

After Tipton's death, the pace of Audie Murphy's life seemed to quicken measurably, even dramatically. He seemed to court danger. He volunteered for patrol after patrol. Even when not commanded to, he would go along for the fight, tagging after other patrols that were no concern of his - 'just in case'. The twenty-year-old was always in the forefront of the fight. Even in 1945 when he had been awarded the Medal of Honor and had been wisely drawn onto the staff, away from his company, so that he would not be killed before he received that high award, he simply could not stay away from combat. When his Company B was bogged down during the Battle of the Siegfried Line, who turned up in their midst, spick and span in his staff uniform, to rally them? Audie Murphy of course! More than once in those last weeks in Germany, with every side road filled with hidden dangers - lurking Hitler Youth, desperate for some final glory; bitter, hard SS men armed with their deadly panzerfausts; the lone Tiger, waiting for some unsuspecting fool of an *Ami* to walk straight into the trap - Audie Murphy, alone in his unarmed staff jeep, would be found driving along, as if he were back in a peacetime Texas. What was he doing? Why, he was on 'liaison duty'.

Was he trying to die? Had something snapped within him after Tipton's death that made him court death so recklessly? We do not know. On that subject, although he made many pronouncements about his combat career afterward, Audie Murphy kept discreetly silent.

But if he did want to die, he was unlucky. Audie L. Murphy, however flawed, was destined to become a living hero. Death could wait.

NOTES
1. R. Martin, ed. The GI War. Boston: Little, , 1967
2. Murphy, op. cit.
3. Murphy, op. cit.
4. Murphy, op. cit.
5. Ibid.
6. Ibid.
7. Ibid.
8. Taggart, op. cit.
9. Murphy, op. cit.
10. Ibid.
11. Ibid.

18

What was to follow was called later 'the Champagne Campaign'. For at a cost of five hundred men wounded and killed, Gen. Alexander Patch had put ashore two whole Corps of some 66,000 men. In contrast the 100,000-odd men that Eisenhower put ashore in Normandy on June 6, 1944, suffered 10,000 casualties, nearly a ten percent rate. Now, as the Americans started to proceed inland, virtually all resistance vanished, and the happy GIs were welcomed not by German bullets but by cheering Frenchmen of the Resistance, firing a *feu de joie* into the brilliant blue sky of the *Provence*, and by happy smiling dark-eyed beauties handing out kisses, fruit, wine and occasionally something more

Retreating skilfully, General Wiese allowed the Russians, Ukrainians, Turcomen, and half a dozen other Soviet nationalities who had been incorporated into the Wehrmacht to drift away. He had but one aim: to preserve the bulk of his German-speaking units for the battle to come in the Reich.

After the fleeing Germans, came the Americans and General de Lattre's French, fighting their way up the few valley roads, forced by the terrain to stick mainly to the valley of the Rhône River.

Manoeuver was difficult for the Allies, scenting an easy victory. For the valley of the Rhône was not more than a dozen miles broad in some places. The secondary roads leading down from the mountains on both sides of the valley were steep, winding, and narrow: little use for the Allied armour. Still, as the Germans retreated, harassed all the time by the partisans of the French *maquis*, who dominated the mountains, General Patch did attempt to cut them off and bring Wiese to fight a pitched battle.

Time and time again, General Wiese of the German Nineteenth Army managed to slip out of the trap set for him. His infantry he could afford to lose. Without transport they were becoming a hindrance anyway. However, the German general was determined to rescue his armoured and motorized units. So his infantry was sacrificed at place after place along the long road that led north to Lyon, while his armour slipped away.

Murphy, during this time, as August gave way to September, experienced 'a great exhilaration. For there is nothing so good for the morale of the foot soldier as progress. Long ago we came to believe that our only way home lay through the Siegfried Line; and each mile that we move up the Rhône Valley of France is another mile nearer America'.[1]

It would be another year before Murphy could return to America, but for now, under the broiling hot September sun, the 'Champagne Campaign' was easy - save for those at the point. Up there men still fought and died daily - in their scores!

A little further back, it was roses all the way. The Krauts were on the run, the natives were friendly, and the local girls were willing. Half drunk with the good red wines of this bountiful area, which had suffered little under the two years of German occupation*, the purple evenings would find the dusty young soldiers sprawled out in the shady village squares, watching the old men in their floppy black berets playing their *boule* and eyeing the dark-eyed girls in their wooden platform heels and short floral dresses drinking their *rouge* and *Ricard* in the sidewalk cafes. As the historian of the 3rd Division wrote of that advance, it was 'the longest advance in the shortest length of time that it (the 3rd) had ever made - or would ever make - in Europe'.[2] By the first week of September, the progress of the U.S. 3rd Infantry Division through southern France was little more than a drunken, triumphant road march.

Then the 3rd reached Montelimar, some hundred miles or so inland. Montelimar's only claim to fame was that it was the centre of the production of nougat, that sticky tooth-breaking sweetmeat. But for a while it hit the headlines. Here Wiese decided to make a stand. The French city was ideally suited for defence. It blocked the main road heading north and filled the valley, with its sprawl of dingy, stucco bungalows shaded by trees, spreading out to the foothills and the Rhône River. Choked with white dust at this time of the year, the skinny-ribbed dogs lying panting in the gutters, the roads radiating out from Montelimar's medieval center could be easily defended by a determined handful of infantrymen.

'Iron Mike' O'Daniel did not seek a head-on confrontation with the Germans. Instead he encircled the city and then sent in his infantry in a surprise attack. The 15th infantry was given the task of attacking the northwest. Here Company B was to assault a strongly dug in German infantry position, which was supported by two 88mm guns.

Unable to depress their fearsome weapons sufficiently, the German gunners fired above the attacking infantry's heads. Still the German infantry fought on, unsupported, until finally the supporting American tanks appeared; Shermans, their cannon twitching back and forth like the snouts of predatory monsters seeking their prey. At this, the Germans had had enough. They threw up their hands and climbed out of their holes.

For a day and a half, the 1st Battalion, to which Murphy belonged, continued the struggle for the French city. The Marnemen combed through the smoking city, over which the sweet smell of nougat hung like a pall, rooting out the last-ditch, suicidal snipers.

Carrying a tommy gun, which he preferred for house-to-house fighting, Murphy led his platoon cautiously. He hated snipers and for most of his combat career showed no mercy when he came upon them. More than once he had shot German snipers out of hand.

*The South of France had only been occupied in November 1942 after the Allies landed in North Africa, while the rest of the country had been occupied since June 1940.

One day, as he wrote later, he leaped 'from the sunlight into the dim rooms', waiting for his eyes to adjust to the change. 'As we stand in one house, the door of a room creaks open. Suddenly I find myself faced by a terrible looking creature with a tommy gun. His face is black, his eyes are red and glaring. I give him a burst and see the flash of his own gun, which is followed by the sound of shattering glass'.[3]

As always, Murphy had been tremendously fast on the draw, but this time there had been no need for that lightning-fast reflex. For 'the horrible thing that I shot at was the reflection of my own smoke-blackened self in the mirror!'[4]

Behind him Sergeant Kelly, his friend, cackled and quipped, "That's the first time I ever saw a Texan beat himself to the draw!"[5]

By the afternoon of that same day, the fighting in Montelimar ceased. It had been an easy victory for Murphy's 1st Battalion. At the cost of a handful of casualties, they had killed or captured 1,200 of the enemy and, as the divisional history records, captured or destroyed, 'at least 500 vehicles and an estimated 1,000 horses'.[6]

One day later, when the 3rd started its advance up the *Route National 7*, the progress was slowed down by the debris and carnage that the dive-bombers of XII Tactical Air Command had caused. The bloated corpses of the dead Wehrmacht horses stank in the hot sun, so that the advancing GIs called the stretch of highway that led to the next important town, Loriol, 'the Avenue of Stenches'.

The pressure was on from above. Corps Commander Lucien Truscott urged his men forward to make the linkup with the armies advancing out of the Normandy bridgehead deep into northern France, commanding, 'if you run out of gas, park your vehicles and move on foot'.[7]

But the steam was running out of the Allied advance, both in the south and in the northwest. For both armies - those of Eisenhower and those of Devers* - were finding it difficult to bring up the supplies, especially of gas, which their highly motorized army groups needed if they wished to continue advancing.

In the north, the Western Allies were still without a major supply port, and the one they would soon capture - Antwerp - would not be opened completely until October. Gas was running out rapidly, and Patton was forced to steal some intended for the U.S. First Army in order to keep his own Third Army rolling. The situation was a little better in southern France, but Marseille, effectively sabotaged by the Germans, was still not functioning; and the other harbors in American hands were not really suited as major supply ports.

Meanwhile, General Wiese was extricating his battered army from the south with remarkable skill. Using the Swiss border as a hinge to protect his

*General Jacob L. Devers, Commander of the U.S. Sixth Army Group.

left flank from encirclement, Wiese swung his horse-drawn columns north-east, heading for the celebrated Belfort Gap in the Vosges Mountains, that would take him down to the Rhine plain and the safety of the Reich. For three days he held up the Third Army at Besançon north of Lyon while his Nineteenth Army withdrew even deeper into Alsace. Here in the medieval city, Murphy had a second taste of action during the 'Champagne Campaign'.

'A German truck lumbers around a curve. For a moment I do not move as the wonderful feeling of relief floods through my body (Murphy and his comrades had thought the vehicle was a German tank). Then I set my sights on the windshield and pulled the trigger. The truck lurches from the road and hits a tree. I keep down long enough to see if anything develops. Nothing does. The stalled motor coughs and dies. I pour another burst into the cab and move toward it cautiously'.[8]

But Murphy had nothing to fear. As always his aim had been deadly. Both Germans in the truck were dead. 'I poke them with my BAR, but they do not react. The vehicle is loaded with supplies. I kick aside what appears to be a strongbox, grab an armload of cognac and bread for the men and take off'.[9]

Later Murphy discovered that the strongbox contained 'several thousand dollars of French francs'.[10] But for the time being 'money is without meaning to the famished men who sit gulping cognac and bread'.[11]

Soon the advancing Americans were reaching the Vosges Mountains, and capturing the villages of Pomoy, Genevreuville, and Mollans. It was at Genevreuville that Murphy received his first wound in combat after being at the front for over a year.

He had been on his way to report to headquarters when he came across a bunch of nervous, raw replacements moving up into the line. Suddenly the air was rent apart by the obscene howl of a mortar bomb. *Thwack!* The bomb exploded nearby in a ball of angry red flame. Murphy yelled with pain and blacked out.

'When I come to, I am sitting beside a crater with a broken carbine in my hands: My head aches; my eyes burn; and I cannot hear. The acrid, greasy taste of burnt powder fills my mouth'.[12]

Audie Murphy had still not lost the luck of the Irish. If the shell had struck home a little closer, he would have been as dead as the two replacements who lay only feet away: bloody, bundles of torn rags, killed before they had even reached the line. But it hadn't. Instead he had suffered a few splinters of steel and lost the heel of his right shoe.

A few stitches, a couple of days in hospital and a new pair of shoes and Murphy was back in the line, as the autumn leaves began to fall, wondering, 'vaguely which of us will still be alive when the new leaves return to the trees'.[13]

Sergeant Kelly, his old buddy of the North Africa days was also struck by a mortar fragment two days later. It didn't kill him but 'clipped off half of his right hand'.[14] Later, Murphy commented, "The wound is sufficient to remove him from combat permanently, but in time will not greatly affect his ability to hoist a bottle."[15]

The tone Murphy affected was light-hearted, but that day as they carried Kelly away for good - for now he had his 'million dollar wound' - the young staff sergeant must have realized that he was all alone now. There was not a single survivor left he original Company B (save for the supply sergeant who was not a combat soldier), except himself. Audie Murphy, that skinny weak-looking teenager, who had joined them back in February 1943, had outlasted them all. The feeling of loneliness must have been overwhelming.

NOTES
1. Murphy, op. cit.
2. Taggart, op. cit.
3. Murphy, op. cit.
4. Ibid.
5. Ibid.
6. Taggart, op. cit.
7. Ibid.
8. Murphy, op. cit.
9. Ibid.
10. Ibid.
11. Ibid.
12. Ibid.
13. Ibid.
14. Ibid.
15. Ibid.

19

Victory was in the air!

While the 3rd Division faced up to the German defence of the Vosges, higher headquarters far behind the lines were heady, almost drunk, with the prospect of victory soon. The Germans were on the retreat everywhere. In Holland, France, Belgium, Luxembourg, they were fleeing back to their own country, a beaten, disorganized rabble. Behind them they left a trail of abandoned equipment, tanks, trucks, cannon - and dead men.

Admittedly, due to the supply position, the steam was going out of the Allied advance. But what did it matter? Patton might complain that 'My men can eat their belts, but my tanks have gotta have gas!'[1] But at higher headquarters the staff officers outdid each other in their predictions. Surely, they maintained happily, we'll be sending 'the boys' home by Christmas. Eisenhower had even wagered a 'fiver' with Montgomery that the war would be over by the end of 1944. It was a bet that he would come to regret bitterly

Meanwhile, at the front the tide of war was slowly changing in the Germans' favour. The weather had begun to turn. In eastern France, the bitter, relentless fall rains had commenced, turning the Moselle-Lorraine area into a bleak series of muddy fields in which the American armour bogged down. Over the border in the Reich, the Germans scuttled into their vaunted Siegfried Line on which the Tommies had wanted to hang their 'washing' back in 1939. Behind it Hitler ordered a massive call-up of his remaining manpower while the factories worked all out, producing new tanks, guns, and aircraft to replace those lost in the debacle in France. In September 1944, the German output of weapons of war was the highest, of the whole war and in the Vosges, General Patch's Seventh Army began to run out of shells.

None of this affected the optimism of the top brass. On September 12, de Lattre's French Army linked up with General Leclerc's 2nd Armored Division of Patton's Third Army coming from Normandy. The two fronts - the one from the northwest and the other from the south - linked up at Chatillon-sur-Seine *seventy-three* days ahead of schedule. Again this confirmed the generals' belief that they would 'take the Krauts on the run' and 'bounce' their way across the Rhine to final victory in Berlin. Soon, as Montgomery's great airborne force prepared for their bold drop into Holland, they were in for a great surprise.

At the start, everything went surprisingly well. In the case of Patch's Seventh Army, now massing at the foot of the Vosges, it was planned that first the Army would take the spa town of Epinal, secure a crossing over the Moselle River, and then advance north-east and force open the Saverne Gap (which separates the High and Low Vosges) into the Rhine plain below For their part, de Lattre's Frenchmen under Devers's overall command, would use the Belfort Gap. Facing the Allies, Wiese had a mere four infantry divisions, all under strength, and two shattered armoured divisions. With this small force he was supposed to defend a huge front along the Vosges stretching from the Saverne Gap to the Swiss border at Bâle. Patch was confident, like all the top brass, that it would be a walkover for the Allies.

Initially it seemed so. One day before the attack on the Moselle was due to start, Seventh Army HQ was informed that mayor of the small town of Raon-aux-Bois wanted to see a senior officer urgently. It was very important. So HQ sent a liaison officer who spoke French to meet the mayor, a Monsieur Gribelin. The latter was a retired naval officer, sixty years old. When he told the American what he knew, the latter was tempted to kiss the ex-naval man, beard and all!

Gribelin told the liaison officer that there was a jeep-wide ford across the Moselle nearby, where the water was only waist-deep. The current was slow and there was plenty of cover at the spot for vehicles, too. Indeed the man used it as a short-cut to the town of Eloyes on the other side, still in German hands, when he went to visit his married daughter every Sunday. He, Gribelin, in spite of his age, would be glad to guide the Americans across if they wished.

They certainly did!

On that dark night, with the rain pouring down in streams, the mayor did exactly that, leading a strange procession of jeeps in single file, filled with tense GIs. They crossed the major water barrier without a single shot being fired at them.

That was the easy part.

Higher up in the foothills of the Vosges, Murphy's battalion now prepared for the tough part. Murphy was back in the line with his 'wounded carbine', as he called it, its shattered stock bound up with wire, he and it ready for action.

The battalion's objective was the quarry outside the village of Cleurie, a rugged, hill-mass, covered with tangles of spiked brambles and trees, which formed the anchor point in the German main line of defence. It dominated the road net that the 3rd Division needed for its advance, and the Germans knew it. They had covered all approach roads and tracks with machine guns so that the only way the Americans could attack was over the ridge line and into the quarry itself, where the German infantry were dug in. Nor could the superior American artillery be used effectively in any attack. It would be too dangerous to shell the area when the 3rd's infantry was close to the enemy. In essence, the Battle for the Cleurie Quarry, which would last for six bloody days, was going to be an infantry fight, pure and simple.

On September 30, Murphy's 1st Battalion was thrown into the attack, probing the enemy front, trying to find an easier way of attacking the heavily fortified place. As usual, Murphy was in the lead when he almost stumbled into a German machine gun position. The Americans reacted faster then the five Germans manning the post. One of his men ripped off a shot - and missed. Audie followed the shot with a grenade. It hit a tree and bounced off, exploding harmlessly.

Now it was the Germans' turn. A German NCO came at Murphy, waving a pistol. Murphy was quicker. He fired from the hip. The German fell down dead. One of the machine gunners sprang up. Perhaps he, too, was going to make an attempt to kill the *Ami*. Murphy didn't give him a chance to try. Again he pressed the trigger of his 'wounded carbine', and the German fell to the ground - dead. Moments later, Murphy's platoon finished off the rest with rifles and grenades, and another German strongpoint ceased to exist. But there were plenty more of them in the confused chaos of the hillside.

By the second day of the battle for the quarry, the Americans were beginning to beat the Germans back, but they were paying a heavy price for each yard of shattered earth that they gained. The enemy fought with stubborn, almost suicidal energy. They fought and retreated and just when the weary men 3rd thought they had finally broken the enemy's resistance and they were at last in full retreat, they would counterattack, and the whole bloody, costly business would commence yet once again.

On the evening of October 1, Capt. Paul Harris, Murphy's Company Commander, was briefing his platoon leaders on the plans for the morrow when suddenly, startlingly, small-arms fire started somewhere close by.

A German patrol had penetrated the 3rd's line yet again!

The startled non-coms and officers doused their lanterns as slugs began to howl off the stout stone walls of the cottage in which the briefing was taking place. Harris yelled an order. Crawling, ducking, the Americans fled the place, but not before Murphy had grabbed half a case of hand grenades.

Now the scared fugitives could hear the rumble of tracks. The Germans were bringing up their feared 'flak wagons', mobile 20mm anti aircraft cannon banked in fours, which when used in a ground role could fire an awesome one thousand rounds per minute!

But Murphy was master of the situation. As the Americans fled up a slope, he continued tossing grenades behind him, and as one of the survivors noted long afterward, 'Murphy... fought off that attack practically by himself. The next morning we found German caps, blood and equipment they left when they withdrew. He did a marvellous job all by himself'.[2]

However, the strain was beginning to tell on the attackers. That same night as Murphy began to prepare to select men for yet another patrol, he scanned their faces and decided, 'Most of them have been under fire since morning and are ready to collapse from strain and weariness. Knowing what I am after, they lower their eyes and keep silent while waiting for their names to be called. It is the same look that we developed as rookies when a non-com entered the barracks to tap men for an unpleasant detail'.[3]

Yet Murphy, who had the responsibility of command too, seemed both indestructible and indefatigable. Next morning, he was fighting fit and ready for action once more when two surprising visitors appeared in the platoon's lines. They were the Battalion Commander himself, bespectacled square-faced Col. Michael Paulick, accompanied by his executive officer, Lt. Col. Keith Ware. And it was indicative of just how grave the situation was that two senior officers came so far forward.

They told Murphy that they wished to find out where the machine gun fire was coming from that was holding up the whole 1st Battalion and had decided to take out a small patrol personally to check the German positions. Murphy didn't like the idea, but 'rank hath its privileges' and how could a twenty-year-old staff sergeant stop two colonels, plus his Company Commander Captain Harris, who was going to tag along too?

So off they went, the three officers, plus four enlisted men, heading straight for the quarry and the dug-in Germans whom Murphy knew to be everywhere. It was too much for the young non-com. Picking up his carbine and some grenades he decided to trail them as a 'security measure'. It was a measure of Murphy's almost pathological desire for action; there were few NCOs in the U.S. Army in the fall of '44 who would willingly have risked their necks for visiting brass who were foolish enough to venture into such danger.

It was fortunate for the two colonels that Murphy followed them. They hadn't gotten very far when a German machine gun opened up close by. Tracer zipped through the air frighteningly. As one, the officers and the enlisted men hit the ground, crawling for the little cover offered by a shallow depression nearby. There they went to ground with the bullets hissing just over their heads. Now it needed only one German with a lucky grenade - and the whole of the battalion's top bass would be wiped out.

But the Germans had not reckoned with Audie Murphy. Hearing the sudden machine gun fire, he guessed what had happened to the small patrol and doubled forward through the undergrowth. When he got close enough, he pressed himself behind a large stone hewn from the quarry and called out the names of the trapped men, one by one, to reassure them that all was not lost.

Then he went into action with his 'wounded carbine', which was becoming famous in Company B, and with grenades. Eleven years after the war, Colonel Paulick recalled the tense incident. 'Machine gun bullets ricocheted around us and the sound of our guns kept our ears ringing. It was then that I heard a familiar voice over the noise of battle It was Audie. I realized then that he must have some sort of plan in mind and that our positions had something to do with it'.[4]

Murphy had!

'Perhaps half a minute later the first of a series of grenades shattered the outpost. After the last explosions we rushed the position to complete the elimination. We found a machine gun, four dead Germans and three wounded'.

'To me the important thing about what I had just seen was Murphy's immediate grasp of the situation, his precise thinking and his uncanny coolness in action'.[5]

It was not surprising, with the Battalion Commander himself doing the recommending, that Murphy was put in for the Silver Star and the Legion of Merit for 'gallantry in action'. He received both.

A day later, Murphy took Lieutenant Colonel Ware and Capt. Merlin Stoker on what turned out to be a sniper hunt on the tip of the ridge overlooking the quarry. He came back grinning all over his freckled face and showed one of his comrades 'a rifle with a very powerful scope on it'. It had blood all over its stock, and when his comrade asked how he had come by the German weapon, a victorious Murphy chortled, "Well, Pyle, I caught a Kraut asleep in his hole and he was the biggest, ugliest Kraut I ever saw." [6] Had Murphy killed the man while he was asleep in cold blood? Murphy never explained.

Four days later Murphy won yet another Silver Star in the Battle for Cleurie Quarry. Leading a six-man patrol forward, Murphy and his men were surprised by the Germans. Four of his men fell down wounded or dead in the first startling burst of German fire. Murphy told the remaining two men to dig in, while he worked his way forward toward the enemy under mortar fire, keeping 'so low (that he) must have dug a ditch down the side of the hill', as he told a newspaperman after the war.

But in spite of the fact, as he told it, that he 'was cold, wet and scared and (that his) teeth chattered so loud (he) was afraid (he'd) give himself away'[7] he tackled and killed two German snipers. But that wasn't enough for Murphy; he called down mortar fire on the rest of the Germans while bullets cut the air all around him. Smoke followed, and as the surviving Germans tried to make a run for it, they were shot down mercilessly by the rest of Company B as they emerged choking and spluttering from the white, chemical smoke.

Thus in less than a week, he had taken out several ordinary patrols, two with high ranking officers, and had won the Silver Star twice over. Virtually every day in the hard fighting for the quarry at Cleurie, Murphy had risked his young life.

Why? What motivated him? He certainly didn't hate Germans. He wasn't bucking for promotion. Already he had been recommended for a commission and had turned it down (as we shall learn soon, he had to be coaxed by no less a person than the Battalion Commander himself into finally accepting one). Nor was he one of those rare combat soldiers one finds in all armies who delight, in killing for the mere sake of killing. Murphy was too sensitive for that.

Was it Tipton's death then? Was it the need to display his love that drove him to take such risks for his fellow soldiers? Was it the need to break out of that overwhelming loneliness that afflicted him now that all the 'old heads' had vanished into the bloody maws of the God of War? Or did he simply want to die - and get it over with, once and for all?

NOTES
1. Farago, op. cit.
2. Simpson, op. cit.
3. Murphy, op. cit.
4. Simpson, op. cit.
5. Ibid.
6. Murphy, op. cit.
7. Ibid.

20

In that same month that his life was saved by the young staff sergeant, Colonel Paulick, the CO of the 1ˢᵗ Battalion, had had enough of Murphy's dickering. One month previously he had called his Company Commanders together and had told them he wanted them to recommend enlisted men for battlefield commissions. There was an overwhelming shortage of infantry officers, and there weren't enough coming from Stateside. He told Captain Harris of B Company that 'there was one man he wanted to see on the list and that was the name of Audie Murphy'.[1]

A few days later the CO was surprised to see that Murphy's name was absent from Harris's list of recommendations. He called in the Company Commander and angrily asked why. Harris said that Murphy had categorically refused to be placed on the list. According to Murphy's own statement, he 'did not consider himself officer material. He was embarrassed by his of formal education and he did not choose to leave the men he had fought with so long'.[2]

Murphy's embarrassment was understandable. His Texan accent was thick and soldiers from the north often had difficulty in understanding him (it would be little different when he first went to Hollywood). He was ashamed of his terrible English and atrocious spelling. 'Squirrell' for 'squirrel', 'parfime' for 'perfume', 'witch' for 'which' and the like. When he wrote home to tell his sister he had won the DSC, he just couldn't manage the spelling of his award and, in his letter it became 'Distgh ser Cross'. In short, Murphy didn't feel that he could tackle the written work and administration that even a second lieutenant would have to deal with.

Paulick was adamant now, however. He called Murphy to his command post and ordered him to accept a commission. Murphy fought back. He told Paulick that 'if we needed him in battle he was willing to continue to command a platoon. He knew he could do that. But for administrative work of a higher order that might come up later, he insisted he didn't have the background. Besides there was the matter of leaving his company'.[3]

Paulick would not take no for an answer. He solved the problem there and then. He told Murphy firmly that his own battalion adjutant would take care of the paperwork and he, personally, would waive the usual policy of having an enlisted man transferred from his current outfit once he was commissioned. Murphy could stay with Company B. Murphy gave in. There was nothing else he could do.

Thus it was that on the morning of October 14, 1944, Audie Leon Murphy was formally discharged from the U.S. Army as an enlisted man. A few hours later, he and two other men from the 15ᵗʰ Infantry Regiment had the gold bars of a second lieutenant pinned on their shoulders by its commander Col. Hallett Edson. According to Murphy, the colonel told them, "You are now *gentlemen* by act of Congress. Shave, take a bath, and get the hell back into the lines!"[4]

Perhaps he did say that. New officers were certainly needed badly enough in the sorely depleted 3rd Infantry Division. Infantry commanders were in short supply at the front. And these three new 'second looeys' would be little different from all of those who had gone before them in this bitter fall, when the life expectancy of a combat commander was just a mere six weeks. Before that time had elapsed, Murphy's two companions would be dead and he would be fighting for his life in a military hospital.

Now, as the Americans pressed deeper and deeper into the Vosges Mountains with the Germans giving 'ground stubbornly, bitterly', as Murphy put it, not only did the terrain become tougher, but the weather too. 'In the mornings the ground is white with frost; snow is already on the mountain tops. The earth freezes and thaws, turning the terrain into an ocean of mud through which we must wallow toward our objectives. At night we shiver and sleep fitfully'.[5]

BBC correspondent Collin Wills, watching the 3rd advance that month, recorded, 'They climb into the hills and cold squalls of rain sweep down on them and drench them and then the rain suddenly gives place to snow - blanketing, blinding snow or a cruel driving sleet that freezes in solid sheets on the windscreens of the trucks. The drivers drive with bare red hands - the gloves can't grip the slippery wheel that whirls this way and then that with every bump and pothole and every slippery skid on the icy roads. On they go, these endless urgent columns crowding on every highway, debouching into the though country tracks that are churned into seething glaciers of mud. Mud surges up in an oily flood on the footboard, mud flies up in a dense spray from the whirling wheels, coating men and machines as completely as paint sprayed from an air gun'.[6]

And as the terrain changed, with the transformation from fall to winter, the people changed too. For the last three months the advancing Americans had been used to cheering crowds. They had been welcomed as the liberators from the Nazi yoke. Up here in the High Vosges, it was different. Here they were more like conquerors than liberators, for virtually every family had at least one male member fighting in the Wehrmacht. Since 1940 these people had been *Reichsdeutsche*, fully incorporated into the Third Reich, and the native language was German. French was the tongue that had been forced on them at school prior to 1940 when the Germans had come.

Down below the Vosges in the towns of the plain, most of the GIs had bought picture postcards of the locals, gaudy, cheaply coloured things, which they had sent back to the folks at home. 'Big-bosomed babes holding bunches of grapes between their toothpaste smiles and wearing picturesque Alsatian clothes', as one disgruntled sergeant described the cards that winter, 'or else pictures of mountain scenery with healthy happy people and an overripe yellow moon in the background.

But, as he went on to complain, echoing the thoughts of many of his comrades, 'the beautiful babes weren't beautiful anymore. The healthy happy people were hungry and thin… As for scenery, that forest full of snow-covered Christmas trees was lousy with snipers; those winding streams running through the valley in soft curves only made their feet wetter and the full moon shone on hills… making the GIs curse, thinking of the long fucking climb and the fucking mud and the fucking mortars on the other side!'[7]

In this mood of quiet despair, with nature itself seemingly conspiring against them, the weary men of the 3rd Division slogged ever higher into the mountains, with the Germans fighting 'their characteristic slow retreat', as Murphy put it. 'They batter our ranks with artillery and mortars; and in the forests, units lie like coiled snakes, striking suddenly and viciously'.[8]

On October 25, Murphy's Company B was ordered to continue the fight in the forests near the battered hamlet of Les Rouges Eaux, a significant enough name for the water of the river on which it lay, the Muerthe, had run red in the blood of both Americans and Germans. That day the company advanced under heavy German shellfire, relentlessly pushing the enemy back through the thick firs. Again Murphy's luck held out, although he was temporarily deafened by shellfire. All around him men died.

Next day, however, after nearly a year and a half in combat, the newly created 'second looey's' luck finally ran out.

Murphy was up front, leading his platoon through the woods, which today were thick with enemy snipers, some tied to the trees, their bodies camouflaged by shapeless green overalls and aprons, their faces streaked like those of Red Indians in a Hollywood B-movie. Directly behind him came his radio operator, a young, wisecracking replacement.

The two of them had just passed the body of a dead lieutenant, his uniform glistening with hoarfrost. The silence in the wood was unreal, treacherous. Just then there was a sharp, dry crack.

Without even a moan, the radio operator was pitched to the ground, dead before he hit it.

Sniper! The word flashed through Murphy's brain as he leaped for a tree, before the German, hidden to their front, got in a second shot.

Too late! Another dry crack like a twig breaking underfoot in a hot, dry summer.

The second bullet ricocheted off the tree and hit Murphy a tremendous blow in the side like that of a 'ball bat'. He yelled with pain and fell to the ground. The slug plowed through his hip and right buttock.

For one long moment he simply lay there, unaware of the pain, but gasping frantically, as if he had just run a long race. Some thirty yards to his front, the German sniper, confident that he had dealt with the first *Ami* who had walked so stupidly into his trap threw back the camouflage net that had

111

hidden him and prepared to finish off the second American who lay helpless in the trail.

For some reason he fired at Murphy's helmet, which had rolled from his head under the impact of the first slug. As Murphy commented grimly, "that is the last mistake he ever makes"[9]

Sick with shock, but still conscious, hardly able to move more than a couple of inches, Murphy raised his carbine pistol-fashion and fired. As always, even now when the world was swimming before his eyes, he didn't miss. Hadn't he been brought up to hit the animal or go hungry'?

The bullet caught the German right between the eyes. He fell back with a howl of absolute, total agony. As Murphy said after the war, "It was his brain or nothing. He would not have missed the second time".[10]

The wounded Murphy tried to rise to his feet. He couldn't. The pain was overwhelming, and his right leg was paralysed. So he simply lay there panting while the others emerged from the trees. One of Company B's non-coms, a sergeant, examined the wound and told the officer, his face now white with pain, that the bone didn't seem broken and that if everything went well Murphy might be able to sit down 'in a month or so'.

He, like all the rest of them staring down at Murphy, was sympathetic but realistic. Murphy was 'out'. He had his 'million dollar wound'. But they were going to have to continue fighting - and dying. So the sergeant, in the unfeeling way of the combat soldier, ignored Murphy's moans of pain and asked if he could have the lieutenant's 'lucky carbine': the patched up weapon that had been Murphy's since Italy.

Murphy said he could. "Thanks", the sergeant said, no doubt hoping the beat-up old weapon would bring him the same kind of luck it had Murphy. It didn't. Next day, he was killed and most of the platoon was wiped out in a savage firefight in the forest.

The men of what had once been Murphy's platoon pushed on into the trees and their own date with destiny, leaving Murphy to be borne laboriously to the rear by the cursing, overworked stretcher bearers. Murphy no longer cared. He was racked by pain. His whole lower body seemed on fire and the first shot of morphia they had given him was not yet working.

He was placed in a box-like ambulance together with other wounded and driven down rutted muddy tracks to the base of the mountains, the wounded crying out in pain every time the ambulance hit a pothole.

Finally they were unloaded at a crude, tented hospital, where Murphy had to wait several hours for attention, while the harassed doctors worked on more serious cases. 'My hip feels as though a white-hot brand had been raked across it; and I feel sick in mind and body'.[11]

For three long days Murphy lay in the company of six other wounded officers in a pyramid tent with duckboard floors, set up in the mud, while the bitter rain beat down on the canvas outside, attended to by medics in helmets and rubber boots who smelled of ether and fresh blood. The fever

In an early photo of four of the Murphy children, Audie,
a typical poor Texas sharecropper's son stands on the right.

The High Vosges mountain range in eastern France through which Murphy's unit fought in the advance on Germany.

The Alsatian town of Neuf-Brisach, known to the GIs as 'Waffle City' on acount of its shape, was the 3rd Division's objective when Audie Murphy won his Medal of Honor.

Tank Destroyers waiting for enemy Panzers.

Entering the village of Holtzwihr.

Great Parade of 42, 45 and 3ʳᵈ U.S. Divisions. April 1945 at Hitler's Nuremburg Stadium.

Major Gerneral John 'Iron Mike' O'Daniel presents 1ˢᵗ Lt. Audie Murphy with the Distinguished Service Cross and Silver Star Medals.

Audie Murphy collects his medals in *'To Hell and Back'*.

Holtzwihr - looking south out of the woods from Audie's point of view.

Holtzwihr - looking north from the German point of view.

118

Parts from the M10 Tank Destroyer found by Marty Back
at the battle site near Holzwihr in 1996/97.

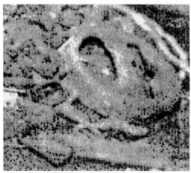

Left Tail Light Lens cover
found at Holzwihr.

View of a Left Tail Light Lens cover.

M10 Tank Destroyer parts.

119

Then and now. Nothing today remains in France to recall Murphy's heroism.

1870 Cannon at Holzwihr.

Murphy and David 'Spec' McClure visit
the beachhead in southern France in 1948.

(Left) Murphy in
'To Hell and Back'.

(Right) A war-weary star relives
his wartime exploits
in *'To Hell and Back'*.

121

Military Promotional Photo.

Audie Murphy and Burt Lancaster in the film *'The Unforgiven'*.

Murphy and his first wife, Wanda Hendrix *(Universal International)*.

Murphy and his second wife, the former Pamela Archer.

Murphy as the Young Soldier in The Red Badge of Courage *(Universal-International)*.

The cast of The Red Badge of Courage assembled for a picture. *(Universal-International)*.

Murphy in *'Gunpoint'*.

Murphy in
'Six Black Horses'.

Last-known publicity photo, Murphy - though approaching fifty - is still handsome and extremely youthful.

Audie L Murphy's grave in Arlington National Cemetery.

NO. 23 OF 45

MOVIE STARS

What current movie star is the most decorated hero of World War II?

SEE DIRECTIONS INSIDE WRAP

1950s collectors' movie cards.

JOIN THE
AUDIE MURPHY PLATOON

Captain Audie L. Murphy
Serve With His Famous
3d INFANTRY DIVISION
(THE ROCK OF THE MARNE)
AT WURZBURG GERMANY

Serve with your friends
in the same unit
Sightsee along the Rhine River
Vacation in Berlin — Paris — Rome

Army Recruiting Poster.

The memory of Audie Murphy lives on.

spread through his torn young body, while beside him 'delirious men moan and curse'.[12]

In the end he was loaded into a long, white-painted ambulance train and taken away from the mud and misery and sudden death of the High Vosges. Already up there it was beginning to snow heavily and would continue to do so all winter till the day he came back.

He was carried south with the rest of the seriously wounded, flushed with fever and worried by the strange smell coming from the great wound in his buttock. As they passed through the places where the 3rd had once fought - Besançon, Valence, Loriol, Montelimar - the female nurses tended him, looking just as worried as he was. The sun started to slant in through the small windows of the coach, and he fought his worries. They were in the Provence, passing through Arles where Van Gogh had once painted, though the young officer knew nothing of the Dutch painter, heading for the ancient capital of the province, Aix-en-Provence, and the Third General Hospital, where he would spend the next two months recovering from the sniper's bullet.

By now Murphy thought his wound had gone gangrenous from the three-day delay in treatment at the tented hospital just behind the lines. The doctor he asked about it said the wound was just infected. Yet the way the medic sniffed at the open wound - for the stench of rotting flesh, typical of gangrene - and then shook his head, told Murphy he was right.

He was. For the next month, the doctors would 'pump me full of penicillin and whittle away dead and poisoned flesh'[13] until finally they had removed five pounds of it, leaving him with a livid nine-inch scar. Murphy suffered it all willingly. He wanted to live, for he was beginning to fall in love.

NOTES

1. Simpson, op. cit.
2. Ibid.
3. Ibid.
4. Murphy, op. cit.
5. Ibid.
6. BBC War Report, op. cit.
7. Martin, op. cit.
8. Murphy, op. cit.
9. Ibid.
10. Ibid.
11. Ibid.
12. Ibid.
13. Ibid.

21

At first Murphy, like the rest of the seriously wounded, lived in the clouded limbo of a military hospital, sleeping, waking, only half aware of the misery and pain all around him; the stench of ether and rotting flesh; the pain of the dressings; the mess of dried blood and pus, green in places; the ritual of Professor Fleming's wonder drug, penicillin, pumped into his skinny, wasted body every three hours, around the clock, day and night.

On November 3, he wrote to Haney Lee, nicknamed the 'General', for whom he had worked back in Texas just before he had enlisted:

> I have nothing to do but lay in bed, so will try to write you a couple of lines to day (sic), if you can read it. I can't set up so I have quite a time trying to write very clearly.
>
> I haven't gotten any mail for a long time now, hope it catches up with me soon. Say, Gen, those Krauts are getting to be better shots than they used to be or else my lucks playing out on me and I guess someday they will tag me for keeps. Nice thought anyway.
>
> Gen, do you ever go hunting? I guess not, to much walking huh. Remember how I use to bug you to (go hunting) with me. Oh well *when* I get home I'll not get out of the house far enough to shoot a sqirrill.
>
> I've seen so much blood I don't think I ever want to shoot anything else except (Krauts and Japs) ha, ha fooled you didn't I. Well Gen can't think of a thing more to write so had better sign 30 for now.
>
> Ans soon
Lt.
>
> P.S. Meant to send you a couple of Kraut PW's to help you farm, but thought before I closed sorry, can't, sorry. [1]

Beneath the banter and the attempt at humour, it was clear that wound had been a shock to Murphy; but like the rest, once immediate pain had cleared up, he chattered compulsively about his battle experience. Each of them explained to the others how he came by his wounds, going into much detail. Then suddenly, they stopped talking about such things. Why recall all the pain?

Now they became reflective. They had come through the shouting, the crash of gunfire, the noise, the chaos of the battlefield. *They had survived!* But underneath they knew their own suffering and experience really meant nothing. By some chance, for there was no reason to it, fate had picked them to survive while their comrades had perished. Why had he, Murphy, been saved when the rest of his platoon had been wiped out the very next day? There were no answers to those sorts of questions.

So they shut up about the fighting. They retreated into their individual cocoons, trying to get well, finding convalescence tolerable, enjoying the weak winter sunshine of Provence. They watched the cheery, superficial movies that Hollywood sent out to boost their morale, read trivial detective stories and cowboy epics, and flirted with the more available of the nurses, all the time waiting for the call that would one day summon them back 'up there'.

In Murphy's ward there was another young officer, roughly his age, who had suffered much more terrible wounds than he. His name was Perry Pitt, and he would remain Murphy's friend until the day the latter died. Pitt had been so badly hit by a German shell that he was a paraplegic, destined to be confined a wheelchair until he died as an old man.

That winter in Aix, he was desperate; his whole young life was ruined. He was no longer a complete man. Time and time again, he ran high fevers, and it was on these occasions that the duty nurse took it upon herself to give the grievously injured young officer special care. Even when she was off duty, she came into the Third General to care for and reassure Pitt.

Her name was Carolyn Price. She was a pretty first lieutenant with a strong determined face beneath dark chestnut-brown hair rolled in the fashionable, practical wave of the time; a dedicated, well-educated twenty-four year old, who had been overseas working in military hospitals for a year now.

It was quite natural that the wounded young hero, who was four years her junior, and whose contacts with women over the last two years had been limited to the fleeting, commercial contacts that were the lot of an infantryman, fell desperately in love with Carolyn Price. Indeed, she was the first American woman with whom he had exchanged more than a few words since 1943 - and that helped, too. And, in the final analysis, Murphy, who admired courage And determination so much, could not but fall for a person who devoted herself to a man like Perry Pitt, whom most people, especially women, would think of as a hopeless case.

Later his friend David McClure would say of him, 'He fell in love with her (Carolyn). That was the story of his life. He was always falling desperately in love with some girl'.[2] But this was the very first time and Murphy did not want the affair to become one of those fleeting encounters that had been his lot up to now. He asked Carolyn Price to marry him.

She turned him down. She had seen enough of what happened to young men like Audie Murphy in war: broken bodies to be patched up and sent to the front once more, never to return. She had no desire to become an instant widow. Besides, she had her job and her dedication to the wounded, broken both in body and spirit, who flooded into Third General day after day, week after week. That selfless task, the tending of these soldiers who had been hurt so much, would continue after Murphy had gone.

After the war had ended, Murphy would say little of his romance with Carolyn Price. Nor would Carolyn Price detail what had gone on between them that winter. She was no Agnes Kurowsky, who tended Hemingway when he was wounded and in hospital in Milan in World War I. She would not write a letter to her lover that included a sentence as fine as the one penned by Agnes Kurowsky to her lover before rejecting *his* offer of marriage. What the nurse in Milan wrote was: 'At least we had our spring'.

Hemingway was tormented by the anguish of that winter love affair for the rest of his life. It forced from him the haunting statement that 'A broken heart means that never can you remember and not being able to remember is very different from forgetting'.[3]

Murphy wrote to her, of course, when he returned to the front, but after he had become famous in the movies, Carolyn destroyed the letters in case they 'fell into the wrong hands'.[4]

Later, when he was on leave in Cannes on VE Day, he called her and asked her to come down to the coast to join him in celebrating the end of the war in Europe. She refused, saying she was on duty. Five months after that, in November 1945, he met Carolyn in San Antonio. She was still in the service and in uniform and Audie was not. Later she told David McClure that the young man who had once loved her 'acted a bit awkward' on account of the difference in their positions. That was the last time they ever saw each other.

Unlike a disappointed Hemingway, he could not write to a friend when it was all over: 'Idealists lead a rough life in this world, Jim. But like hermit crabs they acquire shells. At any rate, I'm now free… and I can fall in love with anyone I wish'.[5] But if Audie Murphy, only one year older than a lovesick Hemingway had been when his nurse-lover turned him down, could not vocalize his thoughts, he could *live* them. He had already acquired one shell. Now he'd put on another. Like Hemingway he would feel free too to love anyone he wished - and he would.

While an unhappy Murphy recovered in hospital in far-off Aix, things were happening at the front. Twelve days before he was finally discharged from Third General, on Saturday, December 16, 1944, the German Army struck in the Belgian Ardennes, taking the top brass completely by surprise. Within twenty-four hours, a quarter of a million Germans were streaming westward through the broken American front, heading for the coast. Day after day, as the last Christmas of World War II approached, the news was black and hopeless. Up north it was defeat after defeat, with the Germans poised to cross the key Meuse River and bolt for the channel ports; and if they managed to seize those, the young officers glued to the radios knew, then the war could go on for a long time.

Three days before Christmas. Patton started to pull his Third Army out of the Saar area, next to the eighty miles of front held by General Patch's Seventh Army, to which Murphy's 3rd Division still belonged. By Christmas Eve the Third Army had gone into the battle, a third of a million men, leaving behind a great gap in the Allied line along the Saar-Rhine front, which had to be filled by spreading out the Seventh Army. Two days later, while de Lattre's French First Army was fully occupied guarding General Wiese's troops dug in, in what was called the Colmar Pocket, Patch's Seventh was woefully thin, manning a line that stretched from Switzerland to just below Saarbrucken in Germany. Where there had been two armies there was now one. It was a recipe for disaster!

On December 28, the day that Murphy was discharged from the hospital to go on a two-week convalescent leave, with the Germans going all out to defeat the 'battered bastards of Bastogne', Hitler called together his Corps and Divisional Commanders at his remote command post in the Gothic castle of Ziegenheim, from whence he was directing the battle in the west. With a trace of his old fire and magnetism he told the generals who would carry out the new attack that they must make a supreme effort. The initial attack into the Ardennes had caught the *Amis* completely by surprise. Now he was prepared to launch a new one into the thinly held line of the U.S. Seventh Army in Alsace.

"I wish to appeal to you to go into the operation with all your verve", he cried at them, "with all your zest and all your energy. This is a decisive operation... We will yet be masters of our fate!"[6]

Then he announced the date for the great new attack, code-named Operation Northwind. In order to achieve complete surprise, Hitler set the time for the beginning of the assault at 11:00 pm, New Year's Eve. The *Amis* would be celebrating. They would be too drunk to know what was happening to them until it was too late. At least, that was what Hitler hoped.

Where Audie Murphy spent that New Year's Eve, the last of World War II, is not recorded. What the young officer did, frustrated in love, perhaps sick at heart and lonely, we do not know. It would be the last time for the rest of his short life that an important event or happening was not documented. Soon his movements would be very definitely 'news'.

But wherever he was that night and however he celebrated the passing of the old and 'the ringing in of the New', he could not have realized, not for the life of him, how the events taking place further north would change everything. Not even in his wildest dreams could this semi-illiterate son of a Texas sharecropper, whose occupation was listed on his Army documents as 'farm labourer', have foreseen what this New Year of 1945 was going to bring for him. His whole future was about to be magically transformed.

This night, the skinny pale twenty-year-old who walked with limp was just another of scores of similar obscure 'second looeys' waiting to go back into the line, doomed to an early death or, if they survived, to the vast obscurity of humdrum civilian life from whence they had come. There, 'in the land of the round doorknob', as they called it in the parlance of the time, they would court, marry, and procreate. And then they would die as obscurely as they had lived. History would not deign to record their passing.

But not this youngster with the limp. Fate had already picked him out.

Adolf Hitler announced over Radio Berlin: "I want, therefore, in this hour, as the spokesman of Greater Germany, to promise solemnly to the Almighty that we shall fulfill our duty faithfully and unshakeably in the New Year; in the firm belief that the hour will strike when victory will ultimately come to him who is most worthy of it, the *Greater German Reich!*"[7] As he did so, the clocks chimed twelve, and the elements of eight German divisions rushed the American lines in the snowbound Alsace-Lorraine area. The last German counterattack of the Second World War in the West - Operation Northwind - had commenced.

It was 1945 - Audie Leon Murphy's year of destiny!

NOTES
1. Simpson, op. cit.
2. Letter to author
3. Sunday Telegraph Magazine. London: April 12, 1986.
4. Letter to author
5. Sunday Telegraph, op. cit.
6. J. Eisenhower. The Bitter Wood. New York: Putnam's, 1967.
7. Ibid.

22

Now - at last - the Germans were on the run in Alsace. By the end of January, days after Audie Murphy had carried out that amazing one-man stand at Holtzwihr and won himself the Medal of Honor, the sadly depleted 3rd Division had taken virtually all their objectives. The capture of Colmar itself and the final elimination of what was left of the Colmar Pocket were only a matter of days away. The Germans were pulling back rapidly from the city, heading for the fortified town of Neuf-Brisach, the Rhine crossing, and the safety of the Reich. General Wiese's Nineteenth Army, which had fought the Franco-Americans ever since the invasion of southern France, had almost ceased to exist. *

The weather had changed, too. The air had become milder and the icy winds from the still-snowbound Vosges had died down. In the Rhine valley the deep snows that had made life so difficult for the combat infantryman were beginning to thaw, turning the fields and the country lanes into a sea of heel-clinging mud and slush.

On the first day of February 1945, Audie Murphy led what was left of his battered Company B and a handful of scared replacements into the attack once more. At the outskirts of the Alsatian village of Kunheim they succeeded in capturing a half-dozen, woebegone German infantrymen, without much of a fight. Murphy ordered them 'searched', which meant in GI terms, searched - *and looted*. His men were just doing this when there was the rusty clank of armour.

Murphy, half-bored, half-amused by his men's activities, spun around at the sound - and gasped. The tanks were German and they were laden with German infantry! As weary as he was, Audie Murphy acted with his old speed and decisiveness. Hastily he grabbed a helmet from one of the prisoners and clamped it on his own head. A few of his men did the same. Then they tensed, their rifles stuck in the sides of their prisoners.

The German tanks came within thirty yards. Murphy swallowed hard, feeling the cold sweat trickle down the small of his back. After nearly two years of combat, was he finally going to be hauled off ignominiously 'into the bag'? He waved hopefully.

It did the trick. The tank drivers turned their noisy steel monsters and the three Mark IVs disappeared into the morning gloom, trailing behind them a wake of pebbles and flying mud. Murphy let his shoulders slump

---

* In the meantime, General Wiese had been removed from his command and returned to Germany. So he never surrendered to the Americans, against whom he had fought so long and so skilfully.

wearily. It had been a near thing. They pushed on.

The fighting was not altogether over yet. At five o'clock in the morning of the same day that Colmar fell, the 3rd's 7th Infantry Regiment attacked toward the Rhine in an attempt to seal off Neuf-Brisach, the last town in German hands. It was going to be the last action of the 7th on French soil after having suffered 10,000 casualties, a staggering three hundred percent loss rate in its last two and a half years of combat.

Just outside the village of Biesheim, the leading elements ran straight into a large force of concealed Germans. The enemy outnumbered the American point four to one. Fierce hand-to-hand fighting broke out. An artillery observer with the 7th, T/5 Forrest Peden volunteered to go back for help. He returned with two light tanks and guided them back toward the old Jewish cemetery at Biesheim, where an eerie battle was taking place among the medieval tombstones. Just as Peden's tank reached a large ditch outside the cemetery, where a large number of the 7th were trapped, it was struck a tremendous blow by a German anti-tank shell. It reeled to a stop and began blazing fiercely at once. The crew bailed out, but Peden died on the deck, consumed in a funeral pyre of burning fuel. Yet another brave man in the 'Rock of the Marne' Division - the third of the campaign - had won the Medal of Honor.

But Audie Murphy was making certain that he would not receive *his* medal posthumously as he led his men through the same area in the attack on Neuf-Brisach. That same night, as he recorded later, 'We creep as stealthily as mice through the strange territory. A brick wall rears before us. We pause, listening intently for the clink of metal, the guttural whisper, or the scrape of a boot. But except for the sighing of the wind through the trees, there is no sound'.[1]

Murphy rolled over the wall next to him and, to his surprise, found himself inside a walled cemetery. He ordered his men inside, too, for the rest of the night. It would make an ideal bivouac for his footsore, weary troops. Not all of them were convinced. One of them said, "The graveyard company finally gets home".[2] Another commented drily, "Move over friends. You got some company!"[3]

Nevertheless, they slept soundly, while Murphy, as weary as they, took it upon himself to stand guard. Twice he nodded off. In the end, he took out his pistol and held it at his waist with both hands. The next time he dozed off, the gun slipped from his fingers, struck him on the foot, and brought him back to consciousness.

Dawn revealed to the sleepy, yawning GIs that they had dug in only a few dozen yards from a group of German infantry who had done the same in the field on the other side of the wall. Murphy could hardly believe his eyes, as he stared through a hole in the wall at the awakening Germans. It was an infantryman's dream. Audie Murphy could not resist such a tempting target. Hastily he ordered up his machine gun crew. They slipped the weapon through the wall and aimed at the Germans. The machine gun burst into frenetic activity, shattering the dawn calm. Four of the totally surprised Germans went down, arms flailing, dead or wounded. The rest flung up their arms, crying "*Kamerad*" in hysterical voices. They wanted to surrender - quickly. The advance of Neuf-Brisach went on.

On February 6, the 3rd had virtually invested Neuf-Brisach, the last German stronghold. Now the GIs of the Marne Division were calling the eighteenth-century fortress 'waffle city', because from the air, with its criss-cross of streets within the fortifications, it looked exactly like a waffle. On that morning, the commander of the 3rd Division's 30th Regiment told the CO of his 1st Battalion, he wanted a 'waffle for my breakfast'. The hint was all too obvious. The 1st Battalion moved in to the attack.

Later Gen. George C. Marshall, the U.S. Army's Chief of Staff, wrote in his account of World War II, *The Winning of the War in Europe and the Pacific*, that 'The climax of the battle was a night assault on the bridgehead town of Neuf-Brisach by infantry of the U.S. Third Division, using assault boats and scaling ladders on the moats and walls of the fortified town, very much after the fashion of medieval battles'.[4]

Marshall had let his imagination run away with him. It was actually broad daylight when the fort was taken, and the moat had been dry for a century or more. There were no scaling ladders and assault boats. The first patrol of the 3rd to enter the place was guided by two scared schoolchildren. The fortification surrendered without a shot being fired and the two French kids were rewarded for their bravery with a handful of GI candy!

The Regimental Commander had his 'waffle' for breakfast, and the brass were pleased. That was all that mattered. The dogfaces of the 3rd Division were too exhausted to concern themselves with the glory of having captured the last German stronghold on the west bank of the Rhine.

The congratulations poured in, but as the survivors of the Colmar Pocket Battle finally reached the Rhine once more,* the only official communication that meant much to them was the one they received on February 10. It read, 'Organized enemy resistance west of the Rhine River between Strasbourg and the Swiss border is reported to have ceased. Order of Battle - *no contact!*'[5]

It had been a bitter hard fight for the 3rd Division. In sixteen days of combat, the division had won three Medals of Honor, captured twenty-two towns and taken 4,200 prisoners, killing an unknown number of Germans and virtually destroying what was left of the German 708th Volksgrenadier Division and 2nd Austrian Mountain Division. But the butcher's bill had been terribly high. The division's 30th Regiment alone had suffered a total of 1,170 casualties, one-third of its strength; while the 7th, which boasted that it always suffered more casualties than any other regiment in the U.S. Army had

*The 3ʲ had first reached the Rhine in November 1944

lost roughly the same number.

Figures for the 15th, Murphy's regiment are not available, but it, too, if Murphy's company is anything to go by had suffered terribly. And so had its twenty-year-old commander. In his immature hand, he wrote on a picture extant, taken at that time, 'Eek horrors, it's me again - have lost some weight and a bit pale, yet'.[6] It shows him in his new officer's trench coat, hair carefully dressed in his drugstore pompadour style, brought with him from his Texas teenage days, head cocked quizzically to one side.

The face is still amazingly youthful, almost childlike and unlined, after what he had gone through. But the eyes are a give-away. They are looking out at a world that would be beyond the comprehension of the recipient back in Texas. They are really the eyes of a youth who *had* been to 'hell and back', as he would one day entitle his autobiography.

They are the eyes already of a man who would never settle, never fit into the cosy, complacent, unthinking world of civilian life. Never! The war had stamped him indelibly. One day he would come back from the fighting, bearing the war with him like an invisible army pack for the rest of his life.

In that second week of February, the 15th Regiment went into reserve, and Murphy took the opportunity of going on leave to 'Gay Paree'.

Apparently he liked Paris, for he praised the place in his letters, though probably all he saw, just as most GIs from the line did, was 'Pig Alley' (Pigalle), with its drinking dens and whores, where the dogfaces were commercially entertained for a few hours before being shipped back.

On March 5, Murphy was called to Nancy where 'Iron Mike' O'Daniel pinned on him the DSC and his Silver Star. It was probably here that he was told that he had been recommended for the Medal of Honor for his valour at Holtzwihr. For on that same day he wrote home to his sister Corinne: 'Well, sis i have been awarded the DSC, the Silver Star and the Distgh ser Cross for Valor and the SS for Gallantry in action. I have also been recommended for the Cong medal of honor. Boy if I get that i will soon be coming home, well not much news over here so will goodbye now. Love to all Audie. PS. The women over here are wearing the same thing in Brassiers this year. Believe it or not'.[7]

That day Audie Murphy's combat career virtually came to an end. The brass, who had lost so many recipients of the MOH in the 3rd Division, decided that Murphy was not going to receive his medal posthumously like so many of the rest. The war had two months to go, and he was transferred to the staff. He became a liaison officer with the 15th. Due to his lack of education he was of little use in a real, working staff job. Instead he was given the task of jeeping from regiment to regiment within the 3rd, keeping the headquarters informed of what the 15th was doing, as it prepared for the last attacks. These were to be launched against the Siegfried Line and the Rhine itself, the last great natural barrier protecting Germany in the west.

Murphy's own feelings about his new post were mixed. 'The constant peril of the front lines is temporarily over', he wrote later. 'There will be small dangers, of course, and moments of minor terror... Eventually I feel that I will go back up; and somewhere, sometime, the bullet bearing my name will find me'.[8]

He still courted danger in his new position. Combat had become a drug that he craved. In that same March, as his former regiment attacked in the Saarbrucken-Zweibrucken area, fighting their way through the vaunted Siegfried Line with heavy casualties, he heard that Capt. Paul Harris, now commanding his old Company B, and two of his company officers had been killed in the fighting, and what was left of the company was bogged down.

Without saying a word to his fellow staff officers, he commandeered a sergeant and a jeep and drove toward the sound of the fighting. Then he got out and walked until he found Company B, huddled in a trench and pinned down by enemy fire. They were commanded by a green young officer and were frightened and trembling.

Murphy coaxed the badly shaken survivors out of the trench, and rallied them enough to take them through the pillboxes and dragon's teeth of the portion of the Siegfried Line that faced them. For some reason, German fire had ceased, and not one shot was fired at them. Having cared for his lost sheep, Audie Murphy left and returned to his staff job. He found he had not been missed in his absence, which was good enough for him. He never mentioned the incident to anyone, and it would have been forgotten if one of the survivors of the bogged-down company in the Siegfried Line had not written about it.

Things were moving fast. The 3rd Division barrelled through Germany, but here and there the fighting was stiff enough for a couple of its members to win the Medal of Honor. There was some talk of a last-ditch stand by the Nazis in the Bavarian-German Alps - 'the Alpine Redoubt' as the supposed fortress was called. The 3rd turned south-east toward the Alps. On April 11, the 3rd took part in a three-division assault on Nuremberg, where Hitler had held his vaunted *Parteitag* in better times. On April 20, the day ironically enough when the Fuehrer celebrated his last birthday in besieged Berlin, the ruined city fell to the Americans.

Again the 3rd pushed on toward the Alps. Now a prestige objective loomed large, Hitler's mountain home, the 'Eagle's Nest' at Berchtesgaden. Although the place was strictly outside the 3rd's zone of operations, 'Iron Mike' reasoned that his division, which had fought so long, should have the honour of taking the place. The U.S. 101st Airborne Division and French General Leclerc's 2nd Armored Division also in the area had been a mere twinkle in the planners' eye when the 3rd had first gone into action back in 1942.

So, in the way that victorious generals play in wartime, the three Divisional Commanders raced for the completely unimportant, bombed-out mountain ruin, each trying to hinder and stop the other. In the end, the 3rd and the 2nd Armored reached the place together. A compromise was agreed upon. Both the American and French flags would be hoisted over the 'Eagle's Nest' in a joint ceremony. For some reason the *tricoleur* fell down (American sabotage?) and pride of place was left to Old Glory. Meanwhile, Eisenhower stepped in and ordered 'Iron Mike' O'Daniel to get on with the job of capturing Salzburg just over the border in Austria.

On May 4, 1945, Mozart's birthplace fell to the Americans, and the war in Europe was over for the 3rd. But Murphy did not join in the massive wingding that took place a few days later to celebrate VE Day. He heard about it in Cannes, where he had gone on a short furlough.

In the midst of that wild, ecstatic celebration that swept Allied Europe on that bright May day in 1945, Murphy felt alone. He was restless and his nights were plagued by evil dreams. In the end he decided to go up to Aix to visit Carolyn Price.

Later Miss Price wrote to Perry Pitt, who was now back in hospital in the States, 'Murphy came to see me last week. He looks great but limps even more as the result of another wound he received after leaving the Third General Hospital. He now has so many ribbons that his chest is beginning to resemble General Marshall's. But he still refuses to wear all that he is entitled'. Miss Price wrote he refused to talk about how he had won the Medal of Honor, but added, 'I do wish he'd accept a discharge… However I am sure he won't. He's dreadfully tired but determined to see this thing through to the end - his or the war's'. His luck has been remarkable but he can't hold out much longer'.[9]

NOTES
1.   Murphy, op. cit.
2.   Ibid.
3.   Ibid.
4.   Taggart, op. cit.
5.   Ibid.
6.   Simpson, op. cit.
7.   Ibid.
8.   Murphy, op. cit.
9.   Letter to author.

23

Audie Murphy would never need to chance that proverbial luck of his again in combat. Although the war with Japan still raged, Audie Murphy had become too valuable a 'property' for the Army to lose him fighting the 'Nips'.

On the afternoon of June 2, Murphy was presented with the Medal of Honor and the Legion of Merit by no less a person than General Patch himself. The ceremony was held at an airfield just outside Salzburg and was watched by eleven senators. It was a foretaste of what was to come.

As the Army Commander, who had been wounded and had won the Silver Star himself in France in the 'Old War', placed the coveted blue, starred ribbon around Murphy's neck, he asked, "I wonder if you are as nervous as I am?"

Murphy wet his lips and replied dutifully, "Yessir, I'm afraid so."[1]

That finished, Patch pinned the Legion of Merit above Murphy's left pocket, while the senators applauded. The presentation of those last two medals now made Audie Murphy, as yet not old enough to vote, the most decorated soldier in the history of the United States Army. And the Army knew it. The razzmatazz could commence…

The United States went to war in 1941 with a very unusual army. Up to Pearl Harbor, it had kept itself in the background. It was hardly mentioned in the media, its officers kept a low profile, and starved of funds as it was (the only limousine allowed in 'the whole of the U.S. Army was that used to transport the Chief of the Army) it was hardly a glamorous organization. All that changed virtually overnight after December 7, 1941.

Within weeks, the Army was flooded with public relations men. Suddenly obscure colonels and majors, who were now Army Commanders, became public figures, featured on the covers of national magazines such as *Life* and *Time*, appearing weekly in the newsreels so that they were known and recognized even in the smallest, most remote township.

At every level, there were PR men, photographers, and 'glad-handers', as they were called at the time, whose full-time occupation it was to 'plug" their general and their outfit. Eisenhower had one, Harry Butcher, a former radio executive, whom Hemingway described maliciously as 'a nylon-smooth captain of the Navy who could not command a cat-boat'.[2] Ernie Pyle, the reporter, was ordered by the same 'nylon-smooth' gentleman to go out and 'discover' General Omar Bradley. He did and Bradley became duly 'the GI General'.

General Mark Clark, Murphy's former commander, of whom British thriller writer Eric Ambler has written, 'No World War II commander of men had worked more assiduously in the field of public relations than General Clark'[3], even had a song composed about himself! It was sung to the tune of some patriotic ditty and was sung before entertainments given to his headquarters troops in Italy. In part, it read, 'Stand up and sing the praise of General Clark. Your hearts and voices raise for General Clark. Red, White and Blue unfurled upon the field. Its message flaunts Clark's sons will never, never yield'.[4] Nauseating stuff, indeed, but typical of the manner in which the Army publicized its own in those days. The 1st Infantry Division - 'the Big Red One' - which never let it be forgotten that the war was being fought by the Big Red One and 'ten million replacements" even had a PR man who sang calypsos!

Now the PR machine of the U.S. Army took up the young 'hero' He was given the chance of staying in the Army of Occupation as a captain or returning home to the States. The Army preferred the latter. The war with Japan still raged, and Audie Murphy would make excellent copy. Here was this handsome youngster with his ready smile and open face, who had won every medal that the U.S.A. had to give and had killed 240 'Krauts' in the bargain, but had emerged from it all unscathed. Wouldn't he be an inspiration to all those other eager teenage hopefuls, ripe for some desperate glory in the Pacific? This was the *real* John Wayne!

So the Army took charge of the youth. The machine set about making him national news, trumpeting his battlefield exploits throughout the States, and in doing so stamped him forever as 'the most decorated soldier of WWII'. It was going to become Audie Murphy's inescapable public image, one that would burden him till the day he died. He would be idolized for his war record, pure and simple, and for nothing else. As World War II receded from the public's mind and was replaced by new wars - Korea, Vietnam - Murphy still remained that 'most decorated soldier".

On June 10, Murphy left Europe to return to Texas and receive a hero's welcome. Three days later, three transport planes, escorted by a mass formation of eighty fighters and bombers, touched down at Ellington Field near Houston. There, as the guns thundered their salute and the brass bands blared, an assorted bunch of top brass and local heroes started to descend from the planes to be greeted by the local authorities.

There was General Truscott, Murphy's old Divisional Commander, who would soon take over Patton's Third Army command in Germany; Lieutenant General Eaker, commander of the Mediterranean Air Force; Gen. J. Lawton 'Lightning Joe' Collins, who had commanded the U.S. VII Corps in Europe; Gen. 'Slim Jim' Gavin, the dashing commander of the 82nd Airborne; General Patch, who had presented Murphy with his MOH the previous week... and Murphy himself, descending last from the plane, looking small, shy, insignificant, and definitely out of place in this assembly as he limped forward toward the welcoming committee of Texan glad-handers.

At four-thirty that afternoon, after the 'victory parade', there was a press conference, where 'this gallant and courageous young Texan'[5], as the Texas House of Representatives officially declared Murphy, was asked by a young woman reporter how he had won his Medal of Honor. Murphy groaned in mock dismay and said, "Oh, no. Not that!" Asked a little later if he would pose for a picture with General Eaker, Murphy replied; "I sure wouldn't want to ask the general to pose for any picture with me."[6]

Eaker, as aware of his personal publicity as the next general, responded immediately. Weren't all four-star generals just ordinary 'Joes', as democratic as the next man? He grabbed Audie's hand and shook it vigorously, declaring, "This is a real pleasure!" It was not surprising that the next morning the reporter of the *Fort Worth Star Telegram* enthused: 'Murphy was a big hit. His youth, pleasant personality and bashful modesty drew people around him wherever he went'.[7]

There were bouquets of flowers and baskets of fresh fruit, complimentary rooms in local hotels, Negro choirs singing 'old favourites', and local groups intoning 'Home on the Range', leis to hang around the heroes' necks, local society ladies from San Antonio's high society - and glad-handers everywhere.

It was all too much for the young man who had left Texas classed as a humble 'farm labourer'. Without saying a word to anyone, he returned to the St. Anthony Hotel where he had been given a free room.

As the formal banquet commenced, where the president of the Chamber of Commerce (who else?) would read out Audie Murphy's war record, prior to a standing ovation, the returned hero did a little private celebrating in the manner the war had taught him. He talked the elevator girl who had brought him up to his room into coming in with him for 'a few minutes', He seduced her without difficulty and then after ordering and eating a thick steak, he fell into a heavy sleep.

As the president of the Chamber of Commerce finished his eulogy to the hero and the crowd waited to give him his 'standing ovation', it was noticed that he wasn't even present. Twice the president called out his name, fat face beaming expectantly, and twice Murphy failed to respond. So in the end the distinguished assembly continued its banquet while Murphy snored on exhausted in his hotel room.

Two of the many newspaper people who were present at the banquet were astute enough to realize that Murphy was the real story. They left and finally found him in his hotel room. One them, Lois Sagar of the *Dallas Morning News*, suggested she would help the reluctant hero to escape the cloying public celebrations in San Antonio; she would drive Murphy to Dallas the next morning. He readily agreed and next morning Miss Sagar got herself a nice little exclusive, coaxing out of Murphy a reason why 'he had risen to such heights in battle'. His and answer made good copy, 'I just fought to stay alive like anybody else, I guess'. But later, she realized there was something deeper than that to Audie Murphy and concluded about him, 'He first bewitches and then bewilders'.[8]

When Murphy returned to Farmersville, which had now been abruptly transformed into his 'hometown', that unknown and long forgotten Army PR man who was directing Murphy's affairs behind the scenes stepped in once more. He recruited *Life* to do a story on the returned hero. Thus while Murphy agonized a little on what he should do next - go to West Point, as the brass was urging (including 'Iron Mike'), or try for college, a *Texan* one, of course, as many of his new-found friends suggested, events were taking place in New York that would change his life dramatically.

In 1945, *Life* was the country's premier magazine, a king among those weekly publications such as *Collier's, McCall's* and others that had the same kind of coverage, appeal, and publicity as TV does today. Throughout the war Life had dramatized and shaped the American war effort, explaining America at war to itself. Daring, imaginative photographers such as Robert Capa, David Douglas Duncan, and Margaret Bourke-White had shaped America's attitude to the war, concentrating especially on the fighting in Europe. It was primarily Life that had created the legend of the 'American fighting man' as being rough, rugged, determined, but also modest, a softie with the kids, whatever their race, imbued with a soft spot for the peoples of 'bleeding Europe'. For the unknown PR man, a *Life* story on Murphy would be the best kind of publicity for the Army.

So *Life* descended upon Murphy in that remote Texan farming community. The men from New York, blasé, worldly-wise, accompanied the returned hero around the haunts of his teenage days, detailing the modesty of the young man who had stopped a 'German advance single-handed'. They photographed him having his 'first haircut since he came back from Europe', from a woman hairdresser, having a 'chat on the front stoop with Miss Hattie', celebrating his twenty-first birthday with his 'orphaned brothers and sisters' before going off to see his 'special girl'. She turned out to be a nineteen-year-old college girl, Myra Lee. 'Audie hopes she is his own girl but isn't quite sure yet because he usually blushes when he gets within ten feet of any girl!'[9]

But it was the cover photograph that appeared on the front of *Life* for July 16, 1945, in which the Murphy 'story' was featured, that was to change his whole life. It shows a freckled face, a little pudgy and unlined, smiling out from beneath a carelessly tilted and too-large officer's cap, radiant above three rows of medals. How innocent he looked! There was nothing of the killer in that handsome face. Could this small-town hick really be a major war hero? Had this youth really won all those medals and killed so many Germans - and yet remained so patiently unscathed?

What the admiring readers of *Life*, who puzzled about that cover photograph, did not know was that Audie Murphy was already showing the first signs of his physical and emotional stress. Though he never reported sick, he was already suffering from delayed combat fatigue. He had all the

144

classic symptoms. He had a 'nervous stomach' for which he was taking the medicines he would take for the rest of his life. He suffered from nightmares. One morning he told his sister Corinne, 'Sis, I didn't sleep a minute last night. I fought the damned war all night long'.[10] He was restless, unable to relax, always tense and jumpy. Once he and some friends were listening to a Victrola when the phonograph needle slipped, 'The sound made Audie hop over the back of the davenport in one fast move'.[11]

Of course, no one but his family knew this side of the returned hero. The general public thought of Audie Murphy in the terms offered by the *Life* photo-article. What did they know of Murphy waking up the household 'shouting out the names of the men in his company',[12] of the fact that when the others went to bed, he would steal out to put on all the lights so that he would keep awake and not suffer from the awful nightmares that plagued him?

At this crucial time in his life, faced with decisions about his future that he hardly knew how to make, Murphy received a telegram, completely out of the blue. It invited him to come to Hollywood, all expenses paid. It was signed 'James Cagney'.

NOTES
1. Simpson, op. cit.
2. E. Hemingway. Over the River and into the Trees. New York: Scribner's, 950.
3. E. Ambler. Autobiography. London: Collins, 1985.
4. Ibid.
5. Simpson, op. cit.
6. Ibid.
7. Ibid.
8. Letter to author.
9. Life. July 16, 1945.
10. Simpson, op. cit.
11. Ibid.
12. Letter to author.

24

James Cagney, born the son of an Irish saloon keeper in New York's Lower East Side, was a short, stocky man who had graduated from being - of all things, in view of his latter career - a female impersonator and chorus boy, to become one of Hollywood's biggest box office attractions. During the war he had radically transformed his public image.

Prior to the war, screen audiences had inevitably thought of him as the archetypal Hollywood hoodlum, who fired off his tough, arrogant wise-cracks with the speed of a machine gun. By 1940, however, Cagney was play-ing new roles such as the tough doughboy in *The Fighting 69th*, in which he was noble enough to fall on a hand grenade to save his comrades in France in the trenches. Then came *Captains of the Clouds*, 1942, a tribute to the Royal Canadian Air Force, and *Yankee Doodle Dandy* of the same year. The latter was a super-patriotic indulgence that won Cagney an Oscar for his rousing performance as showman George M. Cohan. How he revelled in such stir-ring numbers as 'Over There' and 'You're a Grand Old Flag!'.

Naturally, Cagney was a shrewd enough man to know that Holly-wood was using the current patriotic mood to sell its products, but at the same time he was a genuine patriot who believed in his country and its ide-als.

In 1942 he had left Warner Brothers, for whom he had worked so long and, together with his brother William, had set up his own production com-pany, being one of the first of the Hollywood superstars to do so. The ven-ture was not very successful, but all the same James Cagney was by the end of the war a respected performer at the height of his fame. After having seen Murphy's photograph on the cover of *Life* and thinking he looked like an 'all-American boy' (and perhaps also influenced by Audie's Irish name, for Cagney was proud of his Irish ancestry), he had wired Murphy to come to Hollywood at the Cagney Company's expense. Perhaps, if things worked out well, there might be a movie contract in it for the young Texan hero?

But Audie Murphy did not respond to that first telegram. He had al-ready met a couple of movie stars and had had his photograph taken with Gary Cooper and Sonny Tufts. No doubt, he dimly realized that people in the film industry might want to use him for his current fame as a war hero. For several days he agonized, pacing the floor of his sister's home wonder-ing what he should do. Finally a second wire from Cagney, whom Murphy admired, arrived and made up his mind for him. He would go to Holly-wood.

Later Cagney told David McClure that he had invited Audie Murphy to Hollywood on pure impulse. "I saw Audie's picture on the cover of *Life* magazine and said to myself, there is the typical American soldier. There is assurance and poise without aggressiveness".[1] He thought he'd invite this 'latter-day Huck Finn'[2] out to Hollywood for a couple of weeks as a 'houseguest'. He knew Murphy was still in the Army and there could be no question of movie contracts until Murphy left the service.

Perhaps Murphy thought there was more to the situation than that. As much as he liked the Army, he decided now to get out. Finishing his leave on August 18, he set about processing for his discharge, and on August 22 he started his terminal leave of thirty days, after which he would be plain 'mister'. Did he think that the Cagney offer meant that a new movie career was being opened to him?

We do know that he told one of the officers at the 'separation center' that he would appear in a short feature and would 'be given special schooling at the expense of MGM'.[3] He also told newspapermen that he was sick of being treated like a hero. "I'm tired of being a hero. The true heroes, the real heroes, are the boys who fought and died, and will never come home".[4]

Again the newspapers thought that Murphy was being his usual modest self and the *Houston Post* of August 23, 1945, editorialized: 'We cannot foretell what mark Audie Murphy will make in the world. But we can confidently predict that he will go forward with head unswollen and heart unhurt, into a useful and respected career. His conduct sets a gleaming example for other bemedaled veterans to follow'.[5]

Audie Murphy arrived in Hollywood still clad in his uniform, carrying his civilian clothes that he would don the following day, for then he would be out of the Army. Cagney, who welcomed him, had arranged for him to stay at the Knickerbocker Hotel. He was so shocked by Murphy's appearance that he changed his mind. Murphy 'looked green' to him and was exceedingly nervous and run down. He decided to put the young ex-soldier up at his own home, a sprawling twenty-eight-acre estate in Beverly Hills.

It was sometimes maintained that Cagney had fetched Murphy to Hollywood to boost his own flagging career, but as David McClure states, 'Cagney was a very wealthy man... He certainly needed no boost from Audie. It was the other way around, Audie needed a boost from Cagney'.[6]

In those first weeks in Hollywood, Cagney did not concern himself with trying to introduce Murphy to the movies, though he did tell McClure that he had studied Murphy's *Life* pictures and realized that 'Audie could be photographed from any angle'. He saw in Audie 'Poise... spiritual overtones'. McClure, who had yet to meet Audie but knew of him from those *Life* photographs, said to Cagney, "There is something that we could use in our business".[7]

But for the time being Cagney merely entertained the young hero, of whose wartime exploits he knew no more than what he had read in *Life*, ensuring that he had good food, entertainment, and money. Then after three weeks in Beverly Hills, he returned home to Texas, his future career still undecided.

But James Cagney must have liked what he had seen of Audie Murphy during those first weeks, and the feeling must have been mutual. When Cagney telephoned Murphy back in Texas and suggested he return to the coast once more, Murphy agreed without hesitation.

Some time later he said in an interview, "I don't care anything about Hollywood. I just want to make some money and then come back to Dallas to live".[8] And a while after that when his movie career had really begun to take off, "I didn't really want to be an actor, although I am glad I've had the breaks. I never expected to be one. I never thought of acting. I got into it purely by accident so how could I have felt otherwise? I don't think I'd ever find complete satisfaction in life in being an actor".[9]

But now he leapt at the chance of returning to 'Tinseltown', although in a strange interview with the press just before his first visit he had told a reporter that he might be 'going back into the service about Christmastime… he… contemplates going back into uniform if he isn't able to better adjust himself to civilian life'. According to the reporter, Murphy stated. "I can't seem to adjust myself to all of the noise and fanfare".[10]

The doubts that had plagued him then had vanished now, as he was summoned to Hollywood a second time. The war with Japan was over and the United States was at peace. In the foreseeable future there seemed no prospect of another conflict, at least for the United States. The kind of special combat talent that he had developed over the last bloody, bitter years was no longer needed. His career as a soldier was over. Perhaps he could develop a new one as an actor.

A few days after that phone call he arrived back in Hollywood by bus, with exactly twelve dollars in his pocket, full of hope and new purpose. Yet at the back of his mind he knew (as he said wearily much later), "I came to Hollywood because I had no place else to go".[11]

NOTES
1. Letter to author.
2. Ibid.
3. Letter to author.
4. Ibid.
5. Houston Post. August 23, 1945.
6. Letter to author.
7. Ibid.
8. Simpson, op. cit.
9. Collier's magazine. September 1953.
10. Simpson, op. cit.
11. Collier's, op. cit.

FOUR

TINSELTOWN

Sure the exhibitors love me. I'm a two-bag man. By the time I'm through shooting up all the villains, the audience has gone through two bags of popcorn each!

Audie Murphy

25

Hollywood had had a good war.

The years after the surprise attack on Pearl Harbor had been a boom time for the movie moguls. Their films had been the average citizen's prime form of escape from the grayness and grimness of war. At home and overseas, men and women were fascinated by the celluloid dreams provided by Hollywood, in everything from air raid shelters down in the bowels of the London 'tube' to open-air theatres in the rain-soaked forests of New Guinea, with the Japanese only a few hundred yards away.

And the moviemakers had tried to give Joe Public what he wanted, for both patriotic and financial reasons. In the years between 1941 and 1945 they had covered virtually every aspect of the global war. They had covered all the ground from genteel English ladies fighting the German a' la Greer Garson in *Mrs. Miniver* to *Wake Island*, with its semi-documentary account of the fall of that island to the Japanese. "Tell 'em!" says Brian Donlevy to his radio operator who has just received an invitation from the Japs for them to surrender, "*to come and get us!*"

Hollywood had made of the celluloid war a straightforward melodrama, with bad guys and good guys, who were as easily recognizable as the heroes and villains of prewar westerns. For Hollywood, America had been the knight in shining armour who had sallied forth to rescue the damsel of democracy and free the world from the domination of the 'Nip' and the 'Hun'.

As Arthur F. McClure wrote in his essay 'Hollywood at War', for the moviemakers, 'War was an exciting adventure; politics a superior form of romance; morality a matter of morale. In this treatment, death was painless, decorative and even, ultimately, a blessing'.[1] The average American war movie made in those great years for Hollywood was smooth, lively, well made, naively heroic and unashamedly patriotic. But it was totally removed from the real thing. Just as Hollywood had recoiled from the realities of the Depression, it refused to deal honestly with the realities of America at war.

And behind the superficial patriotism of the war years, the old mores and the old corruption still flourished in Hollywood. There was a kind of glamour about Hollywood in the forties and fifties (which covered most of Murphy's career there), which can hardly be imagined in our own more prosaic time. Not only were the 'hicks' dazzled by it, but so were the participants themselves - the actors, the writers, the producers, the directors, and anyone else remotely connected with the film industry.

For the 'Industry' promised not only big money, and fame, but something much more fabulous - *immortality*! Once you had starred up there on that silver screen, you would live on forever, seen and slavishly admired all over the world. It was only later that disillusionment set in, and the realization came that like everyone else - like all those gawping hicks out there in their crummy little towns - you were just as mortal as the next man or woman. Usually thereafter the predictable happened.

After the glamour, the fame, the multiple marriages, the alcoholism, the drug-taking, there was one way out - self-murder. Once the realization came that they were losing their popular appeal, or their health, or, most important of all, their *looks*, it seemed it was time to reach for the bottle of pills, and take a swift, painless trip to that great projection room in the sky.

Many of the men and women who would play alongside Audie Murphy would end their lives by suicide. There was George Sanders, for example, who killed himself in 1972 with Nembutal, leaving behind a note stating, 'Dear World, I am leaving because I am bored. I am leaving you with your worries in this sweet cesspool'.[2]

Another actor who would star with Audie, big burly Albert Dekker, killed himself by hanging in 1962, dressed in ladies' lingerie. In his last moments he had written some rather unpleasant things about himself on his body in flaming-red lipstick. Everett Sloane was yet another. He ended his life with sleeping pills in 1965. Audie's female associates were just as unfortunate. There was Gia Scala, for instance, who starred with Murphy in *Ride a Crooked Trail* in 1958. She killed herself with a massive dose of drink and pills and was found thus by one of the three men who were currently living with her in her Hollywood home.

This then was the strange world that Audie Murphy was to enter in 1945, one that Don Marquis had summed up in his bitter poem 'Ode to Hollywood' as being 'fertile in naught but faking. Futile each season passes. And scrutiny discloses. Thy most prodigious Roses. Are really - Horses Arses!'.

Of course, there were other young men just out of the service who had experienced some of the same trauma as Murphy had and would learn to cope with the false dreams of acting and Hollywood. Telly Savalas, for example, who had fought with an armoured division in Europe or Lee Marvin who had been wounded in the Pacific. Many years later Marvin, the ex-Marine, stated: "Immediately after the Second World War I had nightmares, followed by a long period of turmoil. Then I became an actor - and acting allows you to act out all your fears. But when I was first called upon to fire a gun in a film I was desperately worried it wouldn't be a blank!"[3]

But Savalas and Marvin would be able to find satisfaction and a sense of achievement in their acting careers, which would help them to sublimate the trauma of combat. Audie Murphy never would. He was too much of a realist for that. "Acting is daydreaming", he stated, adding, "As an actor, I'd make a good stuntman".[4]

Later, too, he would become cynical about Hollywood's values and standards. In a letter to David McClure after an appendectomy, he wrote, 'I am still draining. If this keeps up, it may have a longer run than most of my pictures'.[5]

Murphy was hampered in his new career by the fact that he could not toady to the ogres who ruled Hollywood at that time, men like Louis B. Mayer of MGM or Harry Cohn of Columbia, of whom someone once said bitchily, "You have to stand in line to hate him." These men could make or break a star. They could, also, make the American Dream come true. Truck drivers and waitresses could be turned into what passed for gods and goddesses, at their command. All that was needed was good looks and the ability to photograph well. Talent was not needed; that could be learned.

Murphy did not have the talent, but he did have the looks and he was photogenic. As McClure wrote in 1955, 'Audie Murphy came to Hollywood with the greatest star potentiality ever known. He looked like the all-American boy and his name was already famous as the most decorated soldier in WWII'.[6] But McClure noted, he 'would not play up to anybody who could help him in the film industry if he didn't respect them. Audie had a fierce pride, an innate dignity, a quick temper, and devastating sense of realism with which he (viewed) the world'.[7] All attributes that were calculated not to help a budding hopeful to make a career in Tinseltown, where as one cynic has said, 'Strip the phoney tinsel off Hollywood and you'll find the *real* tinsel beneath'.[8]

For the first few months at the Cagney home, Audie Murphy did very little but attempt to regain his health for although the Cagney brothers did not realize that their protege had some deep-rooted emotional problems caused by the war, they could see that he was not well physically. 'We put him in the guest house and just let him do what he wanted to do, working in the garden, that sort of thing so that he began to fill out a bit and lose that awful green look'.[9]

Toward the end of 1945, James Cagney asked him to sign a contract and offered him one hundred and fifty dollars a week, providing he went to school and allowed himself to be tutored in the dramatic arts; although, as McClure noted, Murphy had 'a Texas accent thick enough to whittle with a paring knife'.[10]

So this most unlikely prospect was sent to the Actors' Laboratory, where he was instructed in the rudiments of his future profession - singing, dancing, swordsmanship, riding, and so forth. Naturally his Texan accent proved a great handicap (Cagney had hardly been able to understand him at first) and all that his coach, Margaret McLean, could say of his speech after months of tuition was, 'Audie's precious Texas accent will be good to draw upon for character parts in the future but it is not standard speech for stage and screen".[11] That accent would remain a problem for Murphy right to the end of his career, twenty-odd years later.

During this period the budding actor had his first contact with the true Hollywood. One of his fellow hopefuls at the Actors' Laboratory was a pretty, dark-haired twenty-one year old straight from Ohio University. Her name was Jean Peters and she was possessed of the same kind of temper as Murphy, high-spirited and quick to fly off the handle.

Murphy, who had tried - unsuccessfully - to conceal his identity and war record at the school, found in her a kindred spirit and she, presumably, was flattered by the attentions of the war hero. They fell in love, and their love affair caught the attention of the movie press. Gossip columnists dubbed them, 'America's most romantic sweethearts'. They swore to each other that they would work long enough in pictures for Audie to buy a spread in Texas or a farm in Ohio; then they would 'retire'' from Hollywood.

Murphy had not reckoned with a tall, lanky man in his forties who wore his hat at the back of his head and looked just like so many other hangers-on in Hollywood. But this man was not just 'anybody'. He was the plane-maker turned movie-producer, Howard Hughes, who had a devastating reputation with women. A woman that took his fancy became his - in short order. For in Hollywood, Howard Hughes represented money, power, and screen fame.

Jean Peters left Audie. It was only ten years later, in 1956, that she would marry Hughes, but she always kept in touch with Murphy through his friend McClure. Naturally Hughes, a jealous, possessive man, was not told that she had had an affair with Murphy, so Jean and McClure kept up a little pretence every time they met in the studios where she was filming.

Now Jean and I knew each other. But we pretended not to. Every time I saw her on the set I would ask to be introduced to her. The publicity girl who happened to be with me would say with some hesitation, "That's Howard Hughes's girl". But they would introduce me nevertheless. Jean would be very formal and polite to me. When we were out of earshot of the others she would say, "Well, how is the little sonofabitch?" I'd say, "What little sonofabitch are you talking about?" She would say, "Audie Murphy". And I would say, "Meaner than ever. Do you want me to tell him anything?" She would say, "Tell him I still have a good right hook". Once I told Audie this and he said, "She wasn't kidding. I have felt that right hook many times."[12]

But although Audie Murphy could later philosophize that 'Jean had everything - including over-ambition'[13], at the time it rankled that he had lost his 'girl' to a man twice her age, just because that man happened to be Howard Hughes.

Murphy soon afterward got to know Wanda Hendrix, a pretty, demure nineteen-year-old who was one of Hollywood's most promising starlets. One day she would become his first wife. In the meantime, he waited hopefully for his first role Cagney had him tested for a part, but he was found unsuitable. Indeed, in the end, Cagney never did make use of Audie Murphy for his own company; and although he supported the ex-war hero for two years, eventually paying him two hundred dollars a week, he did not receive any return for his investment, if that was what it was.

Cagney did for Audie Murphy during the period 1945 - 1946 what the Army should have done. He returned him to a fairly decent state of health, though his underlying emotional problems would never be solved, and gave him a new aim in life to replace his old combat career. Years later Cagney was criticized for having brought such an unlikely would-be actor as Audie Murphy to Hollywood in the first place. He was accused of attempting to capitalize on Murphy's wartime record. But there seems to have been no truth in this. 'All I saw him as was a typical fighting Irishman', Cagney related just before his death four decades later. 'Perhaps I imagined there was a little bit of me in Audie. That was about it'.[14]

In 1947, with his own company not doing very well and already considering the possibility of returning to another studio to make movies again, Cagney decided it was time to let Audie Murphy go. The accountants would no longer carry the ex-war hero. Now commenced the bleakest period of Murphy's long career in Tinseltown.

NOTES

1. C. Jeavons. A Pictorial History of War Films. New York: Citadel, 1974
2. K. Anger. Hollywood Babylon. New York: Dutton, 1984.
3. Daily Telegraph. March 3, 1986.
4. Letter to author.
5. Ibid.
6. Letter to author.
7. Letter to author.
8. Ibid.
9. Letter to author.
10. Ibid.
11. Ibid.
12. Letter to author.
13. Ibid.
14. Letter to author.

26

While he had been under contract to Cagney, Audie Murphy had been loaned to Paramount to play a bit part in *Beyond Glory*, which starred Alan Ladd, another actor who would commit suicide (in 1964). In this movie, Murphy had a couple of very small scenes and exactly eight words to speak. In his usual cynical, modest fashion, he said later that it was exactly 'seven more than I could handle'. Thereafter, no one was interested in him.

He had a screen test with MGM, but the spokesman for the movie company said later that he would 'never get anywhere'; and William Cagney, James Cagney's brother, remarked sadly of Murphy that, 'he would get lost in Hollywood'.[1]

Unemployed and depending on his army disability pension, he lived in the gym run by an admirer, Terry Hunt, who owned a gymnasium and body-building salon in Beverly Hills. Here Audie Murphy eked out a miserable existence. He had tasted the good life, and he had no wish to go back to farm labouring. As for the Army, that was behind him, and he couldn't start all over again. It had to he the movies or nothing. But no one seemed to want his services. He simply existed, encouraged by Wanda Hendrix, his new girlfriend, to stick it out, getting by with so little money that he quipped, 'he had a shower for breakfast and a steam bath for dinner'.[2]

It was, however, in this bleak period of his life that he acquired a powerful ally and champion who would remain his best friend till the day he died. Indeed, if any one can be credited with attempting to keep the memory of Audie Murphy alive nearly forty years after his death, it was this man.

His name was David McClure, nicknamed 'Spec' because of the glasses he wore. A small, quick, intense man, he had come from the same sort of background as Murphy. He was of Irish extraction, and his father had died when he was two months old, leaving his mother to bring him and his sister up by sharecropping. Unlike Audie Murphy, however, McClure had managed to go to a university and acquire an education. Thereafter, he drifted for several years, doing many jobs before he finally landed a position with Hedda Hopper, who, together with Louella Parsons, dominated the gossip columns of the time.

In 1942 McClure was drafted and spent two and a half years overseas in the Signal Corps, and it was at the end of this time that McClure had his first-indirect encounter with Murphy. 'About twelve of us Signal Corps men were stationed on an old battlefield and keeping communications going from somewhere to somewhere. We still did not know what the hell was going on. We were bored stiff. Off duty we had nothing to do but read. So we started robbing the mails. The couriers would come by and throw off unlocked mail sacks. We would go through the sacks and steal all of the magazines we needed. One day, we got hold of the *Life* magazine issue that featured Audie. This was the first time I had ever heard of him. But I immediately felt a terrible guilt because he had done so much and I had done so little. He was an INFANTRYMAN, which I had wanted to be'[3]

After the war McClure returned to work for Hedda Hopper and promptly forgot Murphy. He had his own problems. He was an angry man, raging at the way that America had promptly forgotten the war and the sacrifices of its young men overseas. "I was having one hell of a time readjusting to civilian life", he said, "and I figured correctly that Audie was having even a rougher time".[4]

One day in 1947, however, he was doing his usual job, trying to find out a little scandal for his bitchy, possessive boss, who also could make or break reputations in Hollywood, when he got into conversation with one of the well-known character actors of the time, Henry Morgan. The latter told McClure, "They can call me a communist if they like, but when our most decorated soldier has to sleep in a gymnasium, I think that's awful!"[5]

The statement set McClure to thinking. He asked himself, 'What was a smart soldier like Audie Murphy doing sleeping in a gymnasium?'[6] McClure had thought that Murphy was still with the Cagney brothers. He sensed a story and arranged to meet Murphy.

This was while Audie Murphy was trying to say his eight words in the Alan Ladd movie, and he had plenty of time to spare (his contract was for *ten weeks*). So lunch was arranged, with the promise that Wanda Hendrix would come, too.

But when McClure arrived, Wanda wasn't there and Murphy started to curse in that voluble and highly dramatic manner he had learned in the Army. McClure 'felt at home immediately'.[7] Thereafter the disparate pair, the bespectacled writer, who was fourteen years older than Murphy, and the anti-intellectual ex-war hero, became firm friends, going fishing together - 'just to get the hell away from things'[8] - and eating modest meals in McClure's apartment, for the latter suspected that Murphy was broke. He was.

McClure now took it upon himself to further Murphy's stagnant 'acting career'. He saw that 'Audie's nervous system was rather battered up' and felt that 'Audie was somebody worth fighting for. I was determined to get him a break in Hollywood'. For McClure, 'Audie represented the highest ideals of the American soldier. He had put his life on the line time and again for what this country believed in. Now he needed somebody to fight for him. I nominated myself to be that somebody. I didn't figure that anybody else would do it'.[9] And, naturally, in his boss he had a very powerful ally.

Hedda Hopper, tall, thin, elegant, with a sharp staccato way of speech, laced with profanities in spite of her Quaker upbringing, was a failed actress herself, who had taken up journalism as a last resort. Now sixty-two, equipped with a bogus English accent and spending every penny she earned on clothes, she lived off juicy bits of scandal. Once she had printed heavy hints that Joseph Cotton had made love to the teenage Deanna Durbin in the backseat of his car. Cotton threatened that if she added one more line on the subject, he would 'kick her up the ass!'. She did and he did. Another time she reported that Michael Wilding, who was about to marry Elizabeth Taylor, had been kicked out of the Royal Navy because he had had an homosexual affair with Stewart Granger. The resultant court case cost her and her employer three million dollars in damages. Such episodes were typical of her. No wonder she called her elegant white house in Beverly Hills 'the House that Fear Built'.

Now McClure, her underpaid but respected 'legman', set about enlisting her aid to further the career of his new-found friend. He first brought up the subject of Murphy and his future at a gathering that included Hedda Hopper and Esther Williams, the swimming star. The latter mentioned that her husband, Ben Gage, had found it very difficult to find a job after he had been separated from the service. McClure flew in to a rage and snapped, "What about Audie Murphy?"

Hedda Hopper, sipping tonic water as usual (her guests she usually primed with hefty glasses of gin), said mildly, "Now, now, you can't fight everybody's battles".

Hotly, McClure retorted, "Well, by God, this is one battle I'm going to fight!"

Esther Williams was not impressed. She said, "Can he act?" McClure rounded on her. "Esther", he snapped, "you're a fine one to be asking such a question! Where the hell would you be if you couldn't swim!"[10]

There the interchange ended, but McClure's passionate interest in Murphy's welfare had registered with Hedda and thereafter, although her power was beginning to wane, she became a firm supporter of Audie Murphy.

Perhaps it was because of McClure's connection with Hedda Hopper that he was able to land Murphy a small part in the United Artists' film, *Texas, Brooklyn and Heaven* in February 1948. The film starred Guy Madison, and Murphy played the unlikely role of a wisecracking copy boy for a Texan newspaper (at least he had the right accent). He was paid five hundred dollars for the three-day job - and given several dress shirts for endorsing the manufacturer's product during the publicity campaign for the finished movie.

It was a start. But suddenly the war butted into Murphy's affairs once more in the shape of an invitation to France to visit the sites of his old battles and receive two more medals from a grateful French government. McClure, who had talked Murphy into his bit role in *Texas, Brooklyn and Heaven* by calling the director and telling him "How the hell can you make a movie about Texas without Audie Murphy?"[11], promptly appointed himself the war hero's 'public relations expert' and went along with him on the junket; which was paid for by the French government.

For the first time, McClure had an opportunity to assess the full measure of the man he had set himself out to sponsor and make famous. He also came to realize just how callous the American media was toward has-beens.

At the first press conference that Audie Murphy gave in his Parisian hotel room, the place was packed with French journalists. Not one American made an appearance to interview 'America's most decorated soldier'. Angry and bewildered, McClure toured the various American press bureaus in the French capital, asking if anyone wanted to talk to Murphy. No one did. Not even Life, which had been instrumental in launching him in America. The magazine even succeeded in losing the photos of the young hero in Paris that McClure had sent them in the hope that they might at least print one of them!

Official America was little better. At one of the cocktail parties given in Paris in Murphy's honour, a plump, complacent-looking representative of the U.S. Foreign Service appeared. He began to chat to McClure, who was keeping 'well in the background' and asked casually what the party was all about. McClure said it was being given in honour of Audie Murphy. The fat man looked blank. "Audie Murphy?" he asked. "*Who's he?*"[12]

Later Murphy asked his friend who the fat little man had been and what they had been talking about. McClure told him. Audie turned white with anger. As McClure explained, 'He did not care about being insulted himself, but he did not want the U.S. Army insulted by a man who didn't know what the hell he was doing'.[13] There was trouble in store for the U.S. State Department.

As he toured the old battlefields of Europe with Murphy, McClure began to realize just how much Murphy had been through. They went to Ramatuelle, where Tipton had been killed, and for the first time McClure heard the story of how Lattie had been shot so treacherously. They travelled north to Holtzwihr, where three years before he had won the Medal of Honor, and together they examined the old tank destroyer, where McClure counted the punctures that had been made by the shells in the armour; and they visited the American military cemetery at Epinal, where so many young Americans who were killed that winter lie buried. There Murphy stood to attention in front of that sea of white graves set upon the lonely hilltop, tears in his eyes.

He learned too that Murphy's easy, wisecracking manner cloaked a very difficult and temperamental individual. 'His natural good looks are most deceiving', he wrote later. 'Beneath that shy exterior is a keg of dynamite with the fuse lit. Inwardly he is as hard as steel... Typically Irish, his mind is at constant war with his emotions, with the latter usually dominating'.[14]

They returned to New York, with McClure determined that the Murphy story should be told. Already he had an idea for a book on the war hero. In New York they were received by Norman Reader, who was the public relations man with the French Tourist Bureau. He told the two travellers that he had a radio interview set up for Audie and that McClure could stay behind in the hotel. Reader would deal with everything.

McClure agreed and 'ordered a flock of Scotch-and-sodas, being very thirsty'.[15] Some time later Reader and Murphy returned and, in spite of the drinks, McClure could see that something had happened. Reader kept muttering, "I won't be responsible for that interview. I won't! *I won't!*"

Alarmed, McClure asked, "What's wrong?"

"*Wrong!*" Reader exploded. "Audie has just attacked the whole goddamned State Department! I won't be responsible. I won't".

Gradually McClure calmed the other man down, while Murphy glowered in the corner. The taped interview was due to go on the air in an hour's time.

A few days earlier, Murphy had announced that he was going to marry Wanda Hendrix. A reporter had relayed this news to Wanda's mother, who was very ambitious for her movie starlet daughter. She had said, "Wanda's soon leaving for Italy to co-star with Tyrone Power in the *Prince of Foxes*. She'll probably forget about Audie." This statement came through the teletype and was handed to Murphy for his comments just before the interview. His temper had flared up instantly. Remembering the 'fat sweating' representative of the American consulate in Paris, he had launched into a blistering attack on the State Department. As McClure said later, "Audie could be completely irrational when he was angry."[16]

Reader left muttering that the incident would end up on the front page of *The New York Times*. The next morning, Murphy, his temper restored, called Wanda long distance. He asked her if she was going to marry him. She said yes. Murphy grinned, satisfied, and put down the phone. He turned to McClure who had been listening and said, "Do you know any girls in this town, Spec?"

Astonished McClure said, "Yes, but man, you've just got yourself engaged. What do you want with other girls?"

Murphy's grin broadened. "I'm not married *yet!*"[17] he answered.

NOTES.

1. Simpson
2. Letter to author.
3. Letter to author.
4. Ibid.
5. Ibid.
6. Letter to author.
7. Ibid.
8. Ibid.
9. Ibid.
10. Ibid.
11. Ibid.
12. Letter to author.
13. Ibid.
14. Letter to author.
15. Ibid.
16. Ibid.
17. Ibid.

The movie ought to have been a failure. How could a Hollywood producer in one of his wildest brainstorms, have conceived the idea that America's 'most decorated soldier' should play a dedicated criminal? And yet it happened. Audie Murphy was tested for a small role, but won the lead in *Bad Boy*, which was made in 1948. It was his first starring role and the lean years had ended - for a while.

In *Bad Boy*, Murphy played a professional criminal who was arrested and sent to one of the boys' rehabilitation ranches funded by the Variety Clubs International: a group of artists who actually did carry out such schemes in real life. Here, the director of the ranch, played by veteran actor Lloyd Nolan, recognized that there was some good in the young criminal and finally guided him back to the path of virtue.

The film was routine, unoriginal (it had been done before in the thirties), and Audie Murphy lacked acting ability. But in spite of all these defects, *Bad Boy* met with some degree of success. The primary reason for this was that some of the royalties from the movie would go to the Variety Clubs International and this fact induced many exhibitors to show it.

During shooting, Murphy's lack of acting ability had been a problem. He fluffed one scene so badly, and so many times that the angry director, Kurt Newman, told him that the delay was costing precious money. Deadpan, Murphy quipped, "You must remember I'm working under a handicap."

"What handicap?" Newman snapped.

"No talent", Murphy answered with a smile. The reshooting continued.[1]

The success, such as it was, of *Bad Boy* decided Universal-International to star Murphy in another movie. Naturally they stuck to old formulas. Murphy's next movie was *The Kid from Texas*, based on the life of Jesse James, well whitewashed. This would be the first step toward turning the ex-war hero into a major western star. His pictures would be low budget but, as the former vice-president of Universal, Edward Muhl, said later: "I didn't look for actors. I looked for personalities. Almost anybody can be an actor... Audie was an excellent example of the type of personality I looked for. I don't know whether he was a good actor or not. But he was a personality in spades. The average small-budget western that Audie made netted the studio from two hundred to three hundred thousand dollars... They weren't blockbusters, as money-makers. But they all added up."[2] In the end, Audie Murphy became Universal's biggest money spinner.

Around the time that *The Kid from Texas* was being made, David

McClure persuaded Murphy that his story should be told. McClure realized that the 'autobiography' of Murphy, which he intended to ghost, would be a gamble. But he was prepared to take that risk, for he felt a burning sense of indignation at the fact that the American public had not the slightest idea of what men like Audie Murphy had gone through. He intended to write Murphy's story in such a way that it would shock them into some realization of what the real cost of winning World War II had been for the combat soldier.

He had saved two thousand dollars, half of which he gave to Murphy, who was broke yet again. Now he took a year's leave of absence from Hedda Hopper and set to work with a reluctant Audie, remarking later about the enterprise, "I think I can truthfully say that neither Audie nor I were concerned about the profits. We were primarily interested in telling the story of the terrible price paid in blood and agony for victory." [3]

The book was written over nine months in fits and starts between Murphy's sessions at the studio. Occasionally Murphy would jot down little episodes from his fighting career, but mostly he would relate his story to McClure, who had to keep on prodding him. Murphy's memory seemed amazingly faulty and the only written sources that McClure possessed were Murphy's two scrapbooks, his citations for his various awards, and the divisional history of the Third Infantry Division.

Many years later, McClure realized that it was not because his memory had been at fault that Murphy had seemed unable to recollect what had happened to him only a few years previously. The fact was Murphy did not want to relive the traumatic experiences of his combat career. McClure realized that 'Audie had been burned out by the war. He reacted intensely to the death of his friends in combat. I suppose in order to keep from going insane he buried his emotions so deeply that getting them back was difficult if not impossible.'[4] Almost forty years after ghosting the Murphy autobiography, McClure wrote, 'When I reviewed the years that Audie and I spent together I realized what a cruel thing I did to Audie. I was trying to drag out memories that he was desperately trying to forget'.[5]

In 1948 McClure was more concerned about trying to get a book together on the basis of the few facts and incidents that Murphy was prepared to relate. So he was forced to 'use considerable imagination and a lot of guesses', which he later admitted 'were often wrong'. Consequently, the finished book would be, as McClure states, 'About fifty percent imagination or more'. McClure would take a small true incident, 'and stretch it by the use of GI dialogue to get all I could out of it. There was one thing I did know - and that was GI dialogue'.[6]

After he had finished the book, 'I began to wonder what the real Murphy war story was. It had become so confused and often contradictory that nobody seemed to know the truth'.[7] Many years later David McClure would confidently state, that 'the true story is much more interesting, much more terrible than the fiction that went into both the book and the movie'.[8]

By the time Murphy and McClure had reached 180 pages of manuscript, both of them were nearly broke. So McClure took the manuscript to an agent who got a contract for the book with a New York publisher, who didn't know McClure was ghost-writing it. Now they had an advance and a deadline, but such considerations did not worry Murphy. McClure was left to finish the 'autobiography' the best he could. He worked on, doing his best. 'I figured that if I could meet the deadline, the publishers would throw the manuscript back at me and demand a complete rewrite. Then Audie would have to get serious about it'.[9]

Instead, to McClure's consternation, they asked for a few slight changes and put the published work, under the title *To Hell and Back*, on the market. He had created a new Audie Murphy. Perhaps with a view to Murphy's film career in the prudish America of the 1940s, Audie emerges as a nice, decent boy, and there are no references to his sexual activities in war-torn Europe.

What emerged was the typical 'GI' in the popular image of the middle-forties, a tough-talking, wisecracking soldier who goes through hell, but emerges from it bloody, battered, but undefeated, with another hard-bitten quip at the ready. The enemy was the 'Kraut', to be exterminated without feeling. As for the 'natives', they were simple, obliging, pathetically grateful to the American soldiers, and strictly 'European' in the Hollywood mould.

Murphy's comrades of Company B, Brandon, Snuffy, Horseface, Kerrigan, Polack, and the like could have been found in half the war movies of the time, based on the good old American cross-section tradition.

There was only one dimension that McClure added that gave the 'autobiography' a certain depth and feeling. This was the underlying tone of war weariness, apathy, at times, fatalism: a sense of bitter resignation, which made Audie Murphy appear far older than his actual years. This overwhelming ennui is, perhaps, the only insight into Murphy's character that the book gave.

Surprisingly enough when it appeared in 1949, it was greeted with approval. *Publishers Weekly* hyped it up, stating that it had an 'Ernie Pyle flavour' about it, which was high praise indeed then, although Pyle's prose style was definitely suspect. *The Saturday Review of Literature* maintained it 'was a fighter's story of a fighter's war. Stark, grim, straight from the shoulder. *To Hell and Back* is a terrible, powerful book'.[10] *The New York Times* thought it 'vivid, gripping, mature'.[11] Only the *Herald Tribune* thought the descriptions of Murphy's comrades 'overdrawn' and the GI humour 'strained''.

It sold well, too, aided by all the free publicity Murphy's new movie career was engendering. Sales rose to some 130,000 copies, and in the end it went through five printings, which was very good for the time. Later it was published in Britain too, and it continued to be reprinted well into the sixties in both countries.

Whatever its faults, *To Hell and Back* did ensure that the American media were aware of the ex-hero once again, and it also strengthened his position in Hollywood. Only one studio could boast of having 'America's most decorated soldier' on its payroll, and Universal realized that fact would generate free publicity in every city where a Murphy movie was shown.

Within twelve months of the book's appearance, Audie Murphy made three westerns, one after another, *Kid from Texas*, *Kansas Raiders*, and *Sierra*, in which the female lead was played by his new and not very happy wife, Wanda. In all three of these films he played alongside established, even famous actors, such as Brian Donlevy, Scott Brady, and the country singer, Burl Ives. Yet his mentor, David McClure, felt that Audie was becoming typecast and that these B-feature westerns were not helping to advance his friend's career. He needed a role in a non-western, made by a director whose work commanded critical attention.

By chance, McClure had just attempted to read Stephen Crane's *The Red Badge of Courage* that year. He had done so before but each time the classic study of a young soldier's fear had 'bored the hell out of me. But it always left a solid impact'. This time, however, he passed the book on to Murphy telling him, 'If this thing is ever turned into a movie and you get the lead, it should make a star out of you'. He told him to read it, feeling that 'Audie was born to play the role of the Young Soldier'. [12]

Audie read the book and was impressed, pointing out several things about the story that hitherto had escaped McClure. Shortly afterward by an amazing coincidence, the latter learned that MGM was actually going to film the Crane novel and no less a person than John Huston was going to direct.

McClure called Huston immediately and asked him to use Audie Murphy. The latter said, "I would love to use Audie, but MGM wants to use one of its contract players".[13]

McClure was not put off that easily. He took his problem to Hedda Hopper, his boss. She had never read the book and was not about to read it, but she loved a good fight and she liked Audie. Besides she knew that McClure was trying to further the younger man's career. 'So she rolled up her sleeves and started raising hell'. [14]

Although the two of them didn't know it, a power struggle was being waged within MGM at that time between Dore Schary and Louis B. Mayer, whom he was trying to unseat. *The Red Badge of Courage* had become a political football between the two of them. Schary wanted to make it; Mayer was dead set against it. Now Hopper called Schary and told him that with the new Korean War raging, the role of the Young Soldier ought to be played by a real soldier - Audie Murphy. Although Schary hated Hopper with a passion, he took the point. He knew, too, that if he didn't cast Murphy in the role, Hopper would attack him in her widely read columns. As McClure commented later, "This is how things are done in Hollywood".[15]

A few days later, Hedda Hopper announced in her column in the *Los Angeles Times* that Audie Murphy would star in *The Red Badge of Courage*. She gushed, 'The happiest and most appropriate casting of the year took place at MGM yesterday when Dore Schary gave Audie Murphy, the most decorated hero of World War Two, the leading role in *The Red Badge of Courage*, with John Huston directing. For a change we'll have a real soldier playing a real soldier on the screen. It couldn't happen at a better time'. [16]

It certainly couldn't for Murphy. He knew a great deal about the narrow borderline between cowardice and heroism in battle (more than Crane, who had never been a soldier and never seen a battle). The part did not call for a great deal of speaking. Nor would he have to do love scenes, which he detested. Here, almost at the beginning of his career he was going to star in a classic, a serious, up-market film, to be directed by a leading director. It was, as McClure had predicted, his chance to become a *real* star.

But there were certainly imponderables. The film would have no standard plot, no romance and no leading female role, and if Huston had his way there would be no stars. It certainly would not be what Hollywood considered a commercial movie.

Louis B. Mayer had made his position quite clear. As he told *New Yorker* writer Lillian Ross shortly before shooting stalled, "A million and a half. Maybe more. What for? There's no story. I was against it. They wanted to make it. I don't say no. John Huston. He was going to make *Quo Vadis?* What he wanted to do to the picture! No heart. His idea was he'd throw the Christians to the lions. That's all. I begged him to change his ideas. I got down on my hands and knees to him. I sang 'Mammy' to him. I showed him the meaning of heart. I crawled to him on hands and knees. 'Ma-a-ammy!' With tears. No! No heart! He thanked me for taking him off the picture. Now he wanted the *Red Badge of Courage*. Dore Schary wants it. All right. I'll watch. I don't say no, but I wouldn't make that picture with Sam Goldwyn's money!"[17]

Now everything depended upon the man with no heart, John Huston, and he knew exactly what kind of a fight he had on his hands. As he wired Lillian Ross, who was going to follow the whole course of the making of the movie and write a fascinating book about it, 'You'd better get out here for the fireworks. We're going to have the Civil War right here on the coast'.[18]

They were indeed.

NOTES

1. The New York Times, June 1, 1971.
2. Letter to author.
3. Ibid.
4. Ibid.
5. Ibid.
6. Ibid.
7. Ibid.
8. Ibid.
9. Ibid.
10. Simpson
11. The New York Times, July 1955.
12. Letter to author.
13. Ibid.
14. Ibid.
15. Ibid.
16. Ibid.
17. L. Ross. Picture. New York: Limelight Editions, 1983.
18. Ibid.

28

In 1943 when Sgt. Audie Murphy had been hotly engaged in the fighting at Salerno, a newly commissioned captain in the U.S. Signal Corps had arrived in Italy to make a movie. Tall and rangy and very confident, with a voice like melted caramel and the face of an ancient tortoise, John Huston was two years into his career as film director. After doing an outstanding job writing a screenplay about Sergeant York, that other Medal of Honor winner from the backwoods, he had been given a B-feature to produce. It was the *Maltese Falcon* and it made Humphrey Bogart's reputation as well as his own. Now the Army had him, and he had been given the task of making a film on the war in Italy.

It was not a success. Although he knew that he was expected to produce a film on the fighting in the 'Boot' that would encourage the people back home, he would not compromise. Instead of producing the movie the Army wanted, full of tough, happy, wisecracking GIs, John Huston gave them *San Pietro*, in which he committed the unforgivable sin of filming dead American soldiers!

British thriller writer Eric Ambler, who was on the Huston team that year, remembers the battlefield as Huston shot it. 'A whole company had been caught on that patch of stubble and the bodies of the dead were dotted everywhere within overlapping patterns of shallow craters that looked like splashes of brown paint. The shrapnel fragments had ripped through everything, haversacks and equipment, as well as men. Scattered among the dead were their possessions, their tubes of toothpaste and their shaving kits, their toilet paper and their girlie magazines and their clean socks and their letters from home… This was the place where the wounded had crawled… and died. Most of the granaries were barely high enough for a man to stand upright or deep enough for him to lie flat. They were like stone kennels. Yet in some there were five or six bodies. They must have been here for at least two days and nights. Those who had not died of their wounds and the freezing cold had, in trying to find warmth, probably suffocated'.[1]

Not surprisingly the Army didn't want to show a film that included that terrible scene of death. They called the finished film, *The Battle of San Pietro*. It was an antiwar film, and it was not shown publicly till after the war.

That was the kind of man Huston, who was going to shoot Murphy's first important film, was: tough, a little cynical, uncompromising, and perhaps, as Lillian Ross thought when she observed him for the first time, 'strangely empty of all feeling, in weird contrast to the heartiness of his manner'.[2]

A third member of the film team, whose path in Italy had covered much the same ground as Murphy's and Huston's was Bill Mauldin, who was to play the role of the 'Loud Soldier' in *The Red Badge of Courage*. Mauldin had served in the 'Boot' as an army cartoonist for the *Stars and Stripes*, even spending some time with the 3rd Division, and it was in Italy that he created those two war-weary, ill-disciplined GIs - Willie and Joe. They made the twenty-one year old famous and earned him a fortune. He had come up the same way as Murphy, growing up 'in the rural Southwest with coal-oil lamps and wind through the walls, where we shot our meat and could never pay our bills. I shared his terrible need to feel respected, upright and important'.[3] But as Mauldin admitted years later, "I was lucky. My furies weren't as burning as his and I was able to work most of them out on paper. Audie took the hard way, cutting a swath through the Wehrmacht and then trying to do the same in Hollywood".[4]

Now these men who knew something of the horrors of war, in particular that which had been fought in the two-year long Italian campaign, came together on Huston's ranch to film the most celebrated fictional account of battle in American literature; a movie that was already being hotly debated by the studio brass even before one foot of it had been shot. Louis B. Mayer was still maintaining doggedly, 'How can you make a picture of boys in funny caps with popguns and make people think the war they are fighting is terrible?'[5]

Huston thought he had a perfect choice for the lead in Audie Murphy. The ex-war hero was well suited for the role of the swaggering boy soldier who is frightened in his first battle, runs away, gains his 'red badge' by accident, and thereafter becomes a demon of aggressive energy. "He is a gentle-eyed, little killer", Huston said of Audie. "Why in the war, he literally went out of his way to find Germans to kill. Gottfried and Dore* didn't want him at first, but I changed their minds... Greatness is more often a matter of quality than ability. Dad had it**. So has Audie. You take a great horse. Go past his stable and you can feel the vibrations in there. Audie is like that. He vibrates'.[6]

But even at this stage of the film, with the movie already being rehearsed on Huston's ranch, Gottfried Reinhardt, the son of the famous Max, was not so sure about Audie. He wrote to Huston, in a letter that: 'He needs your constant attention, all your ingenuity (photographically and directorially), all the inspiration you can give him. He should not be left alone a single second. Nothing should be taken for granted. At the risk of making myself a tremendous bore, CONCENTRATE ON AUDIE MURPHY! I watched him. I believe he will be good. How good (and the whole picture depends on the degree), depends entirely on the support you give him'.[7]

Huston knew all this. He knew that Audie Murphy felt he was being

---

*Gottfried Reinhardt, the movie's producer and Dore Schary.
**Walter Huston, the actor.

given a great chance and was understandably nervous; and right from the start, he babied the war hero.

Lillian Ross was present at their first meeting on the set and described how Huston treated the twenty-six year old. "Hello, Audie. How are you, Audie?" Huston said gently, as though speaking to a frightened child. "Well, we made it, kid", Huston said and forced an outburst of the "ho-ho-hos."

Murphy gave him a wan smile and said nothing. A slight young man with a small, freckled face, long, wavy reddish-brown hair and large, cool gray eyes, he was wearing tan twill frontier riding pants and a matching shirt, and all that he could reply was, "I've got a sore lip. 'Bout six this morning I went riding my colt. I went riding without my hat and the sun burned my lip all up".

Huston continued to laugh, but his eyes, fastened on Murphy, were sombre. He seemed baffled and worried by Murphy's unresponsiveness, because usually actors were quick to respond to him".[8]

Of course, Huston had only a sketchy idea of the traumatic effect his young star's war experiences had had upon him. He asked Murphy, "Excited, kid?"

Murphy said softly, "Seems as though nothing can get me excited any more - you know, enthused? Before the war, I'd get excited and enthused about a lot of things, but not any more."[9]

"I feel the same way, kid", Huston said hastily.

In spite of this unpropitious beginning, Murphy began to feel a sense of grudging admiration for Huston. He particularly admired the way that Huston gambled to the extreme, just as he himself did. He knew that Huston had made many movie flops, but somehow he had survived and always found new backers. Once McClure asked Audie how Huston did it; how after so many failures he still managed to draw a top salary? Murphy answered, "Oh, that's easy to answer. I'm just a mediocre failure. So everybody notices it. But John is such a colossal failure that nobody can possibly believe it. He's like an enormous slot machine. People can keep putting millions of dollars into it, figuring that it will eventually pay off".[10]

Indeed Murphy's admiration of his fellow gambler grew to such proportions that when years later he was asked to support John F. Kennedy's campaign for president, he replied he would - on one condition. If Kennedy were elected, he would have to appoint Huston as the Secretary of the Treasury. Murphy maintained that with Huston's manner of handling money and playing the percentages, he would have the U.S.A. broke within six months. Then other countries would have to subsidize America instead of the other way around; and that would be a welcome change.

The reply was humorous but typical of Murphy's growing nationalism and a feeling he himself had that he was out of step with the times in which he lived. It was something that fellow amateur actor Mauldin noticed, too. Murphy, he felt, 'wanted the world to stay simple, but nothing came out right. He kept walking on the balls of his feet like a wary little bobcat, lonely and angry'.[11]

Indeed once during the making of the movie, he came on the set with skinned knuckles. He told Mauldin, when the latter asked what had happened, that he had been driving behind a couple of hard-hats, who had been buzzed by two kids on motor scooters. Angered, the hard-hats had tried to run the kids off the road. They had not reckoned with Audie Murphy. He had waded into the two of them, although both of them were fifty pounds heavier than he, and had put them into the hospital. One of the hard-hats reported that they had 'been attacked by a maniac'.[12]

It was little different sometimes on the set. Once he was supposed to confess to Bill Mauldin, as the 'Loud Soldier', that he had run away from battle the previous day. But after several takes he became increasingly sullen. Finally he growled to Mauldin, "I can't do it. I can't confess a thing like that to this rear-echelon ink slinger".

"How about it - if I confess I ran away?" Mauldin suggested, half-amused, half puzzled by the vehemence of Murphy's feelings.

"I like it", Murphy said relieved; so there and then they sat down 'and we re-wrote Stephen Crane'. Audie then allowed that he had been scared, too, 'but only for a minute, mind you'.[13]

So the days passed under the burning-hot California sun. Reinhardt, the producer, was still worried, not only about the unpredictable Huston, who now seemed to be concerning himself a lot with his next movie *The African Queen*, but also about the star, Audie Murphy. More than once he turned up at the ranch to lecture the latter on his role. After all, he had once run an actors' school and had directed. Dressed in pith helmet and breeches, he once told Murphy how to conduct a bayonet fight.

The interference of this pudgy man in his ludicrous gear brought Murphy out of his withdrawn mood. In one of his rare talkative moments, he said that the psychology of the soldier was the same in all wars. He didn't think a raw recruit in the Civil War was any different from a young man in World War II.

Reinhardt looked down at Murphy, dressed as a Union soldier and resting on his long bayonet, and asked in his thick German accent, "You think the German was a good soldier?"

"We had respect for the Germans", Murphy said. "There was none of this blowing-smoke-rings-in-their-faces stuff. It was a mistake to underestimate the German soldier."

Reinhardt affected not to be impressed. He laughed and said grandly, "You know, there are three kinds of intelligence - the intelligence of man, the intelligence of the animal and the intelligence of the military. *In that order!*"[14]

Murphy said nothing but kept shifting his bayonet from hand to hand.

Once when they were discussing the war, after Huston had mentioned his Italian film, *The Battle of San Pietro*, Reinhardt turned to Murphy and asked,

"Did you ever see *K-Rations and how to Chew Them?*"

Murphy shook his head.

Reinhardt tilted his big cigar at a sharp angle and pointed a finger at his fat chest, "*Mine!*" he announced. [15]

Murphy kept his thoughts to himself most of the time. Watching him, Lillian Ross thought he didn't seem there in mind. Physically he was present, but his mind and emotions were elsewhere. He often seemed to be daydreaming. It took all of Huston's efforts to motivate him. Huston often offered to go fishing or riding with him, hoping to keep Murphy happy and perhaps also curious about what made his leading man tick. Murphy seemed happier with the stuntmen and extras, or simply being by himself than he was with the director or the other main players. Ross classed him as a loner.

Murphy had other problems at this time. His new marriage to Wanda Hendrix was in trouble. Although she sincerely loved him and would do so until the day he died (indeed she would show more emotion at his funeral than Audie's second wife) she, too, was attempting to further her movie career. She knew as a professional screen actress that one had to be seen and talked about; one had to go to fashionable Hollywood parties, be interviewed and photographed, and constantly keep oneself in the public eye. Such things were hateful to Murphy. His sole pleasure seemed to be gambling for high stakes. He didn't like parties and he didn't particularly like people. But he did like womanising on the side.

As McClure stated afterward, "The Murphy-Hendrix wedding was brutal... Audie was simply impossible to live with... Audie didn't want the girls to call him at home so he gave them my telephone number. They called me and cited their latest woes. One day, I said, 'Audie, why the hell don't you change that line of bullshit you hand the girls?'." Murphy grinned at the older man and said, "Well, it works, doesn't it?"[16] It did and Wanda, who would break down and weep over Murphy's coffin at his funeral was becoming increasingly disenchanted with the ex-hero whom she had married for love.

Once, during a break from shooting in the San Fernando Valley, Murphy wandered away from the rest of the cast and crew and came across an orange grove. It was a hot day and he was thirsty, so he slipped into the trees and began pulling oranges off them. Suddenly a harsh voice cried alarmingly, '*Thief!, Thief!, Thief!*'

Murphy fled, spilling oranges out of his jacket. At any moment he expected an irate farmer to appear and fire a load of buckshot into his rear end. He needn't have feared. When he got some distance out of the trees he became aware of some of the crew members laughing at him and pointing. He stopped and swung around. 'A beautiful parrot (was) fluttering from one orange tree to another shrieking "Thief, Thief, Thief" '.[17] It was the grove owner's highly original manner of guarding his precious fruit from people like Murphy.

That was perhaps the only light moment in the shooting of what was an intensely serious movie, which was already causing the studio so much concern that even at this early stage they were resorting to cheap tricks to publicize it.

'First, last, and always, it *(The Red Badge)* is entertainment', the publicity guide for promoting the picture announced to the men who were going to do the hard job of selling *Red Badge* to the distributors. Trying to cash in on Murphy's and Mauldin's appeal to the fan magazines, the handout stated that there would be a standard article for wide distribution to these magazines entitled, 'The Audie I know'; while another, written in Murphy's name, would be called, 'I know Bill Mauldin', by Audie Murphy.

A few days later, Reinhardt was surprised to find an advertisement in a trade magazine for *The Red Badge*, depicting Audie Murphy chatting across a fence with a pretty farm girl whose pig was stolen in the film. The idea was obvious; it was to convince the picturegoer that there was some feminine interest in what the studio bosses were telling themselves was not a commercial film. There was only one catch. There was no such scene in the picture!

But Audie Murphy knew nothing of all this. When, for the first time after thirty-odd days of shooting, he saw himself in the rough cut of the finished movie, he exclaimed in both bewilderment and delight, 'Seems I didn't do all that!'[18] But he had, and in spite of all his problems, Audie knew that if the finished product was a box-office, or even an artistic success, he would be saying goodbye to the western and 'the kid' image. His career might really take off.

NOTES

1. Ambler, op. cit.
2. Ross, op. cit.
3. Life, June 11, 1971.
4. Ibid.
5. Ross, op. cit.
6. A. Madsen. John Huston. New York: Doubleday, 1978.
7. Ross, op. cit.
8. Ibid.
9. Ibid.
10. Letter to author.
11. Life, op. cit.
12. Ibid.
13. Ibid.
14. Ross, op. cit.
15. Ibid.
16. Letter to author.
17. Life, op. cit.
18. Madsen, op. cit.

29

One afternoon in February 1951, *The Red Badge of Courage* received its sneak preview in Hollywood's Picwood Theatre, a fifteen-minute drive from Dore Schary's house. All the MGM brass were present including L. B. Mayer, white-haired and bespectacled, sitting in the audience with his arms folded, his face revealing nothing.

After the showing of James Stewart's *Harvey*, there was a gasp from the audience when the second feature turned out to be *The Red Badge of Courage*. They hadn't known in advance what 'the major studio preview', as it was billed outside, was going to be. Lillian Ross, who was there, wrote later: 'Some of the preview goers laughed at the right times, and some laughed at the wrong times, and some did not laugh at all. Several elderly ladies walked out. Now and then there were indecent calls from the balcony; one masculine voice obviously in the process of changing, called out, "Hooray for Red Skelton!" Two or three babies cried During a particularly violent battle scene, Mayer turned to a lady sitting next to him and said, "That's Huston for you."[1] And that was about all he did say that day'.

After the show, the audience was given questionnaires to fill out stating their reaction to the new picture, while the brass, including Mayer, walked out and waited nervously on the curb for the results.

They weren't particularly good. Huston was handed some of the first filled-in questionnaires and read them out loud, craggy face growing darker by the instant. 'This could be a wonderful picture on television', he read. 'With all the money in Hollywood, why can't you make some good pictures?'

Reinhardt realized that there would have to be drastic changes made to the movie if it were ever to be shown to the general public. Even the fact that someone had written in approval of the actor he had not wanted for *The Red Badge* did not appease him. For the unknown viewer had added, 'Audie Murphy is too good an actor to be stuck with such a stinker as this'.[2]

Next morning, at an emergency meeting that was attended by Huston, Reinhardt announced his verdict, 'Mayer has written it off. Dore will back it. It's a good thing this is not a cheap picture. If it were, they would forget it entirely.'

"Did you speak to LB?" Huston asked, rocking back and forth in his chair.

"He wouldn't talk to me", Reinhardt answered and then explained what he intended to do with *The Red Badge* to an apparently bored Huston. He was going to employ a narrator to read selected passages from the novel to link the various film sequences together to give the movie the quality of the classic Crane work. 'Spencer Tracy should do it', he maintained.

"How many passages?" Huston asked wearily.

Reinhardt didn't answer. Instead he said, "John, you have to tell people what the picture is. We should start the narration at the beginning, before the scene at the river. That scene is puzzling. You pay for clever openings. We must tell them, 'Here is a masterpiece.' You've got to tell it to them".

Huston, who obviously didn't like the idea, began to pace the office. But Reinhardt, who knew Huston would soon be leaving for Africa, persisted. "It might make the difference between life and death", he said firmly.

Reluctantly Huston gave in. "It might very well", Huston said, and a watching Lillian Ross noticed he said the words 'without conviction'. "Let's try it, by all means".

"The people must know this is a classic", Reinhardt ended stoutly.[3]

But the people did *not* know it was a classic. The second preview, held at the Pasenda Theatre, Pasenda, on a Friday night was worse than the first. The predominantly teenage audience showed no appreciation of the few changes. The character that several of them liked best was the 'pig', they wrote maliciously on their cards afterward. When asked which scene they liked best, a lot wrote, 'Where the guy went crazy.'

Reinhardt was beside himself with worry about *The Red Badge's* future. He nudged Huston and snorted, "Take a good look at your movie audience".

Huston looked noncommittal. Possibly his mind was already in Africa with Hepburn and Bogart.[4]

Next morning Huston left Hollywood. He telephoned Lillian Ross to say goodbye, but she noted that he made no reference to *The Red Badge*. Instead he said, "Well, now I'm off to Africa, kid. We're going to have a lot of fun making *The African Queen*'. She felt that there 'was nothing in his tone to indicate he believed it'.[5]

That was the end of Huston's role in the movie that he had talked MGM into making. Now Reinhardt was left holding the bag, while the studio tinkered with the film they hated, whittling away at it progressively until it was hacked down to sixty-nine minutes of disjointed narrative, which contained much more action than narrative. Nevertheless, Crane's theme of fear - or better, fear of fear - just about survived, with Murphy giving an uncommonly sensitive performance.

Indeed, Murphy's performance in his first really big role, outside of the westerns, received praise everywhere. One magazine said, 'Audie Murphy proves himself almost as good an actor as he is a soldier... This is Audie's best screen break to date and should do wonders for the kid'.[6] That 'kid' was the sting in the tail, almost as if the reviewer guessed what was going to happen to Murphy's career next.

The *Tribune* thought that 'With war hero Audie Murphy as a raw recruit in Union blue, this seventy-minute vignette is a study of one man's emotional adjustment to an environment chokingly filled with powder smoke and animal horror. There are no concessions made to movie conventions in this film'.[7]

The film critic of the *Post*, however, put his finger on the central weakness of the movie: 'The picture does not become a fully realized experience, nor is it deeply moving. It is as if, somewhere between shooting and final version, the light of inspiration died, Huston got tired of it, or became discouraged or decided that it wasn't going to come off... So they cut losses and cut footage, thereby reducing a large failure to the proportions of a modest, almost ordinary picture... Mr. Huston's product is that of a splendid director who had lost interest, who was no longer striving for that final touch of perfection, who had missed the cumulative passion and commentary on human beings that mark his best pictures'.[8]

From Africa, John Huston wrote happily that he was going to make a lot of money with his *African Queen* - he did - and that 'I'm going to have it all in twenty dollar bills with a rubber band around them'.[9]

Naturally Audie Murphy, who had not been party to the wranglings behind the scenes in the studio, was disappointed with the final product and the poor results that *The Red Badge of Courage* achieved at the box office. Later he would claim that it was one of his two favourite movies (the other was his *To Hell and Back*) and he always intended to buy *The Red Badge* back from MGM and have it reedited in the way that he thought it should be. He never did, for he could never scratch enough money together to do so, in spite of the fact that he earned nearly three million dollars in his twenty-year movie career.

His friend, McClure, who thought *Red Badge* would be the breakthrough for his friend, was devastated by the Reinhardt version. 'The film would have done for him (Murphy)', McClure always maintained, 'what *The Champion* did for Kirk Douglas - start him on the road to stardom with starring roles in big budget pictures... Thereafter, with the exception of *To Hell and Back* and another movie directed by Huston called *The Unforgiven*, Audie did not attempt to act. He seemed content to go through the motions and return to the low-budget pictures in which Hollywood type-cast him'.[10]

Murphy had little time to dwell on the failure of *The Red Badge of Courage*. His personal life was going through one of the first of its messier phases. From the start, his marriage to Wanda Hendrix had been in trouble. As McClure noted, 'His war experiences had rendered him as old as death. He suffered from attacks of acute depression and nightmares among other things'.[11] So the marriage of two young, handsome, and likeable people, which had started out so promisingly, ended after a single year.

Wanda accused Murphy of mental cruelty, and he did not contest the divorce. Divorce proceedings took place in a lawyer's office, not in a court. Surprisingly enough, they remained firm friends to the end of his life. But in a way, Audie ruined her film career. She married a wealthy man soon after her divorce and left Hollywood, as if she couldn't get away from Murphy fast enough. When she got divorced a second time and returned to Hollywood in an attempt to restart her very promising career, she found she had been forgotten. She was never able to start up again.

Meanwhile, Murphy had met someone else, Pamela Archer, a supervisor for Braniff Airlines. She had been a stewardess herself for six years, and was now in charge of training younger girls. Like Audie Murphy she came from a large family and had lost her father early (he had been killed in an oil-field accident when she was a child). Unlike Audie, she had managed to go to college, although her mother had been forced to place five of her children in an institution, just as Audie's long-suffering mother had done.

Two years older than Audie, she had hoped to meet him ever since 1945, when she saw the celebrated *Life* cover. In 1950, she realized that dream. The two of them went out together several times and although he was busy making *The Red Badge of Courage*, Audie flew to Dallas to meet her at the Braniff Air Line offices. On Monday, April 23, 1951, they were married.

Right from the start, Pamela Murphy realized that her new husband, the war hero she had worshipped from afar, had problems. On their honeymoon night, spent in a motel outside Dallas, Pamela was startled to find her husband sitting up in bed, pistol in hand (he always slept with a German pistol under his pillow). He whispered that he had just heard a prowler scraping at the window of their bedroom.

Pamela didn't know whether it was his imagination or not, but she pleaded with him not to shoot. Murphy jumped up and sprang to the door. When he opened it, there was no one there. Was it just a bad dream? Pamela did not know. But she would learn during the hard years to come that living with a war hero was not easy at all.

But for the time being, life seemed pleasant for the newly-weds. Audie had begun filming another western movie, his sixth film, this time called *The Cimarron Kid*. He took his bride with him to California and bought a little bungalow for the two of them just off Sunset Strip. McClure, who would become Pamela's friend for life (although he had felt a great deal of affection for the first Mrs. Murphy) thought that 'for the first time since I've known Audie, he seems to have found the meaning of deep peace and contentment'.[12]

Pamela liked cooking and domesticity. She was from the same kind of humble background as he (she was one-quarter American Indian) and she was prepared to have children, which so many of the actresses Murphy could have married weren't. In the first two years of the marriage two boys were born whom Murphy idolized. It seemed as if he had found happiness at last, with a woman not unlike his beloved mother, Josie.

The money kept rolling in too. In the two years after *The Red Badge of Courage*, he made six low-budget westerns, all of which were forgettable and instantly forgotten. Not that Murphy seemed to mind. He told one reporter at the time that he was satisfied making westerns because, 'All I am required to do is to ride a horse, shoot straight, and look sombre'.[13] Another newspaperman was informed wryly that the only difference between all of the westerns he had made so far was that 'they changed the horse'.

The marriage flourished and Audie was happy, but he still had bouts of black depression. Also, his new wife could not comprehend his cavalier attitude to money. She had been brought up in a very poor home, had paid for her tuition at college by working in a steam laundry, and she was very careful. Audie let the good money he was earning in Hollywood slip through his fingers like sand.

One writer, quoting his gym-owner friend Terry Hunt said, 'When Audie arrived in this town, i.e., Hollywood, you could have sold him 5,000 shares of the Atlantic Ocean. He'd sign anything. Not that he wasn't bright. He was very bright. It's only that he is very trusting. There are a lot of sharp operators in this city. Audie thought they were all men of good will'.[14]

Of course, Murphy's recklessness with money went deeper than that. It was rooted in the malaise that was beginning to creep up on him insidiously, but inexorably.

NOTES
1. Ross, op. cit.
2. Ibid.
3. Ibid.
4. Ibid.
5. Ibid.
6. Simpson, op. cit.
7. Ibid.
8. Ross, op. cit.
9. Ibid.
10. Letter to author.
11. Ibid.
12. Ibid.
13. Ibid.
14. Esquire, op. cit.

30

Toward the end of his short life, Audie Murphy once told an interviewer, "Here I was in the dullest town in the world. So I started betting on horses. I love horses, but this gambling went way beyond that. I got so that four hundred dollars was a minimum bet. Even that was boring. I didn't care whether I won or lost, it was as if I wanted to destroy everything I had built up. I got irritable. I hated everything and everybody".[1]

Murphy was possessed with contempt for the wealth upon which Hollywood society placed such a high value. Yet, as McClure wrote much later, 'He was almost constantly in need of money to divert his feverish mind with some kind of new "toy". The toy might be a forty-thousand dollar boat, a race-horse, or entertainment for a new girlfriend. He was desperately seeking a little happiness, a little peace of mind. But his turbulent mind would give him no rest'.[2]

As McClure and other friends saw it (and, naturally, his wife, too), Audie Murphy's greatest weakness was a compulsion to gamble. "He would bet on damned near anything", McClure recalls, "and the stakes were high. He seemed to have no interest in solid business ventures - something which would bring him a steady income. He wanted to deal in risks! If the risks paid off, the income would be great. If the risks didn't pay off, Audie would just shrug and go on to some other crazy business".[3]

Occasionally they did pay off. During a wild dice game on location, he won seventeen hundred and fifty dollars, a great deal of money back in the fifties. Suddenly Murphy took a fancy to buying a horse - a quarter horse called 'Snuffy'. Having done so, he leased a ranch (which he later bought) and began to breed, raise, and train quarter horses and thoroughbreds.

Raising racehorses was - and is - a tricky business, and his alarmed friends thought that Audie had again made a bad choice, more especially as it was discovered there was not enough water on the ranch. Murphy drilled for more - and struck salt water! It seemed the ranch was finished, but then he turned lucky once again, as he had so often done during the war. A 'sun city' for retired people with money was built next to the ranch. A lot of water was needed for the place and had to be pumped from a neighbouring town. So all Murphy had to do was to tap the main waterline. Abruptly, the price of ranchland soared. Murphy's investment doubled virtually overnight. And in the end, when Murphy got sick of the ranch and of breeding horses, he sold the place to Bob Hope for eight hundred thousand dollars (twice what he had paid for it).

But most of his impulsive purchases and business deals ended in failure and financial loss. Once, for example, he decided to set up his own movie production company, together with a Hollywood money man named Harry Joe Brown. The company was known as Brown-Murphy Productions. Under the terms of their agreement, the one partner, Brown, was to submit two possible film stories to Murphy. If the latter didn't like them, he, in his turn, was to submit a further two stories to Brown.

Almost immediately Murphy became bored with the whole thing. After Brown offered him two scripts, that he didn't like, Murphy sent back as his proposed submission Dostoevsky's *The Idiot* and, of all things, a musical version of *Peer Gynt*.

A serious businessman like Brown didn't see the humour in this, and he gave the Hollywood trade press a field day when he slapped a large lawsuit on his partner, Murphy. Hurriedly McClure was brought in to help out.

McClure happened to know Stanley Fox, a lawyer who acted for both Brown and for Cary Grant, who was then considering suing Hedda Hopper for something that she had recently written about him. Fox told McClure, "You are friends of both Hopper and Murphy. Why don't you persuade them to come to their senses?"

McClure's own temper flared, and he snorted, "You tell Cary Grant that if Hopper gets riled up, she might write *anything* about him! She has the goods on him. As for Murphy, he lived up to his contract with Harry Joe Brown. He submitted his two stories".

"But you know they weren't submitted in good faith", Fox said.

"Do you want to bet?" McClure retorted hotly.

"What makes you think so?"

"A man who will stand up to six tanks and two hundred fifty German infantrymen is not about to back off from such a picture deal"[4], McClure said.

Later McClure told Murphy what he had said to the lawyer, and Murphy replied, "Hell, yes, I'll do both *The Idiot* and *Peer Gynt* in grand opera, if it ruins both Brown and me".[5]

The prospect of Audie Murphy playing in just one of those projects must have done the trick. The lawsuit was quietly dropped and yet another Murphy business ended in ruins.

Today we know that the stresses of combat make themselves apparent not only during the actual fighting, but long afterward. Aircrew with the RAF who lost their nerve during World War II were secretly moved from active flying status, had their documents stamped with the bright red letters 'LMF' (Lack of Moral Fibre), and were swiftly transferred to the infantry.

Those were the ones - only one in ten - who broke down *at the time*. *

Recent research in Britain has shown that many of those who did not

---

*It was no different in the U.S. Eighth Air Force operating from the UK For example, at the end of the war the Swiss government would hand over to the U.S. authorities 118 mechanically perfect U.S. bombers that had been deliberately aborted to the neutral country so that their crews could dodge combat.

crack between 1939 - 1945 were doing so in a non dramatic way three or four decades later! Researchers have discovered that men in their sixties, even in their early seventies, were developing ulcers, becoming chronic insomniacs, and undergoing nervous breakdowns as a direct result of the intolerable strain of those long, frightening nights over Berlin and Cologne. *

Similar research in the United States on Vietnam veterans has shown that there is a kind of post combat fatigue, less dramatic but essentially the same as the one suffered during actual combat. With an estimated thirty-eight percent of Vietnam veterans suffering from personality disorders of one kind or another, more than twenty years after the conflict ended there, it is clear that the stresses of battle do not end when the fighting is over. They are perhaps sublimated, even forgotten for a while, but when the time is ripe they will break out again; and, if the individual cannot cope, will end in the typical symptoms of combat fatigue: crying fits, depression, stomach trouble, restlessness, and a whole range of actual physical disorders such as paralysis of the legs.

Today the psychiatrists call this malady Post Traumatic Stress Disorder, but in the forties and fifties, they knew nothing of such an affliction. When in 1945, in a calibrated case, a Marine veteran - a major who had won two Navy Crosses - came home and promptly slew his father, the action was regarded as either madness or brain damage. The fact that the father had forced his son to leave college and volunteer for the Marines and service in the Pacific, where he constantly lived in fear that his cowardice would be discovered (to disguise this he took more risks than the next man and won decorations for bravery), was not taken into account.

In the fifties, no one, not even his closest friends or his long-suffering wife, Pamela, realized that it was something similar to the Post Traumatic Stress Disorder, from which Murphy was suffering. He was a hero after all, wasn't he? What could hurt the man who had stood up 'to six German tanks and 250 infantrymen'?

Although his wife and his friends knew of his depressions, his rages, and his chronic stomach trouble, they could not necessarily relate it, after all these years, to the effects of the war. Nor could they understand his compulsive gambling. McClure, who knew him better than most, thought that 'For all of his postwar years Audie was to live by the psychology of the infantryman. Live today. Let tomorrow take care of it self'.[6] He thought that Murphy 'was not only uninterested in acting, but also he was uninterested in most everything else. Hollywood bored the hell out of him. Most people bored the hell out of him, too. That was why he tried to avoid people and why he got the reputation for being shy'.[7] It was this overwhelming boredom that, in McClure's opinion, made Murphy gamble so wildly and extravagantly: a

---

*RAF aircrew casualties were 58,000 men, as many as were lost in all the long years of fighting in Vietnam.

kind of gambling that proved to be disastrous in the end.

One immediate consequence of this excessive gambling was that during the fifties he was chronically short of money, in spite of the fact that he was earning a great deal As a result, he was forced to borrow studio money in advance against his salary for the next scheduled picture. So, no matter how bad the script for the movie, Murphy was forced to accept it. If he didn't he would have been suspended, and he simply couldn't afford to be without a job.

Thus he continued to be typecast as the 'kid', and was forced into more and more second-rate westerns, which were no challenge to what talent he had now acquired after nearly a decade of Hollywood acting.

Some actors, realizing that their looks are fading or that the particular genre in which they have made their name is going out of fashion, quietly take the transfer and become a 'character actor', one of those familiar second-string players who are always assured of finding a job. Not Murphy. As McClure had said, "He gave little, if any, thought to transferring from a young western star to a character actor. He could have done this easily if only he had looked ahead. But he just didn't give a damn. He was underpaid and knew it. So he began to raise hell with the studios and got a reputation of being hard to handle".[8]

In 1954, the studios tried to capitalize on Murphy's somewhat dry Texan humour. Although the actor himself thought of himself as sombre and indeed on the set it was difficult for Murphy to force a smile at the director's command, Universal-International thought they'd try him in a comedy. This being Hollywood, the bosses hedged their bets. They would make it a western comedy and they would give him a vehicle that had proved itself a box-office success twice in the past. They cast him as lead actor in the film *Destry*.

In 1932 one of the greatest of cowboy actors, Tom Mix, had starred in the same role, with success. Then in 1939 James Stewart and Marlene Dietrich were the stars of the all-time winner *Destry Rides Again*, the story of a naive young man who is made sheriff of a Wild West city but who finally tames it, more by accident than anything else.

But Murphy lacked the sparkle of James Stewart. Nor did he have a leading lady like Marlene Dietrich, who was at the height of her fame at that time as a femme fatale and drew the audiences, whatever role she played. 'He lacked' McClure wrote later, 'the fast and delicate timing for good comedy… he did not indulge in patter, something essential for professional comedy timing'.[9] Nor did he have the kind of awkward, small-town 'hick' appeal that Stewart had brought to his version. Audie appeared awkward with his leading lady and in the publicity stills he looks much more at home clutching a six-gun than he did one of the bosomy, scantily clad 'western' girls. In fact, Murphy never kissed his 'girl' in most of the forty westerns in which he starred.

However Murphy's foray into western comedy was a box-office success, and it was clear that Universal-International was prepared to keep on featuring him in westerns, though perhaps not comedies, until the audiences became bored with him and the seam ran dry. The 'Kid' had become the acknowledged king of the B-westerns. Others who had hit the same trail with him back in the late forties had retired to boot hill, hung up their spurs, or had been smart enough to head for 'them thar hills' and get out of the genre while the going was good.

But, abruptly, a new project was mooted, one that could well change his whole movie image and lead to better things, if it were successful. This film might just do for him, his friend and mentor McClure opined, what *The Red Badge of Courage* had failed to do: take him away from the stereotyped B-western roles that had become such a bore.

Back in 1950, Universal-International had secured the movie rights to *To Hell and Back*, but after nearly five years, the studio script department had done virtually nothing with the story of Murphy's combat career, in spite of the fact that Murphy had been under contract to the studio for most of the time. Suddenly there was a new interest in war films.

The more realistic films of the late forties, which had examined the motives and feelings of men in combat were now being followed by a new type. John Wayne - predictably - had started the new trend in 1949 with his *Sands of Iwo Jima*, which had almost coincided with the commencement of the Korean War. Wayne had carried the movie. The rest of his movie Marines had been the familiar square-jawed, wide-eyed chunks of American manhood, all talking avidly about women when they were not fighting.

Iwo Jima had been the start of a new vogue of action-packed, flag-waving war films that would outlast the Korean conflict and carry on well into the middle of the very conservative fifties, when a former five-star general, Eisenhower, commanded the destinies of the United States.

In many ways, these new war films were coarse imitations of the movies on the same subject Hollywood had made during World War II: tough, noisy, violent, and jingoistic. There was only one new element added: the emphasis on discipline and leadership. Such movies as '*Submarine Command*', '*Retreat, Hell!*' and '*One Minute to Zero*', all laid great stress on these qualities. The reason for the new dimension was not hard to find.

Several American units had broken down in Korea, notably the first infantry division sent there from the soft life of occupied Japan, and several hundred American POWs had openly supported the enemy communist regime of North Korea. Most of these men had been starved, intimidated, and, in some cases, simply tortured, but their betrayal had still come as a great shock to the American public. As a consequence, leadership and loyalty were regarded (by Hollywood and, naturally, the U.S. Army, who assisted with some of these films) as qualities to be emphasized.

Perhaps the best film of the genre to deal with Korea came at the end of the decade. It was Lewis Milestone's *Pork Chop Hill*, based on a real battle

181

during the conflict. This half-cynical, half-heroic account of the fight for a useless piece of hillside, carried out while the cease-fire negotiations that would end the war were taking place, contained a vignette, in which a harassed captain (Gregory Peck) says to a bleeding and wounded GI about to set off on some self-imposed heroic mission, 'Who the hell do you think you are - *Audie Murphy*, eh?'

Perhaps the line would never have been spoken if the Hollywood brass had not decided to resurrect Murphy's war-time image in 1955. They realized they had been sitting on a tremendous war story, one that was packed with heroics, and one that was a prime example of leadership from a most unexpected quarter, that of a freckle-faced teenage 'kid', born, as the phrase of the time had it, 'on the wrong side of the tracks'. Why hadn't they thought of it before? A movie of the real-life story of Audie Murphy, their own contracted war-hero, could not fail to be a box-office hit!

At the time they didn't ask themselves what might be the effect of replaying those traumatic experiences of World War II on the most obvious choice for the star - Audie Murphy himself.

NOTES
1. Esquire, op. cit.
2. Letter to author.
3. Ibid.
4. Letter to author.
5. Ibid.
6. Letter to author.
7. Ibid.
8. Ibid.
9. Letter to author.

31

In 1955, Audie Murphy had been in Hollywood for nearly ten years. In that decade of his life he had made more than a dozen movies, none of them outstanding, and had made a great deal of money, much of which he had squandered. Now he had one more year of his contract left with Universal-International. He guessed that the studio would renew that contract. Yet he knew, too, that any new contract would condemn him to more of the same repetitive westerns he had come to dread.

Once the gun he had used had been meant to kill. Now he twirled the fancy, gleaming, silver six-shooter and played make-believe. What kind of life was that for a man who had actually killed real men?

He knew his limitations as an actor and knew that if he continued to do what he was currently doing, he would never progress. Of course, publicly he made fun of his acting. "It must be my damned curl", he told the reporter of the *Saturday Evening Post* about that time, pretending to be puzzled by what people saw in him on the screen. As for his fans, 'Most of them seem to be nice middle-aged people. I give away more autographed pictures of Pam, my wife, and my children than I do of myself'.[1]

Yet if he were to continue in Tinseltown - and he could not visualize any other career that would provide him with the kind of money he needed for his life-style and his compulsive gambling - he had to make something better of the profession he had chosen. He knew his acting style was as stiff as ever. His voice was flat and his face usually expressionless. As he told the *Saturday Evening Post* reporter, "I can't make-believe worth a zinc cent!"[2]

How much longer could he stand the sort of fan letter (he received six hundred a week) in which two high school girls gushed that they would see his next movie, 'Friday, Saturday, Tuesday and Thursday' and asked, 'when you said (in his last film) "she ain't got no right to call that filly a lady" did you mean it?'[3] Or another that queried, 'Was it interesting to be in her bedroom (that of his co-star)? Didn't you hurt yourself when you fell from your horse twice and jumped through the glass window?'[4]

Could he stand his movie image any longer? For it condemned him to kill, and kill again, and he knew what killing really was. One fan demanded in a letter written that year, 'Let's have more killing and less kissing'.[5] But he was sick of killing on-screen and off. As he told a reporter, and his words were obviously genuine, "I hate to kill anything but birds and fish… Hell, I even hate to cut flowers in the garden!"[6]

"Maybe everybody thinks of me, even in a Western movie, as the baby-faced killer who shot all those Krauts. What they don't know is that I stalked and watched maybe twice as many - *and never took a crack at one!*"[7]

If nothing changed in the direction of his career, how could he stand the vast boredom of his present life? Admittedly he was happy when he was on his ranch with his beloved horses, but that happiness was limited. Always he had to return to Hollywood and its phonies. Once he told a horrified Hollywood trade magazine reporter that he 'hardly ever' went to the movies. "But I can't print *that!*" the reporter gasped. "Well", Murphy replied, "if I can't tell the truth, what's the use of talking?"[8] Thereupon he said no more.

In truth, Murphy rarely did go to the movies, not even to see his own films (it took him nearly a year before he saw the final version of *The Red Badge of Courage*). The celluloid world with its fake values and standards repelled him.

He had no illusions about how he had gotten into the movies in the first place. The fact that he had been a handsome, young war hero back in 1945 had attracted Hollywood's attention. Cagney had given him a start. He had been the first to see the 'poise, assurance and spiritual overtones' in that famous *Life* cover. Thanks to David McClure, Hedda Hopper had then taken him up and proclaimed his talent in her nationally syndicated columns. She had virtually mothered him and had probably been instrumental in getting him work in three movies at least.

But all this was behind him. He had to stand on his own feet at last and try for something new. Already the papers were predicting that when his current contract with Universal-International ran out, he would be re-hired to make the same kind of movie as he had made before. As the *Saturday Evening Post* wrote: 'There is no reason to believe he will play much different parts. His great talent is the amazing deftness with which he handles all types of firearms, something he has possessed since the age of eight'. "He's a throwback to Wild Bill Hickok", said one enthusiastic writer who tailored a script for him, "or maybe Annie Oakley".[9]

But he didn't want to continue twirling six-guns; he didn't want to be a second Wild Bill Hickok, not to mention Annie Oakley. He wanted to be himself - and true to himself. And what surer way of doing just that - at least on the screen - than by portraying himself in the film version of *To Hell and Back*? But there was a problem. *Would the studio let him play himself?*

At that time, there was another up-and-coming young actor, who had come up the hard way like Murphy, under contract to Universal-International. He had been born on New York's East Side, served in the Navy during World War II, and had graduated from 'bit' part to near-starring roles. His name was Tony Curtis, and Murphy didn't like him one bit. It seemed possible to Murphy that Curtis might be offered the part of himself in the forthcoming movie. In the final analysis, he knew, there were only two young actors under contract to Universal who could play the role, Curtis and himself.

So the intriguing commenced. Long afterward it was believed that

Curtis had considered the lead role in what would be Universal's most successful film ever and had turned it down. But that wasn't the case. Murphy
let it be known that he personally favoured Curtis for the part. Naturally the
studio heads thought differently. What could be more logical than Murphy
playing Murphy, they reasoned? So Curtis was not even offered the chance
of accepting or turning down the part. It went straight to the actor whom the
press called (to his great annoyance) 'the pint-sized Gary Cooper'.

Later he might well say, tongue in cheek, '(It is) the first time, I suppose, a man has fought an honest war, then come back and played himself
doing it'.[10] But whatever traumatic experiences the shooting of the movie
might occasion, he wanted to do it. The Army was interested in the movie,
too. They were prepared to back it to the tune of one million dollars of men
and equipment. As one newspaper correspondent put it, 'The Army officials
hope to use *To Hell and Back* as a vitamin pill for recruiting'.

Murphy hoped the film would give him 'the satisfaction of showing
the infantry like it really was'. It would be, in his opinion, 'the first picture to
do that'.[11]

Meanwhile, the wheels started to roll. General Walter Bedell Smith,
ex-ambassador to Moscow and Eisenhower's fiery-tempered and generally
disliked Chief of Staff during World War II, was prepared to do the introduction to the movie. The Army would place a whole division at the studio's
disposal.

It would be the 44th Infantry, which back in '45 had fought in Alsace at
the same time as Murphy had won his Medal of Honor. Some 19,000 infantrymen, several hundred vehicles, and a large number of artillery pieces
would be available for the movie's producer, Aaron Rosenberg. (Though the
Army could only find five wartime tanks for the Medal of Honor scene at
Holtzwihr.) Finally the Army loaned the training and proving grounds of
Fort Lewis near Yakima. Washington, to Rosenberg to shoot nearly all the
movie. From here, in another age, Murphy's 3rd Division had in 1942 left for
the landings in North Africa.

The training grounds at Fort Lewis were transformed into the battlefields on which Murphy had fought in World War II - Sicily, Salerno, Anzio,
Holtzwihr, and the like - while director Jesse Hibbs directed his 'cast of thousands', courtesy of the U.S. Army, using a flag to signal when to start and
stop. For as he said during the shooting, "To start a battle was a cinch. I just
fired a shot and the guns went into action. But stopping the battle was another matter".[12] His megaphone orders could not be heard above the thunder and the drumroll of the artillery. So in the end the director hit on the
device of using a flag. He had a flagpole erected on his observation post
behind the banked cameras. When he wanted to 'cut' the scene, he simply
ran up the flag and all firing ceased. For even the dumbest artilleryman could
recognize what that flag meant. It was coloured white. It meant - surrender.

The producer had similar simplistic plans for the star. When McClure asked Rosenberg how he intended to play Murphy in his own role and heard that the producer wanted to make Murphy an 'all-American hero' in the John Wayne mould, McClure commented in disgust that Rosenberg wanted to 'play Audie as a young Abe Lincoln!' He *couldn't* do that to his friend. But he did and thereafter, Murphy's longtime mentor and ghostwriter for the original book heartily disliked the movie.

As Audie started to film his combat story, the word was given out by the studio's publicity department that the making of the movie might well have a cathartic effect upon the star. By reliving the traumatic experiences of his violent, bloody combat career, he would be able to rid himself of the lasting impressions left by the death of his buddies in Company B. It was the sort of gush that fan magazines loved. McClure however, felt that these scenes did not affect his friend one bit, for Murphy 'knew the difference between play-acting and the real thing'.[13]

Still, there were moments when Murphy *the actor* was strangely disconcerted in those scenes where he played Murphy *the soldier* in moments of desperate combat. 'This strange jerking back and forth', he told the reporter of *The New York Times*, 'between make-believe and reality, between fighting for your life and the discovery that it's only a game and you have to do a retake because a tourist's dog ran across the field in the middle of the battle'[14], was somehow uncanny, even disloyal to those who were long dead, buried out there in Europe these ten years and more.

He later remembered his reaction at the start of shooting 'Looking down at the make-believe Anzio battlefield on the Yakima firing range, I began to feel uneasy for the first time. Back at Universal-International months earlier, I'd felt inwardly reluctant to make a movie based on *To Hell and Back*. How else could I feel when most of the men who'd fought beside me never came back, never saw the posthumous medals or big parades, never tasted the bittersweet taste of victory? Still I'd agreed to fight back through the old battles in front of a camera… But what I felt now was a different uneasiness - the kind you feel when your mind plays back something you don't want to hear or see or feel again. Down below me was the usual clutter of movie location apparatus, production crew moving about in the same efficient pre-battle confusion that always used to surprise me during the real war in Europe. Off to one side the same Fort Lewis GIs, dressed as World War II infantrymen, smoked and joked with other Fort Lewis GIs dressed in German uniform. At Anzio when an American and a German got that close to each other, one of them was going to be abruptly dead'.[15]

Could he bring back that young twenty-year-old sergeant who sat in a waterlogged slit trench for days on end at Anzio? Could he remember the shock when the homemade Molotov cocktails bounced off the shot-up German tank that night? Did he see in his minds eye the faces of those young men, lathered with sweat, contorted with fear, who had died so long ago'? What did he really think when he charged up the 'beach' at Anzio, only to be ordered by the director, "Hold it, Murph! Bring the company back! We'll have to do it again - there was too much smoke". What went through his mind?

And what did he feel when he watched his friend Charles Drake play Tipton, called Brandon in the book? Tipton had been 'skinny, long-necked and homely', with a Tennessee accent. Drake was a hefty, good-looking man with a fine speaking voice. What did he make of the difference between the two of them and their lot: Tipton mouldering beneath the ground these ten years in France; Drake, alive and well, looking forward to the good times that the money he earned in the movie would bring him? We do not know.

When Murphy and Drake re-enacted the scene in which Murphy won his Distinguished Service Cross and Lattie Tipton died, the star allowed the writers to put a phrase into his dying comrade's mouth, that had not been current at the time. 'I goofed, Murph'. In the end the scene was thought 'too corny' anyway

In a piece, which was probably ghosted for him, which he wrote for *Collier's* in September 1955, just after the movie was finished, he stated; "Finally the picture came to an end. The uniforms went back to the wardrobe department, the actors went home. Leaving Yakima on the last day of production I looked back at the 'battleground'. Already the production crew was clearing the field of tanks and props, the earth was drying back into its original hardness. I could walk away from it, and when I came back again there would be no scars, nothing to show that the battle of Anzio had been refought here. But what you can't walk away from is what you remember".[16]

We do not know just how genuine the emotion was in that piece, but Murphy's emotion was genuine enough when, before the shooting was over, the Army gave the ex-war hero the rare honour of a full-scale divisional review. For one hour and a half, the whole 44th Infantry Division complete with vehicles and artillery, over twenty thousand men, plus hundreds of trucks and jeeps, would file past Murphy and General Sink, the commanding general, on the review stand. Before the parade started, Murphy was asked, in view of the length of the affair, whether he wouldn't like to sit down as it passed. He declined stiffly, stating, "I'm not sitting down while these men march for me".[17]

So the long review commenced. Here and there Murphy's trained eye could spot an officer or an older non-com, whose chest bore the ribbons of the European theatre and who had been young men when the Germans had struck their positions along the Blies River in France on that freezing Sunday New Year's Eve so long ago. But even the young soldiers, as green as the growing corn, chests bare of campaign ribbons, impressed him. As one observer noted, 'Audie was visibly touched by the tribute'. [18]

Nevertheless, when it was all over, the man who had been America's most decorated soldier could not allow himself to be seen as a sentimentalist. As he departed for the waiting car, he cracked to a friend out of the side of his mouth, "I think I'll reenlist"[19]

NOTES
1. Saturday Evening Post, The. September 1953
2. Ibid.
3. Ibid.
4. Ibid.
5. Ibid.
6. Ibid.
7. Ibid.
8. Simpson, op. cit.
9. Saturday Evening Post, op. cit.
10. Collier's, September 1955.
11. Ibid.
12. Ibid.
13. Letter to author.
14. The New York Times, September 15, 1955.
15. Collier's, op. cit.
16. Ibid.
17. Simpson, op. cit.
18. Ibid.
19. Letter to author.

32

In stark contrast to *The Red Badge of Courage*, the death-or-glory sentiments of *To Hell and Back* grated. The movie re-creation of Audie Murphy's brave exploits in Europe was a display of heroics of the most elementary and uncomplicated kind. The film said nothing revelationary about Murphy as an individual, about what he thought and felt. It could well have been just another John Wayne, only John Wayne would have acted the part better. Further it was cheapened by the introduction of obviously fictional scenes.

Sharing McClure's obvious dislike of the movie, Audie Murphy himself refused to see it until he went on tour with it to New York. There, after seeing it for the first time, he telephoned McClure in Hollywood and told his friend, 'If this movie makes seventeen million dollars - and it looks like it's going to - you were still right, Spec. We missed by a mile!' McClure agreed regretfully, saying, "You remember I told Rosenberg he couldn't play you as young Abraham Lincoln. Well, by God, he did!"[1]

But perhaps in the ultraconservative America of the fifties that was just what the public wanted. Whatever the critics said, the moviegoers loved it. In the end it would take in ten million dollars and turn out to be Universal-International's greatest success in the studio's forty-two-year-old history, making even more money than the tremendously popular *The Glenn Miller Story*.

Understandably, on account of Murphy's background and the patriotic, conservative nature of the 'Lone Star State', it was given its 'world' premier in San Antonio, Texas. Here an estimated 20,000 fans saw it over five days, while Audie Murphy was promoting it in the city. It broke the record previously set by no less a film than *Davy Crockett* (the one that set the fashion for furry tails). During his time there, Audie Murphy led a parade mounted on a stallion, laid a wreath at the door of the Alamo, helped to enlist fifty recruits into the newly formed 'Audie Murphy Platoon', and was greeted by a marching contingent of the 36th Infantry Division, the one whose officers had once planned to bring Gen. Mark Clark before a court of law after the war.

The movie did tremendous business in Chicago, thereafter in Boston, and a few days later in Washington, where Vice President Richard Nixon, representing the President who was not in the capital, shook the hero-actor by the hand warmly.

While in Washington, Murphy visited the Senate, and there Senator Price Daniel of Texas brashly broke into a floor debate and introduced the local boy. Unabashed, Murphy waved to his admirers and was loudly applauded by the members of the Senate and by the visitors in the gallery.

Even in cynical, sophisticated New York, Murphy was well received. *The New York Times*, often so harsh and abrasive in its judgements on matters cultural, gave Murphy's movie a favourable review. The paper's film critic wrote: 'Gallantry has been glorified more dramatically on film previously but Mr. Murphy, who still seems to be a shy, serious tenderfoot rather than a titan among GI heroes, lends stature, credibility and dignity to an autobiography that would be routine and hackneyed without him'.[2] For *The New York Times*, about a movie like *To Hell and Back*, it was a very decent notice.

Naturally the Army, concerned about recruiting, was overjoyed with the success of a movie, that indirectly it had financed. No less a person than the Secretary of the Army himself, Wilber M. Brucker, sent Audie a telegram relaying his congratulations to 'a fine and distinguished American soldier'.[3]

Everyone was happy, even in the end Murphy himself. As McClure wrote afterward, 'When the picture proved to be a smash box-office and critical success, Audie decided that he liked it after all'[4], especially when his share of the gross profits turned out to be four hundred thousand dollars. It was the largest amount of money he ever earned with a single film, and this time he invested it wisely. He finally bought the ranch that later he would sell for eight hundred thousand.

As was customary in Hollywood at that time, an attempt was made to capitalize on the success of *To Hell and Back* by putting another movie on the same subject into production as soon as possible. 'The public is fickle and forgetful', the studio moguls reasoned, 'so let's get a second "Murphy" into the 'can' as quickly as possible'.

Universal-International decided that they would make a film of Audie's postwar life, an unwritten 'story' that Murphy had sold them for one hundred thousand dollars plus twenty percent of the receipts from the movie. Provisionally the sequel was called *The Way Back*. Now a whole battery of writers, including Audie's friend David McClure, was hired to make a suitable screenplay out of the simple idea.

In due course, the title of the follow-up was changed from *The Way Back* to the more dramatic *Helmets in the Dust*, and although Murphy balked at the idea, the writers dealt a great deal with the difficulties the war hero had faced readjusting to the tameness of civilian life after the violence of combat. In particular, the screenwriters dwelled on his mental and emotional problems during the period 1945 - 55. Then one of the writers came up with what he thought was a bright gimmick. 'This was', as McClure remembered long afterward, 'that Audie had rid himself of all his war neuroses by reliving the war in *To Hell and Back*. This, I believe, is called catharsis by the psychiatrists'.[5]

Murphy refused to be a party to such a cheap trick. He knew and they knew that the recent movie had had no such effect. His problems were far too deep-rooted to be eradicated virtually overnight by a piece of celluloid make-believe. The screenwriters were sent back to the drawing board.

A few days later they came up with another gimmick to enliven a movie that they and the studio bosses knew lacked the action of the current box-office success. This time it was David McClure's turn to protest. In this version the writer had 'Audie finding salvation', as McClure remembers, 'by saving McClure from the fate of a gutter drunkard'.[6]

As McClure stated at the time, 'If this had been true, I wouldn't have minded. But it was strictly false and I threatened to sue the studio if it was used'.[7]

It wasn't. Now in despair, the studio bosses turned to Audie and asked him if *he* wouldn't prepare the new shooting script, together with his friend McClure. For a while they toyed with the idea, but Murphy knew he would have to reveal too much of his personal life, including his current problems with his second marriage (after the first two years of his marriage to Pamela, he had begun to leave home for longer and shorter periods regularly, just as his father had done in the thirties) That was something he did not wish to make public.

For his part, McClure realized that it couldn't be done. He was against revealing Murphy's private life and he knew better than most just how sick his friend was. As he wrote years later, 'Murphy was still a sick boy, and I knew it. I had no idea whether he would ever get well. So I refused to put a phoney happy ending to the script and fast handed in my resignation'.[8]

So *Helmets in the Dust*, which if it could have been made and made right might well have been an extraordinarily interesting and revealing film, was never made.

However, with *To Hell and Back* still doing well and Murphy still the studio's major earner, other attempts were made - for a while - to get him out of the western rut, which he hated with a passion now. One year after the *Helmets in the Dust* fiasco, Audie went to Japan to film *Joe Buttefly*, together with screen veteran Burgess Meredith and Keenan Wynn, plus another World War II soldier of some fame: Marion Hargrove of *See Here, Private Hargrove* whose comedy of pre-Pearl Harbour army life was a best-seller in the early forties.

Joe Butterfly was a comedy, with Murphy playing a photographer for *Yank* magazine. It did well enough at the box office, but earned the star poor reviews. One movie magazine reported that Murphy had 'turned in the worst comedy performance of the year', and the critic of the *New York Herald Tribune* wrote bluntly: 'Audie Murphy is not at his best in farce. His countenance and temperament are too contemplatively serious for this; and in a love scene he is not liable to the outward expression of inner torment suitable in such a situation'.[9]

A year later the studio was still trying by placing Audie Murphy in the screen version of Graham Greene's *The Quiet American*. One wonders what Greene must have thought of Murphy, if he ever saw the movie; for the English writer was still then banned from entering the United States. It would be more interesting to discover what the super-patriot Murphy thought of a novel that quietly damned the initial involvement of America in Indochina. But we don't know. All we do know is that, in spite of fine supporting acting from Michael Redgrave, the picture went under without making too many waves.

In 1958, Universal-International tried again. They had already filmed Hemingway's 1934 *To Have and Have Not* back in 1944, with Humphrey Bogart and twenty-year-old Lauren Bacall. The film had borne little relationship to Hemingway's book, but the finished product was a success. Even forty years on, people still remember Bacall giving a sideways look over her shoulder at Bogart and saying huskily, "If you want me, just whistle. You know how to whistle, don't you Steve?"

In *The Gun Runners*, as the Hemingway novel was now called, Audie Murphy was not so fortunate in either his scriptwriter or his leading actress; though he did have good support in the shape of veteran character actor Eddie Albert. The film was made on a low budget by action director Don Siegel and vanished quickly after its release.

Murphy did a little better in *Night Passage*, in which he co-starred with James Stewart, and then in *The Unforgiven*, which was released in 1960. For the second time Murphy worked with Huston, though this time he wasn't the star. That didn't matter so much to him because, as he told a trade reporter, "When I work with Huston, I always seem to get a fresh and invigorating incentive for this job of acting, call it respect for what I am doing if you will… He charges me with ambition to give an imaginative, first-rate histrionic performance and that's something for I (sic) who have never had an actor's background, let alone training, and subsequently I've always held certain sort of reticences toward acting even though I've always tried my best."[10]

As usual Huston needed money, in this case 'three hundred grand', to pay for the restoration of the noble pile he had just bought in Ireland. Although he was discussing with Arthur Miller the shooting of *The Misfits*, which would star Miller's new wife, Marilyn Monroe, and Clark Gable, he squeezed in *The Unforgiven*, which he stated was his first western, albeit a superior one, for it was to star Burt Lancaster and Audrey Hepburn, with Murphy playing a supporting role as Burt Lancaster's quick-tempered brother.

The Unforgiven was not one of Murphy's usual low-budget western - the cost ran to nearly four million dollars - and it had a story that was not the usual run-of-the-mill theme. There was a hint of miscegenation in the plot plus the odd whiff of incest, with the plot hinging on whether or not the adopted daughter of a Texas family (Audrey Hepburn) is really an Indian or not.

But the story, in spite of Huston's attempts to give it a certain poetry, humour, and inventiveness (cows grazing on the roof of a sod house), never came off. Murphy, however, was generally stated to have played very well in it and held his own with seasoned stars such as Lancaster and Hepburn. Houston, too was convinced that Murphy had the talent to become a fine actor. "He's got the ability to win audiences", he said. "He arouses the maternal instinct in women and the fraternal instinct in men. Not many actors can do that".[11]

But *The Unforgiven* turned out to be long and rambling and did not do well at the box office. The climax, which was an Indian attack on the home of the Texas family, was strictly formula western in which every white bullet found a black, Indian heart.

It was Huston's fourth 'turkey' in a row, but for John Huston, as always, there was something new waiting around the corner - in this case, Arthur Miller's *The Misfits*. Like the rich in Fitzgerald's *The Great Gatsby*, he could drop things and walk away without bothering to pick up the pieces.

Murphy couldn't. As the end of the fifties approached and with Murphy's second contract with Universal-International a bare two more years to run, he realized he had made a lot of money in the last decade, but in his chosen career he had hardly made any progress whatsoever. The studio had given up trying to take him out of the rut. They were quite content to feature him in B-movie westerns, knowing that each film would make a tidy profit, with a star who was admittedly awkward but who at the same time, did not demand the astronomic sums that some of his fellow stars did.

Although he was a very youthful looking thirty-four (he would never really age until almost the end of his life when he seemed to grow old overnight), he felt that 'You get older. It shows up on the screen. That's the truth - age is the worst thing of all. Time is what's chasing you'.[12]

It was not only time that was chasing a disgruntled Audie Murphy, as the fifties gave way to the 'swinging sixties'. Now the traumatic experiences of the war, which somehow or other he had managed to keep at bay for nearly fifteen years, were finally beginning to catch up to him. Audie Murphy's decade of life was going to be the same kind of 'Hell', to which he had gone so confidently and bravely as an eighteen year old - *and returned*. From this particular hell there we be no return.

NOTES
1. Letter to author.
2. The New York Times, September 15, 1955
3. Letter to author.
4. Ibid.
5. Letter to author.
6. Ibid.
7. Ibid.
8. Ibid.
9. Simpson, op. cit.
10. Ibid.
11. Masden, op. cit.
12. Esquire, op. cit.

FIVE

A TIME FOR DYING

I was proud of being a tough soldier.

Audie Murphy

It was the dawn of the 'swinging sixties'.

The decade brought tremendous and unprecedented prosperity to the West; and freedom of choice - unhampered by the restraints of poverty or of conventional morality - unknown to the average man and woman hitherto. There was virtually full employment everywhere. Indeed, labour had to be 'imported' from the Third World to keep pace with the demand.

There was a new concern for the rights of groups that up to that time had had precious few rights, or none at all. There were rights for blacks, rights for the Indian, rights for gays, rights for single parents (i.e., unmarried mothers), rights for battered women, rights for senior citizens, rights for everybody.

But together with many useful changes and a general pleasing air of liberation came many developments to which some might give the dubious honour of having corrupted what was left of the twentieth century. There was a general negation of values - including hard work and self-discipline - by which many older Americans had lived and there were new and disturbing forms of hedonism. Full employment and the confident knowledge that if one 'dropped out' there would be no need to starve critically weakened the sense of personal responsibility on which societies are based.

Pot and the Pill were only the soft outer fringe of a whole new pleasure-seeking, antiauthoritarian subculture. For the young people of the 1960s, the values that the 'squares' accepted as unique, unchangeable, unshakeable were outdated, repressive, sometimes laughable. They were very definitely values that they, the young, could not - and *would* not - accept.

Naturally, old-fashioned pride in one's country was anathema to these rebellious youngsters. 'Old Glory' was burned in the streets. Draft cards went the same way. Vietnam had become an issue - if not the issue - of the decade, and many young Americans of draft age refused to serve their country in the Armed Forces. Thousands fled to Canada.

In the end the sixties became a self-indulgent, rebellious, violent time, where for the first time since the hungry thirties there was mass rioting and fighting on the streets of America's cities. It was a time of bitter criticism, rejection of traditional values, and doubts about the future. Not only on the part of the young, but also on that of the older citizens of the country. For a while in that decade there seemed to be two Americas, distinctly opposed to one another.

Naturally the changes in attitudes and the way America was going was a matter of concern and anger for Audie Murphy who, in 1960 at the age of thirty-six, definitely belonged to the 'squares', For in spite of being a movie star, Murphy remained all his life a simple patriot of the old school who saw no grays, as far as his country was concerned, but distinct blacks and whites. 'My country, right or wrong'.

It was not just because he was a national hero that he viewed things the way he did. It went deeper than that. Though he had had precious little to be grateful for back in the hungry thirties in rural Texas, Murphy had had his belief in his country bred into his very bones. Even Hollywood, with all its moneyed cynicism, could never change that.

In spite of his movie commitments, Murphy had promptly joined the National Guard at the outbreak of the Korean War and had continued to serve for years afterward, attending the annual camps and training new recruits just like any other part-time soldier. He was often quoted as having said that he believed that 'nobody likes for his life to be disrupted. But when the country calls, they need you'.[1]

During the fifties, he could always be relied upon to give simple, patriotic, homespun speeches on the subject of America to officers' groups and the like when called upon. They were never great rhetoric, and the sentiments were trite, but the words, even if a ghostwriter had had a hand in composing them obviously came from Murphy's heart. "The true meaning of America, you ask?" he declared in one typical speech. "It's in a Texas rodeo, in a policeman's badge, in the sound of laughing children, in a political rally, in a newspaper… In all these things, and many more, you'll find America. In all these things, you'll find freedom. And freedom is what America means to the world. And to me".[2]

Pure corn, but clearly sincere.

But now things were changing dramatically and not at all to a patriotic Murphy's liking. "It's outmoded nowadays", he stated, "to be patriotic. If you show patriotism you are considered a subversive".[3] The logic was a little suspect, but the feeling was there all right. When he heard that there had been a big demonstration in New York against America's involvement in the Vietnam War, he shook his head and said, "Gee, I'd hate their guts if they had any". For him the solution was simple. "It'll take one million troops (to win the Vietnam War). But I say - we go in, we do the job. Then we get out. There's no other way!"[4]

As Bill Mauldin would assess his attitude later, 'As he grew older, Murphy wanted the world to stay simple so he could concentrate on tidying up its moral fibre wherever he found himself. But nothing came out right. His country got into wars that heroes couldn't win. Murphy's kind of gallantry faced a buyers' market'.[5]

With the changing times came a change in taste. The same youngster who would soon be demonstrating against the Vietnam War, was discovering that the American Indian had been consistently exploited throughout the nineteenth century, and did not take kindly to the kind of 'history' propagated by Hollywood's B-westerns. As the fifties gave way to the sixties, the

'King of the Westerns' found that he was no longer in much demand as the 'Kid'.

Hollywood had always thought that the western was a genre that would never lose its appeal. But in the swinging sixties it definitely did. Murphy, who had always complained that, in these detested westerns he was forced to make, he had been making the 'same old movie' over and over again, was now beginning to find it difficult to even do that.

Indeed, Hollywood itself was in decline. 'The dream factories' were slowly dying one by one. Film was steadily losing ground to television. Worried studio bosses cut their budgets and tried to make movies that would appeal to young people.

Outwardly, Murphy's private life and public existence seemed intact and thriving. In June 1961, *Banker Magazine* featured Murphy 'at home' on his 848-acre farm, 'where he breeds thoroughbred and quarter horses' that provide 'in some measure a release for his tensions. Born and raised on a farm near Kingston, Audie has always known how to handle horses. He genuinely loves them. Most of his horses are high spirited and he spends hours making friends with them'.[6]

'Horses don't talk', he was quoted as saying, 'which Audie finds an admirable quality '[7]

Murphy, still as handsome and as youthful as ever, was shown riding around on one of his thoroughbreds, trying to humour a new and frisky pony, and holding a shotgun. He told the interviewer that he was currently writing a movie script himself - 'the first sentence of a story is the hardest to write', which will relate 'the seldom-told story of what happens to the serviceman when he comes back from war'. As he explained, 'Those (combat soldiers) who put the most into it (the battle) often take the longest to come back. A good soldier lives for the day, or even the hour'.[8]

The script, *Among the Missing*, was the same old sequel to *To Hell and Back* under another name. The fact that Murphy was now tackling it once more after five years was indicative of how badly things were beginning to go for him.

Next to a picture of Murphy fondling one of his prize quarter horses, the caption read: 'These days when Audie isn't at his ranch, which he calls AM Farms, he is usually occupied in his career of acting. He is under contract to Universal-International for two pictures a year and currently is appearing in a television show called 'Whispering Smith'. If the book he is presently writing proves to be a good seller, he plans to have it made into a motion picture. Preliminary production arrangements have been made with a major studio'.[9]

The last piece of information was blatantly untrue. Murphy had neither a publisher for *Among the Missing*, nor had he found another studio (Universal had long dropped the idea of filming Audie Murphy's postwar life) to tackle the project.

The situation was little better with the TV series, which the admiring magazine writer mentioned. In 1959 when his popularity had begun to decline and the cinema was steadily losing its audience to TV, Murphy had decided to take the plunge. He would go into television. At that time, while the western was failing on the big screen, western series, such as 'Bonanza' and 'Gunsmoke' were flourishing on television. Murphy decided that he, a major western star, might as well cash in on the boom; for, as always, he needed money desperately.

The vehicle he picked was a series based on a movie that Alan Ladd had starred in ten years previously. It was a mixture of western and detective built around the exploits of a real-life Denver railroad detective name Whispering Smith, the role Audie picked for himself.

After NBC accepted the idea, things began to go wrong almost at once. One of the supporting actors fell from his horse and broke his arm. Shooting had to be held up till he recovered enough to ride again. Another actor, who played Murphy's superior in the series, committed suicide. Again work was held up. Finally when the first episode was completed, it was denounced by the Senate Juvenile Delinquency Committee for being 'excessively violent'.

NBC hesitated. Two years after the shooting of the series had commenced they finally decided to show it in 1961. The first half-hour episode was screened one month before Murphy gave his interview to the magazine writer from *Banker*. Even while Murphy boasted of his television series to the reporter, he knew that it was in serious trouble. The ratings were low and the newspaper reviews were tepid. In the end, only a handful of the twenty-six episodes was shown, and the whole series was cancelled by NBC in the fall of 1961.

Murphy's other business ventures were doing little better. From the time he had signed his second contract with Universal-International in 1956, the studio had allowed him to make one movie a year for other companies, or by his own company, for he had formed yet another production company, named Terrania Productions. Supposedly the firm was given the name after the Mediterranean, where Murphy had 'first slogged ashore' as a young eighteen-year-old soldier. This firm would fail like all the other firms he formed, but before it did, Murphy did manage to borrow large sums of money for his film projects.

As was customary in the independent movie business, the producer handled the money. But, as McClure, who knew his friend Murphy only too well, stated: 'Putting Audie in charge of money was like putting a gang of rabbits to guard a cabbage patch!'[10]

In the 1960s Murphy convinced two Kansas oilmen, Jerry Spellman and Rick Clinton, to put up six hundred thousand dollars for a movie he would produce. In no time Murphy had spent the money and asked for more. The two businessmen obliged, giving him a further two hundred thousand. That went speedily enough. He asked for more. The two refused. Till the day he died, Murphy would be looking for further financing to complete the film. He never found it. Aptly enough, it was titled, *A Time For Dying*.

But Murphy was not yet dead. As the magazine writer for the Banker had noted, he was still a youngish man with a future, living happily with his family and successful in his chosen career. He wrote, 'Audie, his wife and two children live in North Hollywood. To his friends he has changed little during his years since the war, except that he operates on a big scale. The quality which others admire most in him is his loyalty through thick and thin. And with his temperament his future is always bound to be thick and thin'.[11]

How 'thin' it was soon to become, the writer could hardly visualize. Everything that Audie Murphy had been able to build up in his sixteen years in Hollywood was about to fall apart. And in the process, the traumas that he had fought off for so long were finally going to catch up with him.

NOTES
1. Simpson, op. cit.
2. Profile of Audie Murphy. New York: 3rd Division Association, 1976
3. Esquire, op. cit.
4. Ibid.
5. Life, op. cit.
6. Banker Magazine, June 1961.
7. Ibid.
8. Ibid.
9. Ibid.
10. Letter to author
11. Banker, op. cit.

34

In 1962 Audie Murphy's contract with Universal-International was terminated. After nearly fourteen years, the studio was not prepared to renew the contract of the 'King of the B-Westerns' for a third time. From now on, Murphy would have to rely upon personal productions or whatever work other studios were prepared to offer him in a market that was steadily declining.

Although by now Murphy was heartily sick of acting, this termination of his contract came as a blow for him. His own production companies were failing, and his first attempt at TV - the 'Whispering Smith' series - had just suffered a quick death. He needed fresh money - desperately. All that he had left in real assets was the ranch.

Money - or the lack of it - was causing serious trouble in his marriage to Pamela Murphy, too. He had walked out on her and the two boys several times during the fifties, and it was often reported by the gossip columnists that they had separated or were about to be divorced. The fact that he was never discreet about his many affairs with other women didn't help. But by 1962 the major bone of contention between the two of them was money.

Pamela deeply wanted to save money, to prepare for that rainy day that did not seem to be too far away now. Murphy only wanted money so that he could spend it recklessly or gamble it away. One gossip columnist of the time reported Mrs. Murphy as saying, 'He goes off on spending sprees and buys everything he sees'. On the other hand, according to the journalist, 'Pam's nagging at Audie for spending money bothers him, and when she speaks sharply to him, he retreats into a stony silence'.[1]

Now, in 1962, their relationship was not helped by the fact that the failure of the TV series had cost him a quarter of a million dollars through loss of other work and he had been forced to borrow another one hundred thousand dollars with which to repay the advance he had received from the production company.

It was not surprising, therefore, that Murphy was very much on edge that year and that he would exhibit the first signs of irrational behavior, landing him in one of the first of his several brushes with the law during the sixties. For a man who believed in law and order, Murphy was all too often tempted to take the law into his own hands, just like one of those 'Kid' characters he played in his films.

Two weeks before his thirty-eighth birthday on June 3, 1962, Audie Murphy approached two eighteen-year-old youths who were sitting in a car parked outside the apartment of Murphy's current girlfriend. The woman had lately been troubled by a series of obscene phone calls and several anonymous letters of the same kind. Now Murphy, with blood in his eyes, advanced on the youths and flashed his honorary sheriff's badge. Obviously he suspected that the youths had something to do with the calls and the letters. It was completely irrational behavior of course. There was no reason to believe that these two youths were the cause of the trouble.

Murphy, however, demanded roughly what their business was and why they were parked there. According to the boys (when they told their story to the police later) when they had not answered as the stranger had wished he had struck them. For his part, Murphy said they had become 'abusive' and so he had 'struck him (one of the boys) across the cheek'.

Fortunately, although the boys signed an assault charge, they did not make a formal complaint. Perhaps they were impressed by Murphy's war record or the fact that he was a well-known Hollywood actor. At all events, they did not press charges. But the newspapers got hold of the story and had pictures of Murphy showing his honorary sheriff's badge.

By now it was quite clear that he was seriously disturbed emotionally. As he told an interviewer five years later, "There was a nightmare, a recurrent nightmare. A feeling of exasperation. I would dream I am on a hill and all these faceless people are charging up at me. I am holding a M-I Garand rifle, the kind of rifle I used to take apart blindfolded. And in the dream, every time I shoot one of these people a piece of the rifle flies off until all I have left is the trigger guard! The trigger guard!"[2]

In order to combat these terrible nightmares that plagued him, he began sleeping with the lights on all night so that 'when I woke up from the dream, I'd know where I was '.[3] The result was that he could not sleep at all. He developed a severe case of insomnia, another symptom of what was one day to be recognized by doctors studying the problem of Vietnam veterans as a Post Traumatic Stress Disorder. He turned to the doctors for help.

They gave him a synthetic tranquillizer. 'I could sleep three or four hours, taking one pill each night. But then I had to take more. I built up the stuff until I was half asleep all the time day and night'.[4]

The tranquillizer was a sleep-inducing drug named Olacidyl. It was very effective, if used correctly, but it could become addictive. Since the drug was a nonbarbiturate, Murphy felt, like a lot of other people who used Olacidyl, that he could kick the habit easily.

He was wrong. As David McClure, who had seen the horrible effects of the drug on a friend who had been hospitalized for three weeks, strapped to his bed so that he could be weaned off it, said, "The drug kicks back in a horrible way".[5]

One of its side effects was that after the patient's body became saturated with the drug, it tended to reverse its effects. Instead of acting as a sedative, it became an intoxicant. In that state, the victim's brain races and he sometimes falls into a state resembling a delirium. Then when the drug level in the body falls, terrible, crippling body pains follow.

"I lost twenty-two pounds", Murphy explained later. "I was so tranquillized I didn't care about anything. I was a zombie. I dissipated all my money. I gave it away. I was not interested in anything. If a bus got in my way while I was driving on the freeway, I'd just force it to the side of the road. I sold off my airplane, my boat, my car, over six hundred acres of land, my ranch, all my horses - *everything*!"[6]

Murphy could not bear having his wife, Pamela, and the two boys see him in this state, so he moved out of the house and took a small apartment in Burbank. This set the gossip columnists writing that he had now made his final break with Pamela. It wasn't true, for Murphy was in no state to concern himself with marital problems, imagined or otherwise. Indeed all the while he was on the drug (nearly two years), his wife would go to the apartment to pick up his soiled clothes and bring him fresh ones.

Murphy continued to take the drug right into 1964 because he was desperate for anything that would grant him the blessed boon of sleep. As he told a reporter at the end of the sixties, 'Beginning eight years ago - up to last year - I had seven years of insomnia. *Seven years!* Outside of cancer, I don't know anything that can be as bad as that. It was just all of a sudden. I could not sleep. I'd be half-dazed. The furniture in my room would take on odd shapes'.[7]

In spite of the drug, Murphy, like all people addicted to Olacidyl, never seemed to get enough sleep. What he didn't know was that when the drug turned intoxicant, it kept him awake. As a result, Murphy took to wandering about, especially to the horse races that he loved. By now his walk was unsteady, his speech slurred and his eyes glazed. People who knew him thought he had become an alcoholic, even though they knew that all his life Murphy had been a very light drinker indeed.

His friends began to avoid him. As he told an interviewer in 1967, 'Well, it was sure interesting how my friends reacted. It was like going on patrol and some damn machine gun opens up on you and you look around and all the green troops are gone and only the seasoned troops are left. I sure found out who were the seasoned troops among my friends and not very damn many, either!'[8]

There were other problems too. Not only did he have hallucinations (the furniture taking on strange shapes), acute insomnia, and nightmares, he also found he had begun to hear strange noises. "It was the *noise*", he told the 1967 interviewer. "In combat, you see, your hearing gets so acute you can interpret any noise. But now, there were all kinds of noises that I *couldn't* interpret. Strange noises!"[9]

These noises worried the war hero so much that he had the garage of his family home made into a bedroom, because he felt he could better protect himself from noise there.

Writing in 1984 on the psychological aftermath of combat in Vietnam in their book *Wounds of War*, authors Herbert Hendin and Ann P. Haas noted that in Vietnam veterans there was 'frequent delay between traumatic events and the development of stress, which results from the soldier's need to suspend and control the overwhelming fear and rage stimulated by life-threatening experiences. The delayed stress reaction is, in a sense, the price he later pays for suspension of his emotions in the service of effective combat'. [10]

The two authors selected Audie Murphy as a prime example of this delayed reaction, noting that 'His waking life was also marked by preoccupation with his combat experiences Audie Murphy had developed many of the posttraumatic stress symptoms that we are now commonly seeing in Vietnam veterans'.[11]

There is no evidence that Audie Murphy went to see a psychiatrist about his problems. Probably his background and temperament would have made him sceptical about the 'section eight feather-merchants' and 'trick cyclists'. Instead he tried to do something about his afflictions by himself, with the loyal support of friends like McClure and his wife, Pamela.

First he withdrew from Olacidy, which was a dangerous procedure. He might have gone into convulsions, which could even have been fatal. As he told McClure, who had also been addicted to the drug, "I had almost rather have cancer than go through *that* again!"[12]

Then he moved back with his family, though not into the house. Instead the double garage attached to the family home was renovated for his use by his wife. As David McClure has written, 'It had a private telephone, a desk, a private shower, a television set, a record player - the works - all that a man could ask for. Audie was sick when he came home Pam suggested he sleep in the garage apartment until he got well. She knew a lot of people would be in and out to see Audie; and she didn't think that Audie, in his condition, should be climbing stairs to the master bedroom. This suited Audie. He was still having difficulty with his sleep. If he wanted to be alone, all he had to do was to go into the apartment and shut the door. If he wanted to be with the family, all he had to do was to open the door and walk into the living room'.[13]

Although Murphy had parted ways with Universal-International, he still got most of his business mail through the studio post office. So it was that McClure would pick up his friend's mail twice a week from Universal and take it to the garage apartment. There he would find Audie, 'Often lying in bed. He would tell me, "I'm just like an old bear. I'm too poor to move. So come on in here" '.[14]

McClure, who had known Murphy for nearly all his career in Hollywood, would stare down at his old friend a little helplessly. 'Murph', America's most decorated soldier, was reduced to living the life of a sick old man. And he was barely forty years of age.

NOTES
1. Simpson, op. cit.
2. Esquire, op. cit.
3. Ibid.
4. Ibid.
5. Letter to author.
6. Esquire, op. cit.
7. Ibid.
8. Ibid.
9. Ibid.
10. H. Hendin and A. P. Hass. Wounds of War. New York: Basic, 1984.
11. Ibid.
12. Letter to author.
13. Ibid.
14. Ibid.

35

In mid-1967 an *Esquire* writer, Thomas B. Morgan, out in Hollywood on another assignment, decided on impulse to try to interview a forgotten man - Audie Murphy. Through a friend this was arranged, and one evening after dark Morgan went to visit Murphy at his home on Toluca Road.

Somewhat tongue-in-cheek, the journalist described the two-story brick-and-shingle Murphy home as being in 'a good defensive position... The rear was guarded by the Los Angeles River, the river flank by the Lakeside Golf Club fairway, the left flank by a long carport, and the front by a white iron grillwork fence'.[1] Outside, long-stemmed 'Audie Murphy' roses (named after the star in the fifties) flourished near the flagpole and a 'big scary police dog named Eric' prowled.

The journalist's impressions of the ex-star war hero, six years after the confident interview Murphy gave to the writer of the *Banker*, are very interesting. For not only was Murphy completely frank with the writer, but there is an underlying tone of self-pity about his revelations. The easy optimism and superficiality of the earlier interview had now vanished and were replaced by a reasoned and almost brutal self-assessment. It seemed Murphy no longer felt the need to hide his traumas and could vocalize them.

Morgan found Murphy playing pool in the game room with a friend named Jerry for four dollars a stake, while his wife was taking her evening Bible class at the local Methodist church. He remarked about the lack of mementos of Murphy's wartime career; even his medals didn't seem complete. Jerry explained that Murphy had gone to some pains to de-emphasise 'the whole deal'. He had given some of his medals away to 'local kids'. He belonged to no veterans association, stayed away from parades and avoided ceremonies where he might have to wear his medals. Indeed, he had refused to attend President Kennedy's White House party for all living Medal of Honor winners. At first sight, it seemed, Murphy wanted to forget the war.

Morgan was introduced to Murphy, who was 'heavier and older ' than he expected. The ex-star had 'an undeniable and undisguised paunch. His face was full, threatening to become round. He combed his red-brown hair up and back with a kind of kid-next-door flourish He had a petite quality so that he really didn't look forty-two, except at the corners of his moody blue eyes. He was still boyish, but a much older boy'.[2]

Murphy asked Morgan if he just could finish the game of pool with Jerry, saying, "I got a passion for this game. We sacrificed this room - the dining room - for it. Now we eat all our meals in the kitchen and don't miss the dining room. We don't entertain often, that's for sure. Tell you the truth. I've never gotten along with Hollywood. Hollywood people and they don't get along with me".[3]

At that moment Murphy must have seemed to the writer a nice modest sort of person for a movie star and ex-war hero: playing pool for a four-dollar stake with a working man in what had once been a dining room, eating all his meals in the kitchen just like millions of other ordinary Americans.

Murphy's first answers to his preliminary questions were quite reasonable and ordinary, too. Murphy told him, "If I hadn't been in the movies, I might have been a farmer. Ha, ha! A happy farmer" and then went on to say he had made three movies in the last two years. His last picture had been made in Israel. The budget for the movie had been kept very low and 'I had to do all the stunts myself. I had to do everything, except pack my own lunch!'[4] Murphy ended with a laugh, declaring, 'Me, Murphy, I'm a middle-sized failure (when compared with John Huston, about whom he had just been speaking) That's why I'm off to Algeria'.[5]

Just then Mrs. Murphy - 'a good-looking woman with fine cheekbones and a softly harassed manner' - arrived back from her Bible class. She introduced her two shy teenage boys to the writer and then left herself, saying at the door, "You want to know about me? I'm a coward and I admire courage".[6]

Morgan asked why Murphy hadn't stayed in the Army. The latter answered, "Wasn't my decision. West Point turned me down (which wasn't true) because too much of my right hip was gone. I can't swim because of it. I've got other ailments besides. Fifty percent disability - shrapnel in my legs, a nervous stomach, regular headaches. So listen, I didn't want to be an actor. It was simply the best offer that came along".[7]

The matter of his service disabilities started Murphy talking about his postwar health problems, which in the end he solved (according to his account) 'by locking himself in a hotel room and throwing away the pills. I stayed in there for five days, having withdrawal pains just like a junkie. I had convulsions. But I quit. I stopped the pills and I quit gambling. This past year I feel like I've been starting my life all over again. I've been sleeping lately - most nights, anyway. But I won't take any more pills. Not one'.[8]

From his withdrawal problems, Murphy harked back to his service days and a listening Morgan had the impression the star had been happy then, confident, knowing exactly what he was doing. "There's this to say about combat", he maintained firmly. "It brings out the best in men. It's gory and it's unfortunate, but most people in combat stand a little taller".[9]

'You have a comradeship,' Murphy explained, 'a rapport that you'll never have again, not in our society anyway. I suppose it comes from having nothing to gain except the end of the war. There's no competitiveness, no money values. You trust the man on your left and on your right with your life, while, as a civilian, you might not trust either of them with ten cents.'[10]

Murphy stood up, arms folded across his chest and was 'suddenly as shy as his own two boys as though he might have seemed too proud'.[11] Morgan thought it was time to go. He made an appointment to meet Murphy once more on the following morning.

"I guess what all that says", Murphy summed up the interview for the *Esquire* man, "is that I really identified with soldiering. That's my problem, I'll admit. To become an executioner, somebody cold and analytical, to be trained to kill and then come back to civilian life and be alone in the crowd - it takes an awful long time to get over it. Fear and depression come over you. It's been twenty-odd years already". Murphy shrugged. "Did you know that doctors say the effect of all this on my generation won't reach its peak until 1970? So, I guess I got three years to go".[12]

Apart from what that 1967 interview revealed about Murphy's ailments and his bitter, impoverished childhood ('No one can know how harsh it was who hasn't lived through it' he told Morgan. 'You'd hear your brothers and sisters crying hungry at night'.[13]), it also made clear that the only part of his life that the movie star had really enjoyed had been those two years in combat in World War II.

The truth is, that in spite of the suffering it had caused him even at the time, Audie Murphy had *loved* the war. He had been young, impressionable, had come from a boring, impoverished rural environment. Suddenly, he was pitched into violent adventure in remote countries on the other side of the globe. Like so many others who later pretended they hadn't wanted to go, but who secretly had been glad to escape the cloying ennui of their daily routine, Murphy had been only too eager to leave a life in which the high spot of the week had been double-dating at a drive-in movie theatre on a Saturday night.

He had burned for glory, and he had found that there is a kind of wild, heady, atavistic thrill to battle. The tremendous noise, the destruction, the fear, the courage, the anger - a whole range of emotions run wild - and the knowledge that you may die and that, if you want to, you can kill, raised life to a pitch of intensity to which *nothing* in ordinary civilian life can compare.

"Sergeant Murphy was an eager beaver, there was no doubt about that", one of the many replacements who went through Company B recalled forty-odd years later. "I was only with the platoon four or five days before I was hit the first time, but there was no denying the fact that Murphy liked battle. I can't recall all the incidents now - that time for me was confused even then - but Murphy was different from the rest. He actually wanted to go in and fight. Most of us, the old guys and replacements like myself, just wanted to keep out of trouble. Not Murphy. He went looking for it deliberately!"[14]

Was there a greater sensation for a youth of Murphy's temperament and background than that of lining some unsuspecting German up in his sight, trying to control his breathing, finger curling around the trigger of his Garand, taking first pressure, the knuckle whitening, heart thudding with excitement, and then that final pressure? The satisfying thump against his right shoulder and another life vanished, just as easily as snapping his fingers? We cannot know for sure. Nonetheless, violence does not seem to have been something that Murphy only learned to love by going to war, and the killing he did does not ever seem to have been the part of the war that disturbed him.

Could anything really replace that ultimate thrill? Could Hollywood with all its eager and willing females offer a substitute for it? Weren't all those westerns he made a silly kind of make-believe that never approached the real thing? They only provided him money so that he could gamble it away and momentarily re-create some sort of excitement.

In addition to the traumas and the very real ailments that had plagued him since 1945, Audie Murphy was suffering from the greatest affliction of all. For the last twenty-odd years since his combat days had come to an end, he had been totally, overwhelmingly *bored!*

On the day following his first interview with Murphy, Morgan met the actor again and they had lunch together. Murphy looked cold, as though he had been up all night. Morgan asked him if he'd slept and Murphy assured the writer he had had a good night. Morgan 'thought he was lying'.[15]

Thereafter they drove to an automobile garage and showroom called Barris's Kustom City. Murphy said he liked to hang around here when he 'couldn't think of anything better to do… It's a way to beat the boredom', he said.[16]

Morgan thought the place was like a child's toy shop, 'with half a dozen cars on display, each tailored like a teenager's dream of superpower with enormous hoods, jazzed-up interiors and phallic tail fins'.[17] There, while the writer observed, Murphy watched a mechanic at work for twenty minutes, got into a Cadillac, punched some buttons, and climbed out again. "Nice", he commented and then asked Morgan if he were bored. The latter replied he wasn't. But Murphy decided he was. He said he'd go for a steam bath and rubdown at the gym run by his old friend Terry Hunt, explaining, "Well, it's what you have to do in a dull town… if you want to kill an afternoon and you don't play golf".[18]

So Murphy 'killed' the afternoon and said goodbye to the writer with 'a look of terrible weariness' on his face, leaving Morgan to reflect that Murphy was 'more than the most decorated soldier of World War II, more than the war hero of our time. He was also a casualty - so much of his spirit, in fact, had been killed in action'.[19]

A few days after the *Esquire* interviews, Murphy set off for Algeria, where he would shoot his last contract movie on a location where production costs could be kept low. He hated to go, but he needed the money desperately.

With him on location, shooting a cheap spy movie titled *Trunk to Cairo*, was another actor who was as weary as Murphy was. He too knew that shooting a movie in Algeria for a minor studio (American-International) meant that he had reached the end of the line.

His name was George Sanders, the fifty-two-year-old arch-cad of the movies, who had gone through four wives - and seven psychiatrists. Most of his latter movies were rubbish, and the one-time Oscar winner* knew it only too well. Like Murphy, he was in a fly-ridden, primitive, middle eastern country, one which had barely recovered from the protracted war there, strictly for the money.

Sanders was as cynical off the screen as he was on it, and, unlike Murphy, he was prepared to draw the ultimate conclusion. Was there any way out of the endless boredom of third-class movies, made solely for money so that he could continue to be bored? There was one way, and he took it in the shape of five tubes of Nembutal, leaving behind a suicide note that commenced, 'Dear World: I am leaving because I am bored…".[20]

NOTES
1. Simpson, op. cit.
2. Ibid.
3. Time, June 14, 1971.
4. Simpson, op. cit.
5. Ibid.
6. Ibid.
7. Ibid.
8. The New York Times, September 15, 1970.
9. Simpson, op. cit.
10. Time, op. cit.
11. Simpson, op. cit.
12. Letter to author.

* For his supporting role as Marilyn Monroe's acerbic lover in *All About Eve*.

36

In the fall of 1968, Audie Murphy was declared bankrupt. In spite of the fact that his low-budget westerns - two a year - had been earning him one hundred thousand dollars per annum, even in the sixties when his career had started to go downhill, he was virtually broke. Indeed, the man who had once been a millionaire (for a few months at least) could not pay back a trifling thirteen thousand dollars that he owed to the First National Bank of Dallas. Texas, which had so honoured its native son in his days as a war hero. Now it wanted its money back.

The news was even reported in the Eastern dailies such as *The New York Times*, and for a few brief days Murphy's name was back in the headlines. Then he sank back almost immediately into his old obscurity, a virtually forgotten man. Still he did take a stab at making one last movie, to be produced by himself. He told a newspaper reporter that it 'was an outdoor film but not a western… I'm just not interested in doing another of the films which I made as an actor for Universal. The same picture - *twenty times!*'[1]

In fact, however, it was a western, and Murphy had assigned himself a small 'cameo role' in it. The role was that of Jesse James - yet another version of the 'Kid' - but Murphy, his paunch visible beneath the tight-fitting black shirt he wore, hardly seemed suitable for the part anymore.

In the end the money ran out and his dissatisfied Kansas backers refused to put up any more. Although Murphy announced to the papers confidently that he intended to release the movie by Christmas 1969, it was never shown. And unlike most of the other potboilers Murphy made, it has never been shown on television either. But the tide of Audie Murphy's last movie did prove prophetic. It was called *A Time for Dying*.

Still Murphy, bankrupt and without another project in view, struggled on. Perhaps like those green replacements who had landed with him at 'Bloody Anzio' all those years before, he now felt a dull dread of what had to come. There was no other emotion that a dogface could feel.

He was arraigned before a bankruptcy court and he told it that he had lost a quarter of a million in Algerian oil, after that country had nationalized its oil fields as a result of the 1967 Six Day War. Murphy was asked whether or not he obtained money from his old movies. He replied that they were, indeed, being shown on TV, but he didn't receive a cent from them, because the State of California took the monies due to him to pay off long overdue income tax payments. Murphy was well and truly broke. Perhaps in his heart of hearts he knew it was time to die.

But in spite of all his other faults and his bouts of black depression, Murphy had never been one to give up. As he once remarked: 'I want to succeed in the thing I started out to do. I hate failures! I hate quitters!'[2] He began mapping out a very unusual TV series, which would combine two things: his love of war and his love of animals. The series was to centre on a war dog in World War II. But what form it was going to take is not known now; for Murphy died before he got beyond the general planning stage, and it is recorded that the U.S. Army only once used war dogs, toward the end of World War II during the winter of 1944/45 in Europe.

It was about this time that Murphy's love of animals, in particular, dogs, brought him back into national prominence for one last time before he died.

Murphy had always kept dogs. At the age of five in the impoverished rural Texas of the thirties, he had kept a pooch named Wheeler, one of those indiscriminate breeds that Texans used to call 'a curbstone setter'. As soon as he was settled after the war, he began keeping them again. Huston gave him a pedigree Weimaraner pup (which he had bred himself) during the filming of *The Red Badge of Courage*, and Murphy spent two thousand dollars trying to prevent it from dying. Thereafter, there was a series of pedigree animals. One of Murphy's last public appearances was as the guest of honour at the annual 'Dog and Dog Owner Parade' down Tinseltown's Hollywood Boulevard in November 1970.

Six months before that event, however, Audie Murphy had featured in another incident concerning dogs, but on this occasion he had been anything but the 'guest of honour'. In fact, he had been the accused in a court of law, charged with 'assault with intent to commit murder'.

It had all started when Murphy telephoned a Burbank dog trainer, David Gofstein, a big burly man of fifty-one who trained dogs for people. Murphy was speaking on behalf of a current girlfriend, who had complained to him that Gofstein was charging too much for training her pet. Murphy passed on the complaint in his usual quick-tempered fashion, which didn't suit the dog trainer one bit. According to Murphy's story, Gofstein told him over the phone that he, Murphy, was 'a phoney movie hero and a pip-squeak', plus several other indelicate names that Murphy felt ought not to be published in a family newspaper.

Murphy decided to take the law into his own hands. For some time now Murphy had voluntarily acted as a special officer with the Port Hueneme Police Force. Having taken a powerful aversion to drug peddlers, possibly on account of his own experiences, he had helped the police track down and arrest dealers on several occasions. As *Time* magazine described Murphy's role as a part-time law officer at the time, 'As the world got faster and faster in the '60s, it left him (Murphy) farther and farther behind. Murphy played a kind of grown-up cops-and-robbers game as a special officer of the Port Hueneme, Calif., Police Department and as a source of Mafia intelligence for the Los Angeles County district attorney's office'*.[3]

The part-time law officer decided to teach Gofstein a lesson. On the night of May 18, 1970, Murphy, his girlfriend, and a man, identified afterward simply as 'a former boxer', set out for the Gofstein Kennels at Burbank. Their aim, as Murphy stated it later, was 'to seek an understanding '. They reached the kennels just after dark. Mr. and Mrs. Gofstein were wheeling out their garbage on a cart made for that purpose.

Murphy challenged the big dog trainer (he weighed two hundred pounds). One word led to another. According to a newspaper wire service report of the time, Murphy's trouble started when Gofstein 'threw a garbage trolley at him, bruising his ribs'.[4] Thereupon Murphy pitched into Gofstein, pausing only to slap Mrs. Gofstein when she tried to intervene in the battle.

Now the 'former boxer' got into the act, allegedly hitting the dog trainer and striking his wife. As Mr. Gofstein told the story, however, it was Murphy who hit him 'in the eye, knocked him down and kicked him... and then stuck a pistol in his stomach and ordered him to get into the car'[5]

However, Gofstein was not having that. He managed to break away from Murphy. 'He fell down, got up and then accompanied by his wife ran for the house'[6] followed by 'shots' fired by Murphy. Later a witness did testify that he saw 'a man shoot a pistol straight up in the air'.[7] But the neighbour could not state categorically that the person who had fired the pistol had been Murphy.

Frightened, ruffled, and not a little bruised Gofstein filed a complaint. It was investigated, and ten days later Murphy was arrested and jailed for four hours until his lawyers could secure his release. This time the charges wouldn't go away as they had done with the two youths whom Murphy had slapped a few years before. He would have to stand trial; being accused of 'assault with intent to commit murder', a very serious charge indeed.

Immediately the case hit the headlines. The way *The New York Times* reported the incident was typical. The news item placed conspicuously on its front page read, 'Four men and eight women were selected today to try Audie Murphy, World War II's most decorated soldier, on charges of assaulting a dog trainer. The former movie star is accused of hitting David Gofstein, 51, who also says that the Medal of Honor winner, who is credited with killing or capturing 240 Germans, fired a gun during the argument'.[8] How the mighty had fallen!

The trial lasted ten days. Murphy pleaded innocent of the charge of 'assault to commit murder'. Instead, his lawyers maintained that it was a case of self-defence. They charged that Gofstein was the aggressor and that Murphy had just been attempting to defend himself.

On the stand Murphy, soberly dressed, testified he was authorized to possess the blackjacks the police officers had found in his car and house

*Due to his compulsive gambling, Murphy had come into contact with certain dubious characters on the west Coast who may have belonged to the Mafia. Hence the reference to him as a source of Mafia intelligence.

after he had been arrested the previous May. He could possess them because he was a special officer with the Port Hueneme Police Force and a deputy with the Dallas County, Texas, Sheriff's office. What kind of a jurisdiction a Dallas deputy had in California was never explained; nor did the prosecutor press the issue. And the jury was perhaps sensitive to his charm or to his record as a war hero or to his fame as a movie star. Could they send a war hero, with the kind of appeal Murphy always had for women of all ages, to prison? They couldn't!

He was finally acquitted and quipped afterward to the waiting press, "I think it is injurious to my reputation to think I could fire at a target as big as Mr. Gofstein - and miss!"[9] Murphy didn't appear to realize what damage he did to his already fading reputation by becoming involved in such brawls. Indeed what was a war hero like Murphy doing, flashing honorary badges and pretending to be a police officer, complete with pistol in his shoulder holster? As *Time* magazine commented: 'The incident marked the depths to which he had fallen. Audie Murphy belonged to an earlier, simpler time, one in which bravery was cardinal and killing was a virtue'.[10]

Time was running out at last for Audie Murphy. His health was failing. He suffered several blackouts. He caught colds easily and found it difficult to shake the infections off. His insomnia came back. In 1970, in the last fall before he died, he visited a prewar acquaintance in Dallas, 'Mama' Woods. She hadn't seen Audie for two years and felt that he appeared 'depressed'. She was struck, too, by the fact that 'he had aged considerably his face seemed bloated and he had lost one of his most wonderful features, the twinkle in his eyes He was not the Audie Murphy that I had known'.[11]

As 1970 gave way to 1971 and Murphy made one last attempt to restore his financial position, he went to visit his old friend McClure in Hollywood. Of late they had not seen so much of one another. McClure's interests were still in Hollywood with the movies, and Murphy's career there was finished. Now they talked together for two hours in an aimless sort of a way, with McClure trying not to reveal the thoughts that were now troubling him. But after Murphy went, for the last time, he wrote, 'He seemed awfully tired - spent. I looked at him and realized that I would not have recognized my old friend had I seen him on the streets... For years Audie seemed to be eternally young and then, as if the raging emotional and mental fires within had surfaced, he seemed to grow old overnight... I never saw him again. Two weeks later he was dead'.[12]

NOTES

1. Simpson, op. cit.
2. Ibid.
3. Time, June 14, 1971.
4. Simpson, op. cit.
5. Ibid.
6. Ibid.
7. Ibid.
8. The New York Times, September 15, 1970.
9. Simpson, op. cit.
10. Time, op. cit.
11. Simpson, op. cit.
12. Letter to author.

37

On May 23, 1971, twenty-seven years to the day from when the 3rd Division had begun its breakout from 'Bloody Anzio', with the divisional brass band playing them into action, Audie Murphy set off on a mission, which was perhaps equally desperate for him. Together with another man, he was to fly to Martinsville, Virginia. Here he was to inspect, for a group called Telestar Leisure Investments, a firm that made prefabricated housing. If he was satisfied with what he saw, he would recommend that Telestar invest in the Virginia firm, in which he had an interest. He hoped that if everything went well, he would recoup the quarter of a million dollars he had lost in Algerian oil.

At ten after nine that morning, the light plane, which was painted blue and white, the same colours as the divisional patch of his old 3rd, set off from Atlanta, Georgia. The plane, which contained Murphy and four other passengers, was piloted by Herman Butler, who had already twice been suspended from flying for aviation offences, though none of the businessmen in the cabin to the rear knew that.

The first two hours of the flight to Martinsville were uneventful. One wonders what was going through forty-six-year-old Murphy's mind during those hours. Did he remember that this was the day the old 3rd broke out after four months of the mud of Anzio? Did he recall that for four long months that winter he and the rest had not dared to poke their heads above the ground; how they had used 'Ration cans as chamber pots, hurling them from the holes like grenades after they have served their purpose?'[1] We do not know, for all the men in that plane were doomed, including Murphy.

At eleven o'clock that morning the plane reached the mountains of south-west Virginia and began to run into trouble. Visibility diminished rapidly. There was low cloud, fog, and rain, and the weather was worsening steadily. Butler, the pilot, who was not qualified to fly on instruments, decided to make a change in his flight plan. He would fly east to avoid the mountains and try to land in the vicinity of Galax, sixty miles from Martinsville.

Murphy, who was a qualified pilot himself - he had bought a plane back in the fifties - must have noticed the change of direction, but presumably he let the man who was in charge, Butler, get on with it.

Down below several people heard the plane, hidden somewhere above them in the fog, desperately attempting to find a safe landing place. One of them, Larry Chambers, a reporter on the local *Galax Gazette*, actually saw the plane momentarily. He reported that he saw a light coloured, two-engined plane seeming 'to bounce in and out of the clouds'. Then after what he thought was an attempt to land 'on the four-lane bypass northwest of the city'[2], the plane, flying at two hundred feet, headed west, disappearing into the fog and the rain. Larry Chambers was probably the last person to see the plane.

At ten to twelve the pilot, Butler, contacted the tower at Roanoke Flight Service Station and asked for the current weather there. He was advised that the 'ceiling was 1,000 feet broken, 2,500 feet overcast, visibility three miles in light rain and fog, with mountain ridges obscured'.[3] Butler said he intended to land at Roanoke. Then his radio went dead.

Time passed leadenly below. At Martinsville itself, the people waiting to pick up Audie Murphy, and the other businessmen who were to inspect the prefabricated building plant, began to grow worried. The plane bringing them was now long overdue and they could see the weather was not particularly good for flying. Finally they contacted the local airport authorities, who in their turn got in touch with Roanoke Field. They reported they had received a radio signal from Butler stating he was going to land there, but since then nothing had been heard from him - and Butler had definitely not landed in the area!

Now suddenly, it was realized that the plane was not just overdue, but was missing, and that it was carrying America's most decorated soldier.

The news was flashed all over the country. It appeared next morning in the papers and was telecast over the national networks, with Audie Murphy's career as a soldier and a movie actor receiving prominence.

Due to the terrible weather, the search for the missing plane could not commence immediately. As the conditions improved, the Virginia Wing of the Civil Air Patrol ordered a saturation search of the area from which the plane was last reported. The Air Patrol made a maximum effort. The Virginia Wing put thirty-three planes in the air, flying some eighty sorties. The North Carolina Wing joined in, with another seventeen planes.

On the afternoon of Monday, May 31, the crashed plane was located by a helicopter flown by a Colonel Hale and a Major Slusser. It had crashed into the heavily forested side of Brushy Mountain some twenty miles from Roanoke. The plane had apparently burned on impact, but the numbers still visible on an unburned part of the wrecked plane matched those of the missing Aero Commander. Judging from the fact that the impact took place only four hundred feet from the top of Brushy Mountain, they concluded the pilot had been trying to make a landing approach to Roanoke's Woodrum Field, twenty miles away.

Ground parties set out for the site of the crash. By late afternoon they had reached it, and at four o'clock that same day they radioed back to the medical examiner for West Virginia that all six men in the wrecked plane were dead. The medical examiner himself, Dr. David Oxley, reached the scene two hours later and order the terribly injured, and in some cases charred, bodies taken back for autopsy.

At the time there seems to have been some confusion as to the number of bodies. State Police Lieutenant Marvin Kent reported that he found *five* bodies on the site of the crash: Murphy; his companion Jack Littleton; Claude Crosby, president of Modular Management; Raymond Fater, a lawyer representing him; and Butler, the pilot. There was no mention of a sixth man. However, on the day following the recovery of the dead men, Dr. Walter Gable, a pathologist and Deputy Chief Medical Examiner for West Virginia, told a news conference that all six bodies had been identified by 4:15 the previous day.

Be that as it may, Audie Murphy's body, which had suffered horrendous injuries, had been definitely identified. The main clue to his identity had been that nine-inch scar on his right hip where they had 'dug out five pounds' of his flesh back in Aix-en-Provence Hospital in the bitter winter of 1944. As Dr. Gable told the news conference, 'Murphy was the second of the six to be identified... He was one of the three thrown clear of the wreckage'.[4] Although the three who had been inside the plane had been 'burned badly', Murphy had not escaped 'massive total body injuries', but had died instantly. That, at least, was a consolation to his wife, Pamela, who now filed a ten-million dollar suit against the owners of the plane in which her husband had died.*

As soon as his death was confirmed, the media reacted. *The New York Time's* announcement of his death was typical. Under the headline 'Audie Murphy, War Hero, Killed in Plane Crash', it stated, 'Audie Murphy, the nation's most decorated hero of World War II, and five other men were found dead today... near the summit of a craggy, heavily wooded mountain'.[5]

The media in Texas pulled out all the stops. *The Dallas Morning News* editorialized, 'The Memorial Day death of Texas-born Audie Murphy comes as sad news for Texas. Yet in the sorrow of losing America's most decorated soldier, there must be a large measure of pride, because he was a hero. He believed in this nation and her ideals and her needs and was willing to fight and die to uphold them. Thus he brought honour and glory to the Lone Star State'.[6]

Gordon McLendon, the president of Radio Station KLIF in Dallas and a score of other stations all over America, claimed, 'Of one thing we can all be glad and that is the certainty that Audie Murphy felt no fear when that little plane went down near Martinsville. He really had been long worn out with fear. The hard luck kid who suffered so deeply during his last year is now dead'. Then the radio executive asked, 'Is there not to be a day of national mourning for Audie Murphy? Or was John Kennedy a greater hero?'[7]

As was to be expected, the establishment lauded Murphy strictly for what he had done between 1943 and 1945. President Richard Nixon eulogized, 'As America's most decorated hero of World War II, Audie Murphy had not only won the admiration of millions for his own brave exploits he

---

* She never got it

also came to epitomize the gallantry in action of America's fighting men. The nation stands in his debt and mourns at his death'.[8]

The tribute was understandable from a worried Commander-in-Chief, plagued by the running sore of Vietnam, who, reportedly, sat that year watching the movie *Patton* over and over again in search of inspiration. Nor was it surprising that General William Westmoreland, whose Vietnam policy was now virtually discredited, stated on this occasion that 'His example to fellow Americans served as an inspiration to all persons during WWII - Americans and Allies alike, at the front and at home. Today also his example should be an inspiration to all Americans - in or out of uniform - at home or overseas - who served in support of the policies of our country'.[9] Audie Murphy couldn't fight anymore but clearly he could still be used to support the failing policies of the time.

Few were the dissenting voices, who spoke out not just for Murphy 'the war hero', but also for Murphy the war victim. *Time* magazine got a little closer to the truth about Audie Murphy than most that June. In an article entitled 'Heroes: To Hell and Not Quite Back', its feature writer stated: 'When Audie Murphy returned from World War II, not yet 21 and the war's most decorated hero, he held the promise of an emerald future... The baby-faced kid was feted by the press and patriotic organizations, courted by business, industry and Hollywood... When his body was found last week in the crash of a light plane outside Roanoke, Va., Murphy, 46, left behind a promise that had dissolved unheroically into business failures, run-ins with the law, and forgettable parts in forgettable movies'.[10]

Bill Mauldin, the cartoonist who had acted with Murphy in *The Red Badge of Courage*, was asked to write a tribute to his dead friend. The magazine that commissioned the article was *Life*, which had launched Murphy's postwar career back in 1945.

In its June 11, 1971, issue Mauldin came as close to the truth as anybody when he wrote of the dead hero: 'Every time he got into trouble, which was often because his judgement was on par with his luck, great numbers of people who knew him rallied to help. This was not because he had won those medals. It was because most of us accept a certain amount of blending as we go along. We adjust, accept, tolerate, temporize, and sometimes compromise. Not Murphy. In him we all recognized the straight raw stuff, uncut and fiery as the day it left the still. Nobody wanted to be in his shoes. But nobody wanted to be unlike him, either'.[11]

But for a brief period still, Audie Murphy belonged to the establishment, and official America was going to dispatch him from this world with due pomp and ceremony.

NOTES
1. Murphy, op. cit.
2. Simpson, op. cit.
3. Ibid.
4. The New York Times, June 1, 1971.
5. Ibid.
6. Dallas Morning News, June 1, 1971.
7. Simpson, op. cit.
8. The New York Times, June 8, 1971.
9. Ibid.
10. Time, op. cit.
11. Life, op. cit.

38

A few years before he died, Audie Murphy went to Washington with a friend. During his stay in the capital, he asked his friend to come with him to Arlington. The friend, surprised by Murphy's desire to view a cemetery, asked, "Why the visit?" Murphy replied solemnly, "I'd like to make a reservation".[1] It was a simple statement of fact.

Of course, his place in Arlington National Cemetery had long been reserved for him. Now the military establishment was going to make sure that his burial there received the fullest possible media coverage. The situation in war-torn Vietnam demanded it. The burial of the last hero might help to rally the shaken, divided nation a little. But first Hollywood had to have its show.

About eight hundred mourners overflowed onto the patio and the lawn at the memorial service for the dead man at the Church of the Hills at the Forest Lawn Memorial Park. After all, Audie Murphy had lived in Hollywood for over a quarter of a century. Once when he had been young and a hero, the great stars had vied with each other to be photographed shaking his hand. He had met them all, Gary Cooper, Jimmy Cagney, James Stewart. Now there were few 'names' among the mourners. The film industry was represented by studio workmen, extras, stuntmen, and the like. Perhaps that was to be expected. As the press reported at the time, 'Murphy was known as a quiet man who rarely socialized with the stars'.[2]

There were, however, two former stars at the ceremony - and both of them were women. One was Ann Blyth, now a mature matron, who had starred with Murphy back in 1950 in that first western that had condemned him to the genre ever afterward - *The Kid from Texas*.

The other was his first wife, Wanda Hendrix. She was now married for the third time, but she was still loyal twenty-odd years later - to her first love: one of the few who were. She lingered for some time at the casket. McClure, who was there, remembers Wanda 'kneeling and weeping beside it'.[3] Later she told a reporter, "That part of him that was a hero and a fine man, I will always remember".[4] Then she was led from the church, still weeping softly.

Pamela Murphy, standing with her two sons not far from the representatives sent to the ceremony by the Army (six of them - all holders of the Medal of Honor), remained composed, as she would throughout the various ceremonies held for her dead husband this second week of June. Perhaps she remembered only too well the many infidelities of the man who, as David McClure knew, had 'seduced more girls than any man I ever knew - with the possible exception of Errol Flynn?'[5] Perhaps it was her stoic Indian heritage*? Or perhaps she was just too numb for any further display of emotion?

There were old comrades present, too, such as 'Iron Mike' O'Daniel, very old and gray now, to listen to the military chaplain who officiated at the ceremony and gave the eulogy. He ran true to form. After detailing the hardships of Murphy's early life in rural Texas, he said solemnly, "The United States Armed Forces recognizes in the passing of Audie Murphy the passing of one of its most courageous warriors."[6]

Was there nothing else to say about him since 1945? It was as if he had never lived any other life but that of a combat infantryman. But there was one old comrade from the war present there that day who did attempt to pay a different kind of tribute to his dead friend.

Once, in what now must have seemed another age, they had lain together in the same ward in that provincial French hospital at Aix-en-Provence: the one fighting gangrene; the other trying to cope with the horrendous mental and emotional stress of knowing that he was crippled for life. Both had come through, though the emotional scars had remained forever. Thereafter, they had remained loyal friends. Now Perry Pitt, whom the war had made into a paraplegic, told the TV reporters: "He (Murphy) gave everything, took nothing; and never forgot who his friends were".[7] It was as fine a tribute as Audie Murphy ever received.

In his will, Murphy, who probably guessed he would be interred at Arlington, had requested that he should be given a 'simple, plain and ordinary burial'. Washington wanted Murphy to be buried with full military honours.

On June 7, 1971 [9] a fine sunny day, Audie Murphy's casket, draped with the nation's flag, was placed on a caisson drawn by six gleaming black horses. Led by the U.S. Army band, marching with muffled drums, the solemn procession came down the tree-lined avenue toward where four hundred mourners gathered to celebrate the solemn occasion. They stood in the morning sun on a green hillside under the great oaks, not far from the amphitheatre of the Tomb of the Unknown Warrior, picked over fifty years before from the unidentified dead of World War I.

To left and right of the glittering military assembly were the rows of simple white crosses, marking the graves of those killed in the wars that had been fought since Audie Murphy had won his medals - Korea, Vietnam, and the like.

Chief of Staff four-star General Westmoreland, who had fought in that 'old war' himself, was there, resplendent in his uniform. He represented the President. George Bush, years later to be President himself, was also present. But there were humbler folks there, too, that day. There was Marty Benson, one of Murphy's gambling cronies, who wore a bright orange shirt and sported one of those straggly goatee beards fashionable at the time. There

* Pamela Murphy was one-quarter Indian (Cherokee and Creek)

was also a pretty young. eighteen-year-old, Karen Lathinghood, who bore the strange title of 'Miss Vet 1971'. Audie Murphy might have laughed out loud at the incongruity of that teenage 'Miss Vet' attending his funeral, if he had been able to. She was surely strictly Hollywood!

As the twenty-three honorary pallbearers, who included the most decorated soldier to come out of Vietnam, Sergeant (now Lieutenant) Joe Hooper came to attention, the Army chaplain intoned the now customary eulogy to the dead hero. Thereupon the first six pallbearers, all very tall men, folded and presented the flag that had draped the coffin to Mrs. Murphy, dressed all in black and tearless still.

The ramrod-straight, immaculately uniformed firing squad snapped to attention. On command, they raised their rifles to the sky. Another order and they discharged the first of three volleys into the still morning sky, sending the birds flying from the surrounding trees squawking in hoarse protest. A loud, echoing silence followed, broken only by the sound of a woman sobbing softly somewhere in the crowd.

Down the alley, a lone bugler raised his gleaming instrument to his lips with a flourish. He began to play the most moving and most poignant of all Army calls - 'Taps'. Sadly those notes, which signify the end of a day - or a lifetime - to a soldier, drifted and filtered through the sun-dappled old oaks: a last tribute from the Army he had loved so much to its most renowned soldier.

It was all over. Audie L. Murphy had been laid to rest. The Army band struck up the jaunty marching song of the 3rd Infantry Division. Murphy's old outfit, as it swung up the avenue back to its barracks, *'Just a dogface soldier with a rifle on my shoulder... eat a Kraut for breakfast every day... So feed me ammunition... Keep in the Third Division...'.**

Hands were solemnly shaken. Gleaming, gold-braided peaks of military caps were touched in parting salute. Flowers were strewn. Cameras clicked discreetly. Eyes were dabbed with lace handkerchiefs for one last time. And then they were gone, drifting away in subdued little groups that got livelier the farther they got from the grave. Behind them they left the heavy, poignant silence of the cemetery - and all those dead young men.

At last America's most decorated soldier was alone with the 'glorious dead'. Now he would rest forever among these young men, many of whom had not yet been born when he had performed his heroic deeds. Next to his grave** was the grave of one of those who had died violently in battle a quarter of a century after Audie Murphy's war was over. He had been a young captain in the Special Forces, half Murphy's age, who had been killed in action in Vietnam just one year before, on June 27, 1970.

---

* 'The Dogface Soldier.
** In the year 2000 Murphy's grave at Arlington is the second most visited one after that of President Kennedy.

When Sergeant Joe Hooper, one of Murphy's pallbearers, died of natural causes in 1979, he had been long forgotten by the general public. Although he had returned from Vietnam as that war's most decorated soldier, with 115 enemy dead to his credit, the holder of the Medal of Honor, two Silver Stars, the Bronze Star, and a staggering *seven* Purple Hearts, he discovered he had fought in a discredited war. Few mourned his passing.

But Audie Murphy's memory is still kept fresh and alive for us today nearly two decades after his death. Various individuals and organizations, particularly in the Southwest, ensure that Murphy will not be forgotten. There is a veterans' hospital named after him in San Antonio. Decatur has an annual 'Audie Murphy Patriotism Award'. In the W. Walworth Library, Greenville, there is an 'Audie Murphy Room'. Here there is a collection of Murphy's medals, letters, uniforms, and other memorabilia. On several state highways in Texas there are 'Audie Murphy markers' indicating where he had once lived or worked. Fort Benning has an 'Audie Murphy Gym'. In the State Capitol Building at Austin, Texas, his portrait still hangs - the smiling, apparently unspoiled young hero, with the Medal of Honor around his neck.

The Lone Star State, which in 1971 voted Audie Murphy to be 'a great American war hero and one of the most famous of all Texans', is making sure that America's most famed soldier will not be forgotten. Rightly so.

But would Audie Murphy, who in later life ceased associating with military and patriotic organizations (though he remained to the end of his life a great patriot), have wanted to be remembered as the archetypal American military hero? Was thirty months spent in combat as a teenager, all that was worthy of remembrance?

He had always hated the fake publicity about himself, spread for commercial reasons by the ballyhoo merchants who latched on to his wartime experiences to make money. Nor had he wished to appear the perfect soldier. He knew he had not been that, however much he had loved soldiering.

When he came back from the war in 1945, the newspapermen, the public relations hacks had been waiting for him in his sister's living room, ready to start the process of hero worship. And Murphy had not wanted to make a living simply from being a hero. He was far too honest for that. He had told the newspapermen that afternoon that he was simply 'a fugitive from the law of averages'. They hadn't listened.

The attempts to make him 'sell' his combat fame had never ceased. When he was almost penniless, living off his disability pension, they had latched on to him to sell: 'commercial thing - a few shirt ads, whiskies, cigarettes. I don't drink or smoke and at that time I couldn't afford a shirt. I turned them down'.[8]

Perhaps then he had told the real truth - before they had turned him into a reluctant movie star - when he had said, soon after returning from the war, that he had wanted to become a farmer because, 'Farmers are happier'.[9]

That had not been for him. He had never been able to realize that dream of becoming a 'happy farmer'. After 1945 he had been unable to escape his destiny as a war hero. Nor bad he had strength or will enough to shake off that 'red sickness of battle' that Stephen Crane wrote of and that he bore with him to his death.

Once for a little while, before he became a hero, he had been happy. Martin Kelly, the hard-drinking, hard-fighting Irishman from Maine; Jim Fife from Oklahoma; 'Lattie' Tipton from Tennessee; and all the rest from that original Company B had adopted him. The skinny freckle-faced orphan kid from Texas, who looked as if he wouldn't say boo to a goose, had found a family at last. He had loved them and the wild, dangerous life they had led.

What had he once said? "You have a comradeship, a rapport that you'll never have again, not in our society anyway. I suppose it comes from having nothing to gain except the end of the war. There's no competitiveness, no money values. You trust the man on your left and right with your life, while, as a civilian, you might not trust either of them with ten cents".[10]

But these good comrades, whom he had trusted with his life in combat, and with whom he had shared the brutal, rough-and-ready camaraderie of the front, had disappeared over the months, the years, one by one. Dead or broken men, they had vanished from his young life. He had been alone again.

The fact that he was a hero and later a star could never fill the void left by their disappearance, could never make him happy again. Nor could the relentless pursuit of women, or the wild gambling. He had been condemned to be a loner in a civilian world, although surrounded by people, many of whom adored him slavishly. A few had even loved him. No matter. The simple, happy past had vanished. He seemed never able to recapture it. Like some latter-day Gatsby, he was compelled to believe 'in the green light, the orgiastic future that year by year recedes before us. It eluded us then, but that's no matter - tomorrow we will run faster, stretch out our arms farther...'

'So we beat on, boats against the current, borne back ceaselessly into the past'[11]

NOTES
1. Letter to author.
2. Washington Post, June 8, 1971.
3. Letter to author.
4. Ibid.
5. Ibid.
6. Simpson, op. cit.
7. Ibid.
8. Saturday Evening Post, op. cit
9. Ibid.
10. Esquire, op. cit
11. F. Scott Fitzgerald. The Great Gatsby. New York: Scribner's, 1925

AFTERWORD

Time's wrong-way telescope will show a minute man ten years hence, and by distance simplify. Through the lens, see if I seem substance or nothing; of the world deserve mention or charitable oblivion. Remember me when I am dead and simplify me when I'm dead.

- Captain Keith Douglas,
Killed in Action, Normandy, 1944

There is little, if anything, to be seen today of Audie Murphy's progress through Europe in the years 1943 - 1945. Age and the times have changed everything. Europeans in the new Millennium no longer seem to want to know anything of that youthful sacrifice in blood that those Americans who came to liberate their continent paid over fifty years ago.

For the most part, the discreetly hidden American military cemeteries are the only indications that the Americans ever came this way. Half a century of prosperity and peace have had their effect. Europe has forgotten those brash, eager young men with their gum and candies, their Lucky Strikes - 'and cigarettes for sister' - who once slogged their way through their villages and towns, grinning boldly, perhaps never to return.

Salerno has vanished into a welter of white-painted tourist 'villas', filled in summer by thousands of sun-hungry tourists from the north. Where once young men fought and died, they lie, packed and oiled like sardines, soaking in the Italian sun. *'Teutonengrill'*, the German tourists call it cynically. At Anzio they sell you pictures of walking wounded from the 3rd Division, 'courtesy Anzio Tourist Office'. It is no different at St. Tropez, where the ribbon development has spread out to embrace Red Beach and Yellow Beach. Who knows there now how 'Lattie' Tipton charged up that hill overlooking the beach, only to fall back dead into Murphy's arms, softly breathing 'Murph'? Below, the talk is of the latest scandal on the *Cote d'Azur* and why 'BB' retired to St. Tropez in the first place. *

Only the weathered cairn and plaque at St. Tropez-La Croix remind anyone curious enough to stop at the roadside that the 'U.S. Third Infantry Division made an assault amphibious landing in this vicinity... August 15, 1944'. But in summer the narrow winding coastal road is always too hot. Not many stop.

It is no different at 'Nougat City', where Murphy fired at his own image in the mirror during the bitter house-to-house fighting and his buddy

---

* Brigitte Bardot.

Kelly quipped scornfully, "That's the first time I ever saw a Texan beat himself to the draw". Montelimar is bigger and uglier and it still prides itself on the production of that tooth-breaking candy. 'Aud-ie Mur-phy? C'est domage, m'sieu mais…'. But then why should anyone remember that little fighting Texan, who gave his blood three times to help to liberate their country?

When you get closer to the dark, brooding mountains of the Vosges, you begin to see the fading signs that war once passed this way. At that quarry at Cleurie where Murphy won his two Silver Stars within five days, the rotting wooden beams, here and there are pocked with machine gun fire like the symptoms of some loathsome skin disease. Here and there among the brambles you come across rusting barbed wire and gas masks, always the first thing that panicked troops threw away, with the letters 'U.S.' embossed above the eyepiece. Yes, definitely, here once desperate young men fought and died.

Down from the mountains and into the Rhine plain, where the 3rd fought its last battle in France, the medieval half-timbered houses in the villages still bear the marks of fighting, too. But the broad, undersized peasants, heavy with their celebrated sauerkraut and sausage meals, are suspicious. They don't want to talk about the war. Yes, they know who Eddie Slovik was. They had seen the film on télévision. Audie Murphy? A shrug of the shoulders and a shake of the head. They were losers themselves, German-speaking peasants in France whose fathers had fought in the Wehrmacht. They could identify with Eddie, the loser. But the hero, Audie Murphy: 'Mir kenne ihn nit'.*

The village of Holtzwihr, a straggle of houses grouped around the church on the main street, is no different from the rest of those German-speaking communities close to the Rhine. A cannon before the church dated '1871' is the only sign that a war ever passed this way. No mention of those twentieth-century conflicts.

But return to the spot where that crippled tank destroyer stood that January, find the scarred tree where Murphy's machine gunners were killed by a tree burst, discover a 75mm shell case, stamped 'WD 1944' in the undergrowth, and again you can sense what once happened here.

Stand on that narrow, third-class country road, surrounded by trees, head cocked to the west in the faint breeze coming from the High Vosges and once more you can imagine the ugly cries of battle, the high-pitched hysterical hiss of the German machine guns and that bold young man defying the might of the Wehrmacht.

Here for a fleeting moment on a quiet fall afternoon, with no sound save the lowing of the cattle in the distance, you feel that something still lingers of that freckle-faced young kid who was to become America's LAST HERO…

---

* 'We don't know him', in dialect.

BIBLIOGRAPHY

BOOKS

Ambler, E. Autobiography. London: Collins, 1985.

Anger, K. Hollywood Babylon. New York: Dutton, 1984.

Blumenson, M. Mark Clark. New York: Congdon and Weed, 1984.

Bradley, O. Bradley: A Soldier's Story. New York: Random House, 1978.

Congdon, D., ed. Combat. New York: Dell Books, 1955.

Crane, S. The Badge of Courage. New York: New American Library, 1952

Eisenhower, J. The Bitter Woods. New York: Putnam's, 1967.

Farago, L. Patton. New York: Dell, 1970..

E. Fellers, ed. From Fedala to Berchtesgaden. Washington, DC: Infantry Press 1947

Gavin, J. On to Berlin. New York: Viking, 1978.

Graham, D. No Name on the Bullet: A Biography of Audie Murphy. New York: Viking, 1989.

Gunther, J. Inside the U.S.A.. New York: Harper, 1951.

Harmon, E. Combat Commander. New York: Prentice Hall, 1970.

Hemingway, E. Over the River and into the Trees. New York: Scribner's, 1950.

Hendin, Hand A. P. Hass. Wounds of War. New York: Basic, 1984.

Huie, W. The Execution of Private Slovik. New York: Signet, 1953.

Jeavons, C. A. A Pictorial History of War Films. New York: Citadel, 1974

Linklater, E. The Campaign in Italy. London: HMSO, 1951

Madsen, A. John Huston. New York: Doubleday, 1978.

Moorehead, A. Eclipse. London: Collins, 1952

Murphy, A. To Hell and Back. New York: Henry Holt, 1949.

Nicolson, N. Alex. London: Pan, 1974.

North Africa. Washington, DC: Department of the Army, 1942.

Profile of Audie Murphy. 3rd Division Association, 1976.

Rickman, E. Soldier. New York: Harper and Row, 1953.

Ross, L. Picture. New York: Limelight Editions, 1983.

Simpson, H. Audie Murphy. American Soldier. Dallas: Alcor Publishing 1982.

Taggart, D. History of Third Division. Linz, Austria: Privately printed. 1945.

Trevalyn, R. Rome '44. London: Collins, 1984.

Truscott, L. Command Missions. New York: Scribner's, 1953.

Vaughan-Thomas, W. Anzio. New York: Holt, Rinehardt & Winston, 1955.

Whiting, C. The Long March on Rome. London: Century-Hutchinson, 1987.

PERIODICALS AND NEWSPAPERS

Banker Magazine. June 1961.
BBC War Report. London, 1945.
Collier's. September 1953.
Collier's. September 1955.
Daily Express. July 1953.
Daily Telegraph. March 3, 1986
Daily Telegraph Diary of the War: The First Quarter. London: 1944.
Dallas Morning News. June 1, 1971.
Esquire, 'Who Made the Difference'. December 1983.
Houston Post. August 23, 1945.
Life. July 16, 1945.
Life. June 11, 1971
New York Times, The. June 1945
New York Times, The. July 1955
New York Times, The. September 15, 1955.
New York Times, The. September 15, 1970
New York Times, The. June 1, 1971
New York Times, The. June 8, 1971.
Saturday Evening Post, The. September 1953
Saturday Evening Post, The. September 1955.
Stars and Stripes, October 1943
Sunday Telegraph Magazine. London: April 12, 1986.
Time. June 1971.
Washington Post. June 8, 1971.
Audie Murphy Internet Links
1st Battalion, 15th Infantry Regiment Home Page
(www.benning.army.mil/fbhome/33/1-15/1-15.html)
The official home page for Audie Murphy's World War II combat unit.
American Cotton Museum (www.cottonmuseum.com/)
Located in Greenville, Texas this museum is the permanent home for many
    of the Audie Murphy artifacts
Audie Murphy Memorial Web Site (www.audiemurphy.com/)
Site for all things Audie Murphy plus many Web Links.
Farmville, Texas (www.farmersvilletx.com)
Audie's birthplace.
Greenville, Texas Chamber of Commerce (www.greenville-chamber.org/)
Excellent source of upcoming Murphy events.

INDEX

231

Printed in the United States
20768LVS00002B/9

9 780953 867707